MAJOR & MRS HOLT'S
Battlefield Guide to the

SOMME

The Memorial Cross,
Lochnagar Crater

MAJOR & MRS HOLT'S

Battlefield Guide to the SOMME

Tonie & Valmai Holt

LEO COOPER

By the same authors:

Picture Postcards of the Golden Age: A Collector's Guide
Till the Boys Come Home: the Picture Postcards of the First World War
The Best of Fragments from France by Capt Bruce Bairnsfather
In Search of the Better 'Ole: The Life, Works and Collectables of Bruce Bairnsfather
Picture Postcard Artists: Landscapes, Animals and Characters
Stanley Gibbons Postcard Catalogue: 1980, 1981, 1982, 1984, 1985, 1987
Germany Awake! The Rise of National Socialism illustrated by Contemporary Postcards
I'll be Seeing You: the Picture Postcards of World War II
Holts' Battlefield Guidebooks: Normandy-Overlord/Market-Garden/Somme/Ypres
Visitor's Guide to the Normandy Landing Beaches
Battlefields of the First World War: A Traveller's Guide
Major & Mrs Holt's Concise Guide to the Ypres Salient
Major & Mrs Holt's Battle Maps: Normandy/Somme/Ypres/Gallipoli/MARKET-GARDEN
Major & Mrs Holt's Battlefield Guide to the Ypres Salient + Battle Map
Major & Mrs Holt's Battlefield Guide to the Normandy Landing Beaches + Battle Map
Major & Mrs Holt's Battlefield Guide to Gallipoli + Battle Map
Major & Mrs Holt's Battlefield Guide to MARKET-GARDEN + Battle Map
Violets From Oversea: Reprinted 1999 as Poets of the Great War
My Boy Jack: The Search for Kipling's Only Son
Revised limpback edition 2001

In *Preparation*

Major & Mrs Holt's Concise, Illustrated Guide to 15 World War One Battles

First published in 1996, Second Edition 1998, Reprinted 1999,
Third Edition 2000. This Revised Edition 2003
by Leo Cooper: an imprint of Pen & Sword Books Ltd,
47 Church Street, Barnsley, South Yorkshire S70 2AS

A CIP catalogue record for this book is available from the British Library

ISBN 0 85052 414 8

Printed in Singapore by: Kyodo Printing Co (Singapore) Pte Ltd

About the authors

Respected military authors Tonie and Valmai Holt are generally acknowledged as the founders of the modern battlefield tour and have established a sound reputation for the depth of their research. Their *Major & Mrs Holt's Battlefield Guides* is without doubt the leading series describing the most visited battlefields of the First and Second World Wars. They have a unique combination of male and female viewpoints and can draw upon a quarter of a century's military and travel knowledge and experience gained in personally conducting thousands of people around the areas they have written about.

Valmai Holt took a BA(Hons) in French and Spanish and taught history. Tonie Holt took a BSc(Eng) and is a graduate of the Royal Military Academy Sandhurst and of the Army Staff College at Camberley. They are both Fellows of the Royal Society of Arts and Science and have made frequent appearances on the lecture circuit, on radio and television.

Contents

Picture credits
The authors and publishers wish to thank the following for the use of illustrations: Canadian National Memorial, Vimy (all rights reserved) p30; Dominique Frère of the Historial for interiors of the Historial, p31; John Huey of Australia, p162; Isobel Swan of Holts' Tours, p259; Dick Goodwin, War Cemetery and Regimental Association photographer, p107. All other photographs were taken by the authors.

ABBREVIATIONS

Abbreviations used for military units and acronyms are listed below. Many of these are printed in full at intervals throughout the text to aid clarity. Others are explained where they occur.

ABT	Australian Battlefield Tour
ADS	Advanced Dressing Station
AIF	Australian Imperial Force
Att/d	Attached
Aust	Australian
BEF	British Expeditionary Force
Bn	Battalion
BWI	British West Indies
Cam	Cameron
CCS	Casualty Clearing Station
Cem	Cemetery
CGS/H	*Conseil Général de la Somme/Historial*
CIGS	Chief of the Imperial General Staff
C-in-C	Commander in Chief
CO	Commanding Officer
Coy	Company
CRP	*Conseil Régional de Picardie*
CWGC	Commonwealth War Graves Commission
DLI	Durham Light Infantry
DSO	Distinguished Service Order
E of I	Empress of India's
FA	Field Artillery
GOC	General Officer Commanding
HLI	Highland Light Infantry
KOSB	King's Own Scottish Borderers
KOYLI	King's Own Yorkshire Light Infantry
KRRC	King's Royal Rifle Corps
L/Lce	Lance
LNL	Loyal North Lancs Regiment
MC	Military Cross
Mem	Memorial
MGC	Machine Gun Corps
MM	Military Medal
Mon	Monument
NSR	North Staffs Regiment
NSW	New South Wales
OP	Observation Point
RB	Ross Bastiaan Commemorative Plaque
RE	Royal Engineers
RF	Royal Fusiliers
RFC	Royal Flying Corps
RHA	Royal Horse Artillery
RI/R d'I	(French) Infantry Regiment
RIF	Royal Irish Fusiliers
RIR	Royal Irish Rifles
RIR	(German) Infantry Reserve Regiment
RIT	(French) Territorial Infantry Regiment
RN	Royal Navy
RND	Royal Naval Division
RWF	Royal Welsh Fusiliers
SAF	South African Forces
SLI	Somerset Light Infantry
SOA	Site of Action
Sqn	Squadron
SWB	South Wales Borderers
VAD	Voluntary Aid Detachment
VC	Victoria Cross
WFA	Western Front Association

Introduction

'The general conduct of the war has been entrusted to incompetent men — there the trouble lies.'
War Diary of King Albert of the Belgians, 5 December 1916

Few campaigns of recent history provoke such emotive opinions as those consequent upon a discussion of *'The Battle of the Somme'* in 1916.

There are two main camps: those who believe the British Commander-in-Chief, Sir Douglas Haig, to have been an incompetent butcher, and those who admire his moral and leadership qualities

Apart from the growing awareness among the general public of the human cost of the two World Wars and the inclusion of these wars in the history syllabuses of British schools, there is the visible evidence of war memorials and cemeteries scattered beside the trans-Europe holiday routes to serve as a lasting reminder and to prompt enquiring minds.

Over the past quarter of a century we have travelled the battlefield of the Somme alone or in the company of hundreds of such enquiring minds, aged from 9 to over 100, each striving to come to terms with the grim statistics of World War I, and in particular with the casualties suffered by the British on 1 July 1916, the first day of the battle, one of the worst single days in the history of the British Army. Some modern historians, like Peter Simkins, formerly of the Imperial War Museum, John Terraine and more recently Lt Colonel Phillip Robinson of the Durand Group (qv), in their careful analysis of the casualty figures for the whole war, are anxious to dispel what they consider to be the emotional myth of a whole generation of Britain's youth being wiped out. But there is no disputing the horror of that single, black day, and its effects in the home towns and villages of the Pals Battalions of the Midlands, the West and the North. Almost 60,000 men were killed, wounded or missing. In a single column, spaced at arm's length, they would stretch 30 miles. Their nominal role would take two weeks to read.

Many of the professional soldiers of the British Expeditionary Force, the 'Contemptible Army' of Mons, le Cateau, Neuve Chapelle and Loos were already dead or had 'Blighty ones'. It was, therefore, on the whole, a brave new army that climbed over the top on that hot summer's morning. It was a citizen army, Kitchener's Army, volunteers all, most new to battle, most young and most to become casualties. One-third of the latter still lie under the battlefield.

In March 1918 the German Army launched 'Operation Michael', a final, all-out attempt to win the war. It nearly succeeded. German forces were stopped just 10 miles from Amiens by British and Australian tenacity and the blame for the near disaster was laid upon General Gough and his Fifth Army. Foch became Supreme Commander, tank fought tank for the first time, the fresh and enthusiastic Americans joined the battle and a final Allied drive to Victory began.

In addition to the host of wartime memoirs, some of which appeared as factual accounts, others disguised as novels, the tradition of guidebooks about the battlefields of the Somme is a long one. As early as 1917 John Masefield published *The Old Front Line*. From 1919 the Michelin series of *Guides to the Battle-fields* were published — with two volumes on *'The Somme'* and a separate volume on *'Amiens'*. In 1928 H. A. Taylor, Capt (retired) Royal Fusiliers and General Staff, wrote *Good-bye to the Battlefields* and in 1935 Lt Col Graham Seton Hutchison DSO, MC, wrote *Pilgrimage*. Seton-Hutchinson, who at the age of 27 commanded a Machine Gun Corps battalion on the Western Front, had also served in Egypt, the Sudan, South Africa and Rhodesia. A friend of Maj Gen Sir Ernest Swinton, originator of the tank, he became a member of the Army Society for Historical Research and fellow World War I soldier, Field Marshal Sir Bernard Montgomery, wrote a glowingly complimentary foreword to Seton-Hutchison's 1945 book *The British Army*.

Since the end of World War II there has been a resurgence in such books. This guidebook conducts the reader to those memorials and sites of both the 1916 and 1918 battles, and the actions of 1917, that have been most requested over the years by our travellers. The brief commentaries at each stop are designed to summarise events and to orientate the reader so that he or she knows broadly who was where, and what happened. A continuous description of the various parts of the Somme battles are given in the Historical Summaries below.

It is also our aim to prompt more questions than we answer: it must not be sufficient merely to tour the Somme battlefield and to say, 'So this is where it happened'. We must ask, 'Why?', and then each seek an answer.

The Commonwealth War Graves Commission's Charter states that the British and Commonwealth memorials and cemeteries should be maintained 'in perpetuity'. Just how long is 'perpetuity'? It is up to those who seized John McCrae's torch to make sure that it means 'forever'.

Certainly the number of new museums, visitors' centres and memorials that have sprung up on the Somme since the last edition of this book would indicate that the flame of interest and remembrance is burning even more brightly than ever. This particularly applies to the 1918 Australian sector and the important new Visitors' Centres at Thiépval and Newfoundland Memorial Park.

Incorporating these new developments and covering (on the journeys to and back from the Somme) some aspects of the adjoining 1917 Battle for Arras and the 1918 American and French sectors has vastly expanded the scope and range of this book to make it a veritable encyclopaedia of the Somme and surrounding WW1 Battles. Of considerable concern was the proposed construction of a third airport to serve Paris, to be sited in the Santerre, which would have a seriously detrimental impact on the Somme battlefield and cemeteries. In July 2002, however, it seemed as if the Mayor of Amiens, and newly-created Minister For Transport, Gilles de Robien, had achieved at least a major postponement of the project.

There are well over 100,000 individual stories of valour, of loyalty and of endurance to tell about this area. By highlighting some of them we hope to bring the battlefield and the memory of the men who fought, and often died, here, alive.

Tonie & Valmai Holt
Sandwich, September 2002

How To Use This Guide

This book is designed to guide the visitor around the salient features, memorials, museums and cemeteries of the Somme battlefield, and to provide sufficient information about those places to allow an elemental understanding of what happened where.

Prior To Your Visit

Before setting out on a visit, read this section thoroughly and mark up the two recommended maps with the routes that you intend to follow. Waterproof footwear and binoculars are recommended.

Choosing Your Routes

The content and sequence of the itineraries are based upon our long experience of visiting the area with interested people. Itinerary One, therefore, contains those features that have been the most requested, and Itinerary Two those next in popularity… and so on. Thus, if you are a first-time visitor, you will probably wish to start with Itinerary One and follow the sequence. This is also the itinerary that you may well choose if you only have one day. American, Australian, Canadian and French visitors will probably first wish to see the sectors where their countrymen fought.

If You Wish To Visit A Particular Spot

Use the Index to locate what you wish to visit. If it is a particular grave, find the location from the Commonwealth War Graves Commission Debt of Honour website before you set out (see below).

The Itineraries

There are five Itineraries. The first three are long – each approximately 8 hours of touring if followed in full – while the fourth, which is short, can be done on a return journey to the Channel Ports. **Itinerary One** contains what are probably the main features of remembrance for the British for the fighting of 1 July 1916 – north of the Albert-Bapaume Road, the Ancre and up to Serre. **Itinerary Two** focuses south of the road on the action at 'the Woods' (Mametz, Bernafay, Trones, Delville and High) and **Itinerary Three** covers the action of the Australians in the 1918 Defence of Amiens, the Allied successes of August 1918, together with some lesser-known and French 1916 sectors in the Somme Valley. **Itinerary Four** covers British, French and Australian actions around Péronne and St Quentin to Bapaume (and extends to Bullecourt) of 1914, 1916,

1917 and 1918. This is followed by **Itinerary Five** which covers some of the American, Canadian and French 1918 sectors. Details of the itinerary routes are given at the beginning of each so that you can mark them on your maps.

Extra Visits

In addition extra visits are described to sites of particular interest which lie near to the route of the main Itineraries. These are boxed so that they clearly stand out from the main route. Estimates of the round-trip mileage and duration are given.

Miles Covered/Duration/OP/RWC

A start point for each itinerary is given, from which a running total of miles is indicated. Extra visits are not counted in that running total. Each recommended stop is indicated by a clear heading with the running total, and the probable time you will wish to spend there. The letters OP in the heading indicate a view point, from which salient points of the battlefield are described. RWC indicates refreshment and toilet facilities. Travel directions are written in italics and indented to make them stand out clearly. An end point is suggested, with a total distance and timing – without deviations or refreshment stops.

It is absolutely essential to set your mileage trip to zero before starting and to make constant reference to it. Odometers can vary from car to car, so your total mileage may differ slightly from that given in this book. What is important, however, is the distance between stops. Distances in the headings are given in miles because the trip meters on British cars still operate in miles. Distances within the text are sometimes given in kilometres and metres, as local signposts use these measures.

Length Of Stay

Some fortunate visitors to the Somme Battlefield may have the luxury of two weeks in the area – in which time a leisurely and thorough coverage of the battlefield would be achieved and all the itineraries and extra visits could easily be made. Most people, in our experience, have between one and three days. The itineraries are designed so that sections of them can be followed at the individual's convenience – you may not be interested in visiting every item that is described on an itinerary. All cemeteries that are on or very close to an itinerary are, at least, mentioned. Reading the descriptions in advance will help you decide whether you wish to stop or to embark on a diversion or not.

Approaches

On the assumption that most visitors reach the Somme from one of the Channel Ports, or the Tunnel Terminus, two interesting approaches are suggested. **Approach One** is short and direct and takes the visitor into the eastern edge of the battlefield, thereby starting the tour by visiting the important museum, the *Historial* at Péronne. **Approach Two** comes in to the western edge of the battlefield and meanders through a series of alternative visits to Amiens. If the Somme tour is to be taken at the end of a holiday, one would arrive from the Paris direction on the motorway at Péronne, and from Normandy at Amiens, via Abbeville.

Maps

The guide book has been designed to be used with *Major & Mrs Holt's Battle Map of the Somme,* and the words 'Map –' in the heading indicate the map reference for that location. Frequent use of this map will also assist you in orientating, give a clear indication of the distances involved in possible walks and show points of interest which are not included in the itineraries or extra visits.

The faces of 1916, now, sadly anonymous

Iron harvest at Serre

Also recommended is the *Michelin No 236 Nord: Flandres-Artois-Picardie* (which, incidentally, will also serve you through Cambrai, Loos, Neuve Chapelle, le Cateau, Mons and Ypres). A warning, however – French road numbers change with distressing frequency. Be philosophical if the road numbers given either in this guide or the map have changed when you reach them.

History Of The Battle

The historical notes given at each recommended stop can in no way be continuous and sequential. It is therefore recommended that the visitor precedes his/her tour by reading the Historical Summary on page 13.

Enjoying The Somme

The *Département* of the Somme is a particularly beautiful region of France and there are some excellent restaurants and hotels in the area. Some handily placed hostelleries are mentioned as they appear in the itineraries. For more information, read the Somme Past and Present (page 270) and Tourist Information (page 269) sections, and consult 'Hotels' and 'Restaurants' in the index.

A Warning

It is most unwise to pick up any 'souvenirs' in the form of bullets, shells, grenades, barbed wire etc that may be found on the battlefield. To this day, builders making foundations and farmers on the Somme when ploughing – especially fields which have been used as pasture for many years – turn up the sad remains of World War I soldiers, bits of equipment and ammunition. The latter are then piled up at a corner of the field to await collection by the French Army bomb disposal unit. During the making of the TGV railway line, 140 tonnes of WWI 'hardware' were collected, and an average year yields 90 tonnes. It is known as the 'iron harvest', and it is extremely dangerous to handle – accidents still often occur. Indeed, in the summer of 1985 several deaths occurred on the Somme from WWI ammunition, much of which is extremely volatile. Leaking gas shells are particularly unpleasant. The authors once saw one smoking in a field next to the CWGC Cemetery at Delville Wood. Cuts from sharp, rusting objects can cause blood poisoning or tetanus. It also seems more fitting for such items to be left where they are, as many of them find their way into local museums, where they can be seen by generations of future visitors. Safe souvenirs can be bought at the Visitors' Centre at Delville Wood.

Historical Summary

1916

The 1916 Battle of the Somme lasted from 1 July to 17 November. It was opened by a 100 per cent volunteer British Army, over half of which was new to battle and had, barely 18 months earlier, answered Kitchener's call to arms.

The Commander of the British Expeditionary Force (BEF) was also new. General French had been replaced by his critic, General Haig, and now the latter had to prove his worth.

At the end of 1915, the French and British planned for a 1916 joint offensive on the Somme, with the French playing the major role. Masterminded by Joffre, the plan was (as far as Joffre was concerned) to kill more Germans than their pool of manpower could afford. But when the German assault at Verdun drew French forces away from the Somme, the British found themselves with the major role, providing sixteen divisions on the first day to the French five.

The British plan was based upon a steady 14-mile wide infantry assault from Serre in the north to Maricourt in the south. 100,000 soldiers were to go over the top at the end of a savage artillery bombardment. Behind the infantry – men of the Fourth Army, commanded by General Rawlinson – waited two cavalry divisions, under General Gough. Their role was to exploit success. Thus, Haig's plan looked very much like an attempt at a breakthrough and not as an attrition battle as conceived by Joffre.

When the early assaults failed to penetrate the German lines, the British Staff set about denying that they had ever intended to do such a thing. To many, their protestations appeared to be attempts to cover up the failure of Haig's plan, and, as the C-in-C continued with his costly and unimaginative attacks, other voices demanded his removal. But he kept his job. He was, after all, a confidant of the King and a pillar of the Establishment.

By the time that the battle ended, British casualties exceeded 400,000. The British secret weapon, the tank, had been used against expert advice in a penny packet operation in September at Flers-Courcelette. Could it have been a desperate attempt by Haig to gain some sort of victory that would offset his earlier failures?

In October and November, piecemeal attacks continued when the heavy rains allowed, and, in a break in the weather on 13 November, the British took Beaumont Hamel. What had been achieved since July? On the ground very little: a maximum advance of 8 miles. Haig said that the battle had been a success and had achieved the aim that he had placed first on his list of aims – 'To relieve the pressure on Verdun'. Certainly the German offensive at Verdun had been stopped, but how could the C-in-C maintain that it had been the prime objective of the Somme offensive when the decision to attack the Somme was made by him and Joffre a week before the Verdun battle began? Again, there is the smell of smokescreen in the air.

There can be no denying, however, that the administrative preparations for the coming battle were very thorough.

Administrative Preparations for the 1916 Somme Battle

In 1915 at Loos, the orders for the attack were contained on some two pages. In February 1916, GHQ issued a fifty-seven-page memorandum setting out the preparations that should be undertaken before large-scale operations. Things had changed.

To prepare for the battle, a mini-city had to be built and supplied. The planning requirement looked for '7 weeks' lodging for 400,000 men and 100,000 horses'. Extra accommodation was set up for 15,000 men per division in wooden framed tarpaulin-walled huts – but only with lying down space of 6ft x 2ft per man. New trenches, roads and railways were constructed. It was estimated that the Fourth Army alone would need thirty-one trains per day to sustain it. Not only was it necessary to prepare roads and railways prior to a battle, but they had to be extended forward to maintain supplies of immediate needs, such as infantry stores, guns and ammunition essential to sustain an advance. Specialist RE units, together with labour and/or pioneer battalions did the work. Following the successful September 1916 attack on 'the Woods', 7th Field Company RE was tasked to build 'tramways' forward, and used 60m Decauville prefabricated track. By the end of October, 8 miles of track had been laid in two lines. One was from Contalmaison to beyond Martinpuich and the other from Mametz Wood to High Wood. The second in command of the company was a Lt Glubb, later to be known as **Lt Gen Sir John Glubb KCB, CMG, DSO, OBE, MC – 'Glubb Pasha'**, Commander of the Arab Legion. Water supply was a particular problem and more than a hundred pumping plants were set up and over 120 miles of piping laid. The range of facilities to be provided for was legion – food, ammunition, medical reinforcements, workshops and postal facilities – all involving movement. A telling measure of the scale of the challenge is given in the *Official History* (1916, p 283). One of the critical tasks on a battlefield is traffic control and a 24-hour traffic census taken at Fricourt three weeks after the battle began lists the following, almost unbelievable, administrative activities:
'Troops 26,536, Light Motor Cars 568, Motor cycles 617, Motor lorries 813, 6-horse wagons 1,458, 4-horse wagons 568, 2-horse wagons 1,215, 1-horse carts 515, Riding horses 5,404, Motor ambulances 333, Cycles 1,043', and this is not a complete list.

The Commander-in-Chief

As pointed out in the Introduction, those who study World War I tend to fall into two main camps: those who are anti-Haig and those who are pro-Haig. But there are those who veer from one opinion to the other, according to the quality of the debate. Was the C-in-C a dependable rock, whose calm confidence inspired all around him, whose far-seeing eye led us to final victory, and who deserved the honours later heaped upon him?

John Masefield, asked by Haig to write an account of the Somme battle, visited him at GHQ in October 1916. Masefield was extremely impressed by this 'wonderful' man. 'No enemy could stand against such a man', he enthused. 'He took away my breath.' He described Haig's 'fine delicate gentleness and generosity ... pervading power ... and a height of resolve .... I don't think anyone could have been nicer.'

Was this the real Haig, or was he an unimaginative, insensitive product of the social caste system that knew no better: a weak man pretending to be strong, who should have been sacked? **Dennis Wheatley**, in his war-time memoirs, *Officer and Temporary Gentleman* opines, 'He was a pleasant, tactful, competent, peacetime soldier devoted to his duty, but he had a rooted dislike of the French and was not even a second-rate General. Many of the high-ups were well aware of that, but the question had always been, with whom could they replace him?'

Many more pages than are available here are needed to pursue those questions fairly and to examine the Battle of the Somme in any detail. But some pointers can be set by a skeleton examination of the battle that, with Passchendaele in 1917, led soldiers, rightly or wrongly, to describe their C-in-C as 'Butcher' Haig.

The Different Parts of the Battle

The Battle is divided into 5 parts:
Part 1. The First Day: 1 July
Part 2. The Next Few Days: 2 July +
Part 3. The Night Attack/ The Woods: 14 July +
Part 4. The Tank Attack: 15 September
Part 5. The last Attack: 13 November.

Part 1. The First Day: 1 July

At 0728, seventeen mines were blown under the German front line. Two minutes later, 60,000 British soldiers, laden down with packs, gas masks, rifle and bayonet, 200 rounds of ammunition, grenades, empty sandbags, spade, mess tin and waterbottle, iron rations, mackintosh sheet, warmed by the issue of rum, 'to each a double spoonful, fed baby-fashion by the sergeant' [Williamson], clambered out of their trenches from Serre to Maricourt and formed into lines 14 miles long. As the lines moved forward in waves, so the artillery barrage lifted off the enemy front line and rolled forward.

Now it was a life or death race, but the Tommies did not know it. They had not been entered. Their instructions were to move forward, side by side, at a steady walk across No Man's Land. 'Strict silence will be maintained during the advance through the smoke', they were instructed, 'and no whistles will be blown'. It would be safe, they were told, because the artillery barrage would have destroyed all enemy opposition. It started on 24 June. Over 3,000,000 shells had been stockpiled but these proved to be insufficient. There were still many duds, despite the outcry of the 'Scandal' about duds after the Battle of Loos. Most of them were due to shoddy and defective workmanship – sub-standard steel casings cracked and burst prematurely; copper driving bands were faulty; the hot summer weather caused the explosives to exude; unburnt fuses remained in the bore and many other lethal inadequacies caused some gun crews to christen themselves 'the Suicide Club'. Despite borrowing guns from the French, the Artillery were short of heavy weapons. The original date for the assault, ('The Big Push'), was 29 June. On 28 June the offensive was postponed to 1 July because of bad weather and there was insufficient ammunition to maintain the same level of bombardment intensity for an extra two days. Because of these factors and the doubtful efficacy of artillery against wire, the Germans were not destroyed, as had glibly been promised. They and their machine guns had sheltered in deep dugouts, and when the barrage lifted, they climbed out, dragging their weapons with them.

The Germans easily won the race. They set up their guns before the Tommies could get to the trenches to stop them and cut down the ripe corn of British youth in their thousands, many on the uncut wire that they had been assured would be totally destroyed. As the day grew into hot summer, another 40,000 men were sent in, in successive waves, stepping over the bodies of their wounded companions ('All ranks are forbidden to divert attention from enemy in order to attend wounded officers or men'), adding only more names to the casualty lists. Battalions disappeared in the bloody chaos of battle, bodies lay in their hundreds around the muddy shell holes that pocked the battlefield.

And to what end this leeching of the nation's best blood? North of the Albert-Bapaume road, on a front of almost 9 miles, there were no realistic gains at nightfall. VIII, X and III Corps had failed. Between la Boisselle and Fricourt there was a small penetration of about half a mile on one flank and the capture of Mametz village on the other by XV Corps.

But there was some sucess. XIII Corps attacking beside the French took all its main objectives, from Pommiers Redoubt east of Mametz, to just short of Dublin Redoubt north of Maricourt. Overall some thirteen fortified villages were targetted to be taken on the first day, but only two – Mametz and Montauban – were actually captured. The French, south of the Somme, did extremely well. Attacking at 0930, they easily took all their objectives. 'They had more guns than we did', cried the British Generals, or 'The opposition wasn't as tough', or 'The Germans didn't expect to be attacked by the French', or 'They had easier terrain'. But whatever the reasons for the poor British performance in the north, they had had some success – on the right flank beside the French.

Therefore, if the attack was to continue the next day, would it not make sense to follow-up quickly on the right where things were going well?

Part 2. The Next Few Days: 2 July +

Other than the negative one of not calling off the attack, no General Command decisions were made concerning the overall conduct of the second day's battle.

It was as if all the planning had been concerned with 1 July and that the staffs were surprised by the appearance of 2 July. Aggressive actions were mostly initiated at Corps level while Haig and Rawlinson figured out what policy they ought to follow.

Eventually they decided to attack on the right flank, but by then the Germans had had two weeks to recover.

Part 3. The Night Attack/The Woods: 14 July +

On the XIII Corps front, like fat goalposts, lay the woods of Bazentin le Petit on the left and Delville on the right. Behind and between them, hunched on the skyline, was the dark goalkeeper of High Wood. Rawlinson planned to go straight for the goal. Perhaps the infantry general's memory had been jogged by finding one of his old junior officer's notebooks in which the word 'surprise' had been written as a principle of attack, because, uncharacteristically, he set out to surprise the Germans and not in one way, but in two.

First, despite Haig's opposition, he moved his assault forces up to their start line in Caterpillar Valley at night. Second, after a mere minute's dawn barrage, he launched his attack. At 0325 on 14 July, twenty thousand men moved forward. On the left were 7th and 21st Divisions of XV Corps and on the right 3rd and 9th Divisions of XIII Corps. The effect was dramatic. Five miles of the German second line were over-run. On the left Bazentin-le-Petit Wood was taken. On the right began the horrendous six day struggle for Delville Wood. Today the South African memorial and museum in the wood commemorate the bitter fighting.

But in the centre, 7th Division punched through to High Wood and with it were two squadrons of cavalry. Perhaps here was an opportunity for a major break-through at last. Not since 1914 had mounted cavalry charged on the Westen Front, but, when they did, the Dragoons and the Deccan Horse were alone. The main force of the cavalry divisions, gathered south of Albert, knew nothing about the attack. The charge was a costly failure, the moment passed, the Germans recovered, counter-attacked and regained the wood.

Then followed two months of local fighting under the prompting of Joffre, but, without significant success to offer, the C-in-C began to attract increasing criticism. Something had to be done to preserve his image, to win a victory – or both. It was done, and with a secret weapon.

Part 4. The Tank Attack: 15 September

Through the prompting of Col Ernest Swinton and Winston Churchill, the War Office sponsored the construction, by William Foster & Co in Lincoln, of a machine that could cross trenches and was both armed and armoured.

By August 1916 the machine, code-named the 'tank' because of its resemblance to a water tank (later christened variously by journalists as 'Diplodocus Galumphang', 'Polychromatic Toad' and 'Flat-footed Monster'), was, following highly successful trials, beginning production. Both Swinton and Churchill considered it essential that no use should be made of the secret weapon until it was available in large numbers. But Haig insisted that he needed them and, late in August, forty-nine were shipped to France. Still very new and liable to break down, only thirty-two tanks assembled near Trones Wood on the night of 14 September for dispersal along the front, and the following morning at 0620, following a three-day bombardment, eighteen took part in the battle with XV Corps. Their effect was sensational. The Germans, on seeing the monsters, were stunned and then terrified. Nine tanks moved forward with the leading infantry, nine 'mopped up' behind. Barely over 3 hours later, the left hand division of XV Corps followed a solitary tank up the main street of Flers and through the German third line. Then Courcelette, too, fell to an infantry/tank advance.

The day's gains were the greatest since the battle began and much jubilation was felt on the Home Front, whipped up by the press. But there were too few tanks and, after the intitial shock success, the fighting once again degenerated into a bull-headed contest. The opportunity that had existed to use the tank to obtain a major strategic result had been lost. Many felt that it had been squandered. Yet the tank had allowed Fourth Army to advance and the dominating fortress of Thiépval finally fell on 26 September, helped, it was said, 'by the appearance of 3 tanks'. At last the British were on the crest of the Thiépval-Pozières-High Wood ridge. But Beaumont Hamel in the north still held out.

Part 5. The Last Attack: 13 November

At the northern end of the battlefield, seven Divisions of the Reserve (Fifth) Army assaulted at 0545 on 13 November. Bad weather had caused seven postponements since the original date of 24 October. V Corps was north of the River Ancre and II Corps was south. The preparatory bombardment had been carefully monitored to see that the enemy wire had been cut, but this eminent practicality was offset by the stationing of cavalry behind the line to exploit success. Apart from the overwhelming evidence of past battle experience that should have made such an idea absurd, the weather's effect on the ground alone should have rendered it unthinkable. The generals were as firmly stuck for ideas as any Tommy, up to his knees in Somme mud, was stuck for movement.

But this time the mines were fired at the right time. On 1 July the Hawthorn mine above Beaumont Hamel had been blown 10 minutes early. The Sappers now tunnelled back under the old crater, which had been turned into a fortification by the Germans and placed 30,000 lbs of explosives beneath it. It was blown at 0545 and covered the German trenches with debris.

The attack went in with a shield of early morning dark and fog, the troops moving tactically from cover to cover. Beaumont Hamel and the infamous Y Ravine were taken by the 51st Highland Division and their kilted Highlander memorial stands there today in memory of that achievement. Immediately to the south of the 51st, the Royal Naval Division took Beaucourt early on the morning of the 14th and their memorial stands in the village.

Fighting continued for several more days and 7,000 prisoners were taken – though Serre did not fall. But, at last, enough was enough. The attack was halted.

The 1916 Battle of the Somme was over.

1917

Although the emphasis when studying the battles of the Somme is upon the preceding and following years, fighting did not, of course, cease in the general area in 1917! In particular, of course, there was the Battle of Arras within which was the Canadian action at Vimy and the Australian assault at Bullecourt. As the sites of 1917 actions on the Somme proper are passed they are described in the main Itineraries of this book.

But just as 'The Big Push' was concentrated in the *Départment* of the Somme in 1916, in 1917 actions moved northwards to the *Départment* of the Pas de Calais and the Battle of Arras. Some aspects of this are covered in Approach One (Vimy and the surrounding sectors) and in Itinerary Four (Bullecourt, see page 241).

1918

See also pages 245-254

On 21 March 1918, following a five-hour bombardment by over 6,000 guns, one million German soldiers attacked, in thick fog, along a 50-mile front opposite the British Third and Fifth Armies. The Fifth Army, under General Gough, who had consistently warned the GOC of the weakness of his position, fell back towards Amiens in the face of the onslaught. Barely a week later Gough was blamed for the retreat and replaced by Rawlinson. Haig asked the French for support and brought the Australians down from the north. On 11 April Haig issued a 'Special Order of the Day', saying that '... There is no other course open to us but to fight it out! ... With our backs to the wall and believing in the justice of our cause, each one of us must fight on to the end.' The German advance towards Amiens finally stopped on 24 April when tank first met tank at Cachy and the following morning the Australians re-took Villers Bretonneux. It was ANZAC Day and the importance of their contribution is well-represented today on the Somme and in this book.

The German offensive, codenamed 'Operation Michael', continued to beat elsewhere along the Allied line, but on 8 August came the 'Black Day' of the German Army. The Fourth Army of British, Australian, Canadian and a few attached Americans, achieved complete surprise by opening their counter offensive at 0420, and co-ordinated artillery, infantry, tanks and air force to such effect that 16,000 prisoners were taken that day.

It was the beginning of the final '100 Days' that led to the Armistice of 11 November 1918.

Some Facts & Figures

'Lies, damned lies and statistics' (*attributed to Mark Twain*)

Casualties

Casualty figures and statistics generally are weapons which can be, and often are, falsified to discourage the enemy, encourage one's own forces or alter a view of events to particular advantage. The Somme figures are given alongside those for Verdun, because only by comparison can the Somme casualties be seen in a meaningful light. We do not claim any absolute numeric accuracy for our figures, which have been deduced from a number of sources, including official histories, which often have a nationalistic bias.

Nation	*Somme*		*Verdun*
	1 July	Total	Total
Britain	58,000	420,000	—
France	4,000*	195,000	370,000
Germany	8,000	650,000**	330,000

* No figures are available, but it can confidently be assumed to be less than half the German total of 8,000

** The Germans did not issue figures. This is the official British figure, but many historians consider this to be British wishful thinking, and that the German casualties totalled much the same as the British.

The Battle of Verdun is often presented as the most horrific conflict on the Western Front in terms of human casualties. Yet even allowing for inaccuracies, the comparative figures above show

• that the British had at least equal, if not greater, losses on the Somme than the French at Verdun;

• that the Germans had greater losses on the Somme than they did at Verdun.

Joffre, therefore, had succeeded in his aim of joining the British and Germans in a battle of attrition. By the letting of so much young blood the British were now firmly in the conflict, Joffre had dispelled the French idea that the British were 'not pulling their weight', and the process of wearing down the Germans had speeded up.

The Fourth Army on 1 July

4 ARMY (Rawlinson)

VIII CORPS (Hunter-Weston)
Hébuterne to Beaucourt
48th (SM) Div (Fanshawe)
31st Div (O'Gowan)
4th Div (Lambton)
29th Div (de Lisle)
III CORPS (Pulteney)
Ovillers to la Boisselle
8th Div (Hudson)
19th (W) Div (Bridges)
34th Div (Ingouville-Williams)
XIII CORPS (Congreve, VC)
Carnoy to Maricourt
18th (E) Div (Maxse)
30th Div (Shea)
9th (S) Div (Reserve)
X CORPS (Morland)
Hamel to Authuille
36th Div (Nugent)
49th (WR) Div (Perceval)
32nd Div (Rycroft)
XV CORPS (Horne)
Bécourt to Mametz
21st Div (Campbell)
17th (N) Div (Pilcher)
7th Div (Watts)

SM = South Midlands
WR = West Riding
N = Northern
E = Eastern
S = Scottish
Formations are shown north to south, with inclusive responsibilities.

Approach One

From Calais via motorways A16/A26/E15 to Péronne
This route passes by St Omer, Notre Dame de Lorette and Vimy Ridge, crosses the Somme and goes direct to the *Historial de la Grande Guerre* at Péronne. **Approximate driving time, without stops: 1 hour 40 minutes. Approximate distance: 100 miles.** Remember that these are toll roads. It will save time if you have the correct change ready – which is indicated well ahead.

From Calais as you leave either the ferry port or the tunnel terminal, follow blue motorway signs A16/A26 signed to Paris/Reims, then fork right following blue/green A26/E15 signs St Omer, Lens, Arras.

There are two possible diversions from the direct route. To enjoy the longer route, set aside a day.

Diversion 1: St Omer/RWC

After approximately 24 miles, take Exit 3 and follow signs to St Omer.

Here was GHQ for the BEF during World War I from October 1914 to March 1916, where Lord Roberts died in November 1914. The young Prince of Wales, fresh from his training with the Guards at Warley Barracks, arrived in France just in time for the funeral, marching 'in the grey morning light behind the gun-carriage bearing the coffin. As the small procession made its way over the cobblestones, led by the pipers playing "The Flowers of the Forest", we were all profoundly stirred.' Sir Pertab Singh, who had also come to honour his old friend, 'climbed up on the motor ambulance that would carry the coffin to the Channel' and 'although it was freezing and the ambulance had no wind-shield and Sir Pertab had no greatcoat, no one could restrain him; and he made the icy, two-hour drive to Boulogne.'

St Omer was the site of many hospitals, as **Longuenesse Souvenir Cemetery** (on the D928 to the south of the town) bears witness. It contains 2,364 UK, 156 Australian, 148 Canadian, 52 New Zealand, 24 South African, 12 British West Indies, 5 Indian, 2 Guernsey, 1 Newfoundland, 64 Chinese, 180 German and 5 unknown burials – showing the polyglot nature of World War I. RFC HQ also moved there on 6 October 1914, well described by Maurice Baring in his book, *Flying Corps H.Q., 1914-1918*. They made 'a fine aerodrome on the top of the hill, once a steeplechase course'. Main memories are of German bombs being dropped on them, and 'A constant stream of guests and

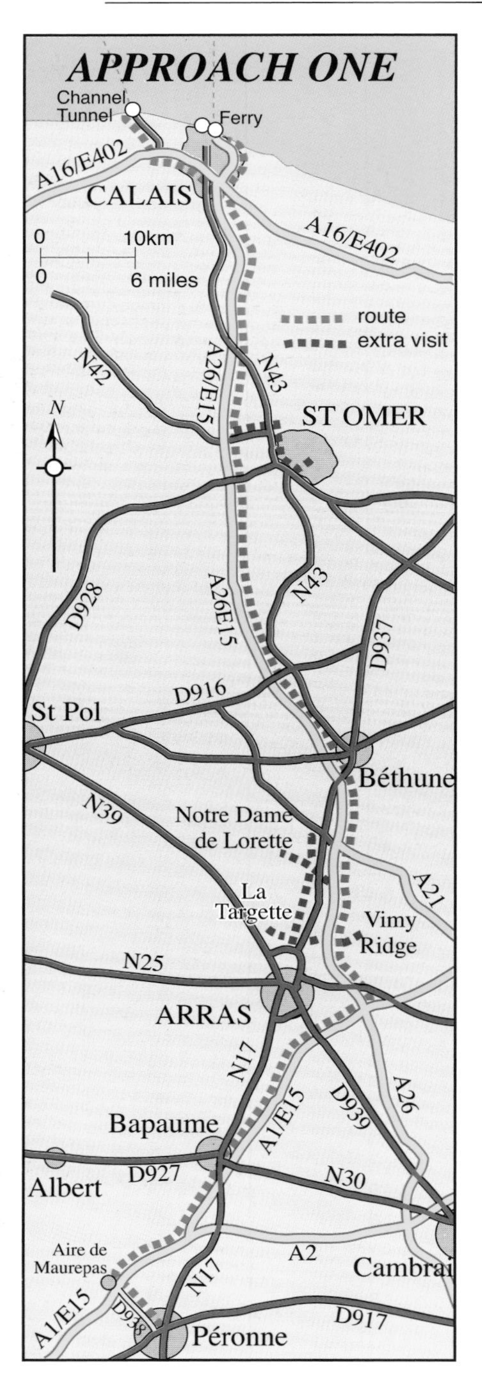

a crowd of people sleeping on the floor; a weekly struggle, sometimes successful and sometimes not, to get a bath in the town, which was always seething with suppliants'.

Today the main square boasts a range of restaurants, and also worth a visit is the cathedral in which Baring heard Mass on St Crispin's Day (25 October), where he 'could not help thinking that Henry V had heard those very same words spoken in the same way just before the battle of Agincourt … not an hour's drive from St Omer'.

Continue. On the left the area of the Loos battlefield, marked by twin slag heaps (the famous double crassier), is passed.

Diversion 2.

Notre Dame de Lorette & French Memorials RWC/OP/ Cabaret Rouge CWGC Cemetery, Czech & Polish Memorials, La Targette–Museum, CWGC Cemetery & French National Cemetery, Neuville St Vaast–German Cemetery, Lichfield Crater CWGC Cemetery, Vimy Ridge Canadian National Memorial, trenches and tunnels/WC

After approximately 58 miles take Exit 6.1, the junction with the A21, fork right and exit immediately signed Liéven, Lens and filter to the right to Bruay en Artois, Aix Noulette. Follow signs to Aix-Noulette, Noeux les Mines. Notre Dame is then signed.

The light tower and basilique can now be seen on the crest to the right.

Continue to the Auberge de Lorette on the right and stop on the left by the memorial.

The **memorial is to the 158th Régiment d'Infanterie**, erected by survivors of the Lorette sector. Before it is the tomb of ***Sous Lieutenant*** **Jean R. Léon,** age 22, 26 May

Statue to Gen Maistre and 21st Army Corps with Notre Dame de Lorette with lantern tower in background

The Basilique and cemetery, Notre Dame de Lorette

Former grave of the Canadian Unknown Soldier, Cabaret Rouge CWGC Cem

Memorial to Gen Barbot and others, 77th Div, Souchez

1915, of the **28th Régiment**, *Legion d'Honneur, Croix de Guerre.*

Walk up the track marked privé to the left to the large memorial on the right.

The **memorial is to *Sous-Lieutenant* Jacques Defrasse**, age 23, 16 June 1915 of the **174th Régiment** and the men of the 3rd Company, killed in the assault on the *Tranchée des Saules* (which was roughly on the site of the track leading to the memorial). One side bears a message from the General commanding the Division praising Cadet Defrasse's courage in the assault on *La Tranchée de Calonne* on 3 May 1915. The other side bears a message from the Corps commander detailing his promotion to *Sous Lieutenant.* Defrasse had only just put his rank stripes on his tunic (to be seen in the Museum at Notre Dame de Lorette) when he was killed.

The memorial is clearly visible from the A21 motorway to the right.

Return to your car and continue to the crossroads signed Notre Dame de Lorette to the right.

The highly painted building to the left houses occasional exhibitions but no longer functions as the advertised European Centre for Peace. Opposite is a former war museum which now contains artisanal artefacts.

Drive up the hill to the Memorials.

At the entrance to the area there is a fine statue to **General Maistre and 21st Army Corps**, erected in 1925.

This vast French National Cemetery, containing 40,057 burials of which 20,000 have individual graves and the rest are in eight ossuaries, is on the site of bitter and costly fighting by the French in 'the Battle of Lorette' from October 1914 to October 1915. It is dominated by an imposing chapel and 52m-high memorial lantern which contains a crypt in which are unknown soldiers and *déportés* from the wars in 1939-45, Indochina (1945-54) and North Africa (1952-62). The 200 steps of the lantern may (when not under repair) be climbed for a superb view over the battlefield and its rotating light can be seen for more than 40 miles around. Between the two edifices is an eternal flame. This is rekindled and the *Tricolore* is raised each Sunday morning after the 1030 Mass in the basilica. The whole area is manned by volunteers from the *Garde d'Honneur de Lorette*, from 0900-1630 in March, until 1730 in April and May, until 1830 in June-August and then until 1630 again until 11 November. There are sixty-four Russians, one Belgian and one Rumanian graves. The first grave on the left as you enter the cemetery is that of **General Barbot** of **77th (French) Div**, whose impressive divisional memorial is in Souchez village. He was killed here on 10 May 1915. To the left of the entrance to the cemetery is an **orientation table** erected in May 1976 by *Le Train de Loos*. It points to Vimy Ridge and to the ruined church of Mont St Eloi (preserved as a memorial) in the valley below. At the far side of the cemetery is an excellent museum with an audio-visual presentation, life-like dioramas and many interesting artefacts and documents.

Recent acquisitions include the complete uniform and personal belongings of *Sous Lieutenant* Defrasse (qv), donated by the family in 2000, a complete Scottish uniform and an immense British naval shell. In the diorama room are stereoscopic viewers, arranged in chronological order of the various stages of the battles in the area, a drinks machine and tables and benches where picnics may be eaten. **Open every day** 0900-2000. ☎ (03) 21 45 15 80. Entry fee payable.

The old cafeteria building nearby was temporarily closed at the time of going to press. In front of the museum is a memorial to **Sous Lieutenant Henri Merlin**, age 24, **10th *Chasseurs à Pied***, 3 March 1915. His citation by the General commanding the 10th Army describes how he fought until his position was overrun by the enemy, made sure that his surviving comrades escaped and then committed suicide rather than retreat.

Return down the hill.

The tip of the Vimy Memorial may be seen ahead and to the right, and the Loos battlefield to the left.

Turn right to Souchez.

On leaving the village is a fine bronze **statue and memorial to General Barbot** (qv) and the 77th Division with plaques to **General Stirn**, 1871-1915 and **General Plessner**, 1856-1914. In 2002 a **memorial** was raised next to it to the **Algerians**.

Continue to the cemetery on the right.

Cabaret Rouge CWGC Cemetery was started by the British 47th Division in March 1916 and used by fighting units including the Canadian Corps until September 1918. The original 'Cabaret Rouge' was a house near the site of the cemetery. To the east were dugouts used as Battalion HQ in 1916 and communication trenches ended here. This large cemetery (with nearly 8,000 burials) was enlarged by concentration of graves from the nearby battlefields after the Armistice. It was from here that the **Canadian Unknown Soldier** was taken on 25 May 2000 from Grave 7, Row E, Plot 8 (and which now bears a headstone explaining the ceremony) and removed to the Tomb of the Unknown Warrior at the foot of the National War Memorial in Ottawa, Canada. To the right under the imposing entrance arch is a plaque to the designer of the cemetery, **Brigadier Sir Frank Higgins, CB, CMG, ARIBA**, who was Secretary to the IWGC 1947-1956. His ashes were scattered here after his death on 20 November 1958 (as were his wife's in 1962).

Continue to Neuville St Vaast.

On the right is the **Czech Memorial and Cemetery**. The Czechs joined the French Foreign Legion in Paris in 1914 and fought with the Moroccans in the May 1915 Artois Offensive as part of the French 10th Army. The memorial refers to the attack of 9 May 1915 on the German strongpoint at Hill 140 in Thélus. The hill was taken but the Czechs had 80% casualties. The memorial was erected in 1925 and behind it are graves from WW2 (including a Captain Aviator, complete with photograph, from 1940).

Across the road is the

Polish Memorial, Neuville St Vaast

Cross and Jewish headstone, with Memorial to 44th Hannover IR in the background, German Cem, Neuville St Vaast

Polish Memorial. The Poles were also part of the Foreign Legion and took part in the same attack on Hill 140. The memorial was inaugurated on 9 May 1935, twenty years after the battle.

Continue to the crossroads in the centre of la Targette village. On the left is

La Targette Torch in Hand Memorial. The memorial was completed on 20 October 1932 and commemorates the rebirth of the village, totally destroyed in May 1916. It is reminiscent of the concept explored in John McCrae's famous poem *In Flanders Fields - To you we throw the torch - Be yours to hold it high.*

On the opposite corner is the well-maintained private **La Targette Museum,** owned by David Bardiaux (who also owns the Notre Dame de Lorette Museum). It contains a superb collection of uniforms, Allied and German gas masks, weapons and artefacts and has several well-presented scenes of trench, aid post and dugout life. **Open everyday** 0900-2000.

If you continue on the D937, La Targette CWGC Cemetery is signed just a few metres off the road to the right.

La Targette CWGC Cemetery, described in the Register as "known until recently" as Aux Rietz Military Cemetery, was begun at the end of April 1917 and used by Field Ambulances and fighting units until September 1918. One-third of the burials are of Artillery Units. They also include 295 Canadians, 3 Indians and 3 South Africans. There is one WW2 burial. Adjoining it is

La Targette French National Cemetery. The perfectly symmetrical pattern of lines of white crosses, which changes from each angle, stretches up the slope to three ossuaries. Built in 1919 it is formed exclusively from concentrations from the surrounding battlefield and other small cemeteries. It contains 11,443 burials (including 3,882 unknown) from WW1 and 593 French, 170 Belgian and 4 Poles from WW2.

Continue to the sign to the German Cemetery on the left.

Torch in hand Memorial, la Targette

German dressing station diorama, La Targette WW1 Museum

Neuville St Vaast German Cemetery. This is on the site of the heavily defended German position known as 'The Labyrinth', graphically described by French writer Henri Barbusse and English writer Henry Williamson. It contains 37,000 burials with 8,000 in a mass grave. In the centre is a stone monument erected by the old comrades of the **4th Hannover Inf Regt, No 164** with the inscriptions *Ich hatt einen Kameraden Ein Bessern findst du nicht* (I have a comrade whose better you could not find) and *Sei getreu bis in den Tod* (Stay true, even unto death). There are WCs to the left of the entrance.

Lichfield Crater CWGC Cem

Return to La Targette crossroads. From La Targette crossroads take the turning (to the right if you have been to the German cemetery, to the left if you haven't) signed to the Canadian Memorial. Continue through Neuville St Vaast to the sign to the right to Lichfield Crater.

Lichfield Crater CWGC Cemetery is one of the most unusual on the Western Front. It is in one of two mine craters (the other being Zivy crater) used by the Canadian Corps Burial Officer in 1917 for bodies from the Vimy battlefield who all died on 9 or 10 April 1917. It was designed by W. H. Cowlishaw and was originally called only by letters and numbers - CB 2A. The grassed circular cemetery is essentially a mass grave and contains only one headstone (to **Pte A Stubbs,** S Lancs Regiment, age 25, 30 April 1916) found after the Armistice. It is surrounded by beautiful stone and flint walls and the Cross of Sacrifice is on a raised level. Below it is a memorial wall on which are the names and details of 41 Canadians soldiers who are buried here. There are also 11 unidentified Canadians, 4 completely unidentified men and 1 unidentified Russian.

Return to the main road, turn right and continue to the well-signed entrance to the Vimy Ridge Canadian Memorial Park.

N.B. Note that you are now travelling in the direction of the well-planned and successful Canadian attack on Vimy Ridge, strongly fortified and held by the Germans for the first three years of the war, despite several brave and costly attempts by the French to take it. Following a well-timed artillery barrage the attack went in at daybreak on 9 April 1917 with all four divisions of the Canadian Corps fighting together for the first time under General Byng. By mid-afternoon they had taken the entire 14km long ridge except for Hill 145 (the highest point upon which the Memorial now stands) which they captured three days later. The price was 10,602 casualties, 3,598 of which were killed.

Turn into the park and drive past the parking area for the Tunnels/Trenches and park near the Interpretative Centre.

Vimy Ridge Canadian National Memorial & Park/WC

By the parking area is an information kiosk where guides can be found. These are well-trained Canadian students who compete eagerly for the honour of telling their Nation's proud story at Vimy and are available between 1 April and 30 November from 1000-1800. There are also public phone boxes and washrooms here.

The commemorative area is divided into three: the Interpretative Centre, the Memorial and the Tunnels/Trenches. It is recommended to visit the former first. Opened in 1997 (and a bronze plaque outside commemorates this) the **Centre** has informative panels and photographs, some trench periscopes, a circular audio-visual explanation of the battle with video screens and commentary in English, French and German and a small book stall. **Open every day (except two weeks around Christmas) 1000-1800.**

Next the imaginative **Memorial** should be visited. Designed by Canadian sculptor Walter Allward (who also designed the Superintendent's house and who said the design came to him in a dream) it was the winning entry for a Canadian Memorial competition (originally to be reproduced wherever Canadians fought with valour, but then considered to be too expensive to duplicate elsewhere). The front of the memorial, with its towering twin pylons representing the Anglo-Saxon and French elements of the nation and/or the sacrifices made by both Canada and France in taking the position, depicts a mourning figure overlooking the Plain of Douai. It was carved from a single 30-ton block of stone. The memorial stands on Hill 145, the last feature to fall. It was unveiled on 26 July 1936 (it took four years longer to build than was at first estimated) by King Edward VIII, his only official overseas engagement as King. A $30 million restoration project for Canadian memorials and sites will include major repairs to this memorial using the original high quality stone.

Drive round to the parking area for the Tunnels/Trenches.

En route on the right is passed the **Moroccan Division Memorial** commemorating the 9 May 1915 battle here. Bronze panels around the stone monument list the ORBAT of the Division (motto *Sans peur, sans pitié* - without fear, without pity) and also recognise the contribution of other foreigners, including the Jews, Greeks, Sudanese and Czechs.

To the right **Canadian Cemetery No 2** and **Givenchy Road Canadian Cemetery** are signed.

It was generally believed that each of the trees which grow in abundance here represents one of the 66,655 Canadian soldiers (their dead for the entire war) whose names are listed on the Memorial and that they came from Canada. But the entire region is well-populated with these trees, which are actually Austrian firs, as three containers of seed for them arrived by train after the war as part of Germany's repatriation price. Beneath the trees, shell-holes, craters and lines of trenches you are passing are a series of German and Allied tunnels which were packed with mines and then exploded. The 100-hectare memorial park is full of unexploded and highly volatile materiel and most areas are out of bounds. There is a constant threat of erosion to this historic area presenting great problems of preservation to the Canadian Ministry of Veterans Affairs which administers it. Much dangerous work has been undertaken by the Durand Group (see page 265) to render known unexploded mines harmless to the thousands of visitors who walk and drive above them each year.

Park near the **Lions Club International Memorial**. Here there is another information kiosk where guides to the tunnels may be found (times as above) and telephones and washrooms. The underground tour is through the impressive **Grange Tunnel** (not for the claustrophobic) and the nearby **preserved trenches** (by concrete sandbags) give a clear impression of a WW1 trench, complete with fire steps and sniper posts. Beyond is the immense crater by whose further lip are the German trenches.

Turn right out of the car park and first right signed to Vimy. Follow the road

Grange Tunnel tour

Preserved trenches

The imposing twin pylons of the Canadian National

through the battle-scarred woods of the Park and at the T junction turn right signed Arras/A26 on the N17. Pass the **Canadian Artillery Memorial** *(unveiled by General Byng on 9 April 1918) on the left at Thélus crossroads, drive under the motorway and rejoin the A26/E15 direction Reims/Paris and continue with the main itinerary, being careful to take the A1/E15 Paris/Amiens fork to the right when the motorway splits.*

There is now a further choice of route. It may be considered useful to start one's tour of the Somme battlefield by visiting the *Historial* at Péronne. However, this involves a considerable detour from the area considered to be of greatest British interest, which centres around Albert, and a direct route to that town is also proposed for those with limited time.

Alternative 1. Direct to Albert:

From the A1 at approximately 86 miles take Exit 14 signed Bapaume. In the town take the D929 which leads direct to Albert which is reached after some 100 miles from Calais.

Alternative 2. Via the Historial:

From the A1 exit at the Aire de Maurepas, signed Albert/Péronne, take the D938, signed to Péronne and the Historial.

At the first roundabout is a large sculpture entitled ***Lumières d'Acier*** (Steel Lights), an imaginative comment on the war by sculptor Albert Hirsch, with an explanatory signboard on the road near it.

Cross the Canal du Nord, enter Péronne, follow signs to the Historial and park.

Historial de la Grande Guerre Péronne, exterior (above) and interior (below)

Historial de la Grande Guerre/RWC

This costly and ambitious project, which aims to show World War I in an entirely new light and act as a centre for documentation and research, was funded by the *Département* of the Somme, and opened in 1992. Its façade is the medieval castle, behind which is the modern building, designed by H. E. Ciriani. There is a book and souvenir shop at the entrance and then the great exhibition halls chart the years before the war, the war years – and in particular 1916 – and the post-war years, from the British, French and German points of view, both civilian and military. There are many audio-visual presentations with some rare contemporary footage and, most importantly for the British, a film featuring veteran Harry Fellows (qv), changing temporary exhibitions on subjects such as 'The Cinema and the Great War' and occasional concerts and lectures.

One impressive display shows the *'Zone Rouge'* – the area that was 80-100% destroyed during the war, from Albert in the north to Péronne in the east to Villers Cotterets in the south and Soissons to the east. This was the area which was originally intended to be abandoned to woodland, like similar sites in Verdun. The home-loving, land-loving Picard had other ideas!

There is a basic cafeteria on the ground floor. At the main entrance is a Ross Bastiaan bronze *bas relief* plaque inaugurated by the Australians in 1993.

Each year the Museum stages a stunning array of vintage cars, meeting here for the *Rallye de la Belle Epoque*, around the weekend nearest to 21 June. The *Historial* works closely with the *Conseil Général de la Somme* on projects to preserve and promote the Somme battlefield by acquiring historic sites, putting up descriptive signboards in sites of particular interest (indicated with CGS/H in the text of this book) and signs for a *Circuit de Souvenir* (Remembrance Route) (see page 267 for more details) and provides or approves guides to the area.
Open every day 1000-1800, though closed on Monday, 1 October-31 May. Annual closing mid-December-mid January. ☎ (03) 22 83 14 18. Fax: (03) 22 83 54 18. E-mail: df17@Historial.org Website: www.Historial.org

Péronne/RWC

The town is well worth a closer look. It has been a fortified town since the Roman invasion and the massive ramparts were built in the ninth century (of which only the Brittany Gate now remains intact). Besieged and heavily damaged in 1870 in the Franco-Prussian War and invaded by the Germans in August 1914, it became to the Germans what Amiens was to the British – a centre of activity and leisure. Many dramatic German notices and posters appeared around the town, some preserved in the *Historial*. The most famous is that which was put up on the Town Hall (on which there is still a sign 'Rue de Kanga'(!)) on 18 March 1917 *'Nicht ärgern, Nur wundern!'* ('Don't be angry, only wonder') left by the Germans as they retreated to the Hindenburg Line. The Warwicks retaliated with their own sign, affixed to a lamp-post, '1/8 Warwicks Entered Péronne at 7 a.m. 18/3/17'. The town was re-occupied by the Germans during the March Offensive of 1918 and retaken by the 2nd Australian Division on 2 September 1918. Their divisional flag is in the town hall, which every day at noon and at 1800 hours plays the *Poilu's* favourite song, *Le Madelon* on its carillon. The church of St Jean still bears marks of bullets and shells on its walls. Damaged again in 1940, the town bears two *Croix de Guerre* and the *Légion d'Honneur* in its coat of arms. It is twinned with Blackburn, which adopted it after World War I. The town's war memorial is unusual as it shows the figure of a belligerently gesticulating woman 'Picardy cursing the War'.

(Alternatively Péronne and the *Historial* may be visited on Itinerary Four.)

Approach Two

From Calais Ferry Port/Eurotunnel to Amiens.

Alternative 1.

The most direct route if you wish to get to Amiens by the quickest method.

From Calais Ferry Port *take the A16/A26 signed Paris. After 4 miles fork right signed Boulogne on the A16.*

From Eurotunnel *(Exit 13a) join the A16 and deduct 9 miles from the total mileage. Continue on the A16 round Abbeville to Amiens.*

Approximate driving time: 1 hours 30 minutes. **Approximate distance:** 113 miles

Alternative 2.

If you can set aside a day and wish to make the approach an interesting and pleasurable experience, with frequent stops along the way, the route to Amiens goes **via Wimereux, Boulogne, Etaples, Montreuil, Hesdin, Doullens, Louvencourt, Warloy Baillon, Querrieu to Amiens, with alternative routes via the Château of Val Vion, Vert Galand and Bertangles**

From Calais take the A16/A26 signed Paris. After 4 miles fork right, signed Boulogne on the A16.

At Exit 14 is the good shopping facility at Cité Europe.

At Exit 9 the ***Cimetière Canadien*** is signed.

Take Exit 4, signed Wimereux-Nord, then the D242 over the railway to the large, ornately landscaped roundabout. Take the exit signed Cimetière Sud and follow those signs to the entrance.

The CWGC plot is a walled enclosure within the main cemetery wall.

Open: 1 Nov-31 March 0800-1700, 1 April-31 Oct 0800-1900.

Grave of John McCrae, Wimereux

To the left of the CWGC cemetery entrance is a plaque bearing some biographical details about McCrae. Standing with one's back to the plaque the Napoleon column (see below) can be seen at 11 o' clock. Some lines from his famous poem, *In Flanders Fields* are inscribed in the memorial seat set in the internal wall to the right of the cemetery. The headstone of this compassionate Canadian Medical Officer is laid flat, as are all of the headstones in this cemetery. Col John McCrae died on 28 January 1918, at No 14 General Hospital of complications to pneumonia and was buried here with full military

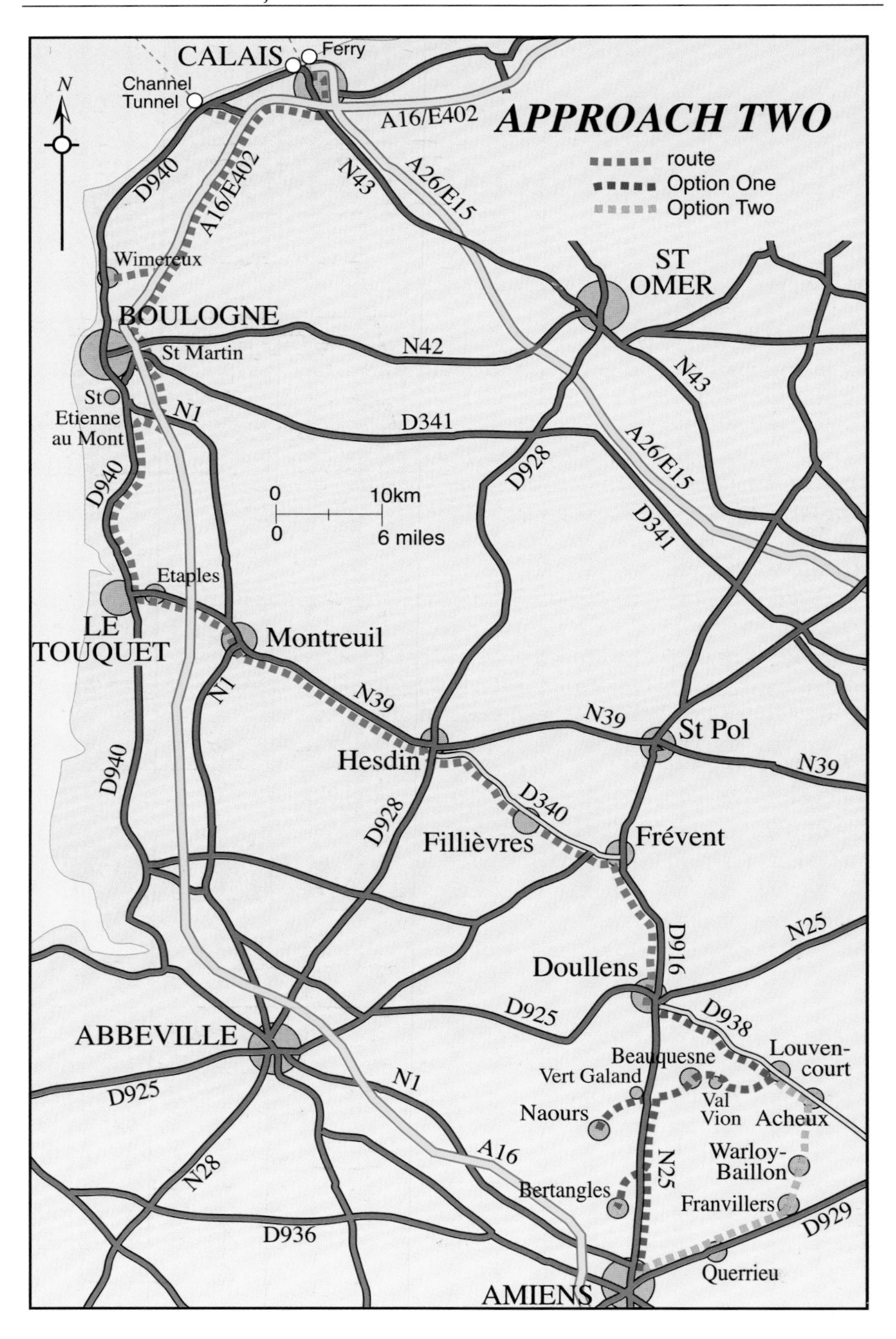
APPROACH TWO
route
Option One
Option Two
N
0
10km
0
6 miles
CALAIS
Ferry
Channel Tunnel
A16/E402
D940
N43
A26/E15
Wimereux
BOULOGNE
St Martin
St Etienne au Mont
N1
N42
D341
ST OMER
D928
Etaples
LE TOUQUET
Montreuil
N39
Hesdin
St Pol
D340
Fillièvres
Frévent
D916
N25
Doullens
D925
D938
ABBEVILLE
Beauquesne
Vert Galand
Louvencourt
Val Vion
Acheux
Naours
Warloy-Baillon
A16
N28
Bertangles
Franvillers
D929
D936
Querrieu
AMIENS

honours. His appointment as Consulting Physician to the First British Army had just been announced.

Continue to the bottom of the road and turn right following signs to the A16. Rejoin it and continue directions to Boulogne.

The imposing *Colonne de la Grande* Armée may be seen ahead and then passed on the right. Surmounted by a figure of Napoleon it commemorates the first issue of the *Légion d'Honneur.*

Continue to the district of St Martin.

At this point a visit could be made to Boulogne Eastern CWGC Cemetery, in which are buried the poet **Julian Grenfell and L/Cpl Short**, shot for his role as ringleader in the Etaples Mutiny (see below), by taking Exit 31 and following green CWGC signs.

Continue to Exit 29 and take the N1 signed Abbeville le Touquet/St Leonard/Montreuil. At Pont de Briques take the D940 to Le Touquet/St Etienne au Mont.

On leaving St Etienne au Mont, a striking pagoda can be seen in a cemetery on the hillside to the right. This is the **Chinese Memorial** in the **St Etienne au**

McCrae plaque, Wimereux CWGC Cemetery

St Etienne au Mont CWGC Cem: Chinese Memorial

Chinese headstone

Mont Communal Cemetery. Surrounded by Chinese graves, it was erected by their comrades in December 1919 in memory of the Chinese labourers who died on service during World War I and are buried in this cemetery. The graves are from 1917 to 1919. In this fascinating cemetery there are also three graves of the SA Native Labour Corps from September/October 1917 and three Chinese sailors from **HMT *Montilla*** (launched in February 1917, later renamed *Gaelic Star*) from October 1918 – a Donkeyman, a Fireman and a Greaser – who died of 'flu. There are members of the RASC Canteens, a **Major Houssemayne du Boulay**, DSO, RE of the RAMC Labour Corps and 3 RAF graves from 31 August 1944. In the civilian cemetery that one passes through is the grave of Mme Rufin, Victim of the Bombardment of St Omer, 28 April 1942.

Continue towards Etaples through Camiers.

It was here that the stockade of the Etaples base court-martial prison and detention camp was situated. Here the various delinquents, deserters and absentees that hid in the dunes as they attempted to get back to Blighty were rounded up. Many of them were desperate men, some of them out and out criminals who preyed on the soldiers training at the Bull Ring with gambling games and robberies.

Continue towards Etaples and stop at the large cemetery on the right just before entering the town.

• *Etaples CWGC Military Cemetery/Bull Ring*

The large cemetery (of 11,436 burials and covering 59,332 square metres) originally contained soldiers, sailors, airmen and civilians from the UK, Canada, Australia, New Zealand, South Africa, British West Indies, Newfoundland, India, USA, Belgium, China, Germany and Portugal (who were later re-interred), with eleven special memorials. The burials were made by ward, therefore officers and other ranks are segregated. Several nurses are buried here. The cemetery was started in May 1915. Its striking entrance complex with fine stone flags was designed by Sir Edwin Lutyens. It overlooks the vast area of dunes that was occupied by extensive hospitals (eleven general, one stationary, four Red Cross and a convalescent depot, which could collectively cope with 22,000 wounded or sick), stores, a railway, and the infamous 'Bull Ring' training ground, site of the 'Monocled Mutineer' episode. The ringleader, L/Cpl Jesse Short, was tried, found guilty, shot for mutiny on 4 October 1917, and is buried in Boulogne East CWGC Cemetery (see above). Vera Brittain served as a VAD in No 24 General Hospital in 1917 and mentions the mutiny in *Chronicle of Youth*. She sometimes nursed the Portuguese officers and, rather to her bewilderment, the Germans. Among the many harrowing and tragic experiences she endured in the wards, the haunting Last Post, with its 'final questioning note' inspired her to evermore 'sacrifices and hardships' and to write a poem called *'The Last Post'*, published in her 1917 collection *Verses of a V.A.D.* In his fictional account of his own war-time experiences, *The*

Golden Virgin, Henry Williamson describes how the hero, Phillip Maddison, arrives at Etaples ('What a –ing hole') in 1916, for three days training en route for the Somme. The Bull Ring 'lay beyond a sandy road past hospitals and rows of bell tents, upon an open area of low sandhills where trenches were dug, bayonet-fighting courses laid out, with Lewis gun and bombing ranges'. He recalls the 'scores of sergeant-instructors ... the barrack-square drill ... physical jerks; firing of rifle-grenades, throwing of Mills bombs; filing through a gas-chamber, wearing damp P. H. helmets ... under coils and over knife-edge obstacles of barbed wire, down into the trench, to stab straw painted crudely grey and red.' Most Bull Ring trainees remembered the brutality of the experience. Robert Graves in *Goodbye to All That* also describes bayonet practice and the words of the instructors with 'their permanent ghastly grin. "Hurt him, now! In the belly! Tear his guts out! ... Now that upper swing at his privates with the butt. Ruin his chances for life! No more little Fritzes!".' Like Williamson, Graves was 'glad to be sent up to the trenches'.

Continue into Etaples.

Along the north bank of the mouth of the River Canche are a variety of delightful fish restaurants, notably Aux Pêcheurs d'Etaples, ☎ (03) 21 94 06 90. It is very popular and therefore advisable to make a reservation in advance.

Continue along the quay.

To the left in the main square, Place Gen de Gaulle, is the **Musée Quentovic** in which there is a small exhibition on the **Bull Ring Camp**. ☎ (03) 21 94 02 47 for opening hours.

Take the N39 to Montreuil and follow signs to Centre Ville and then Ville Haute. Continue to the Place du Théatre.

• *Montreuil/RWC*

From March 1916 to April 1919 the old walled town with its encircling ramparts housed the British GHQ, General Haig staying in the nearby Château de Beaurepaire (about 2 miles south on the D138 near St Nicholas). In the market square, in front of the theatre, is a post-World War II replica of an equestrian statue of Haig on Miss Ypres (who, on closer examination, appears to have undergone a sex change). The statue was raised by national public subscription in memory of Marshal Haig and of the collaboration between the British and French armies, and Franco-Britannic friendship. Montreuil is an ideal place for a lunch break, with several interesting possibilities around the square itself. An alternative is Hesdin, near the Agincourt battlefield.

Take the N39 (D349) towards Hesdin, then the D928 signed to Frévent, following the path of the Canche through a picturesque valley. Continue to Galametz.

In the centre of the village to the right is a Memorial to **Francois Lesur**, FFI, Groupe de Fillièvres, age 19, *'abbatu lâchement'* (killed in a cowardly fashion) by the Germans on 3-9-44. Erected by his brothers.

Continue following the path of the Canche to Fillièvres. On leaving the village watch out for the green CWGC signs to the right.

On the right is the **CWGC British Cemetery at Fillièvres**. It contains some interesting burials, including **Lt E. F. Baxter, VC** of the King's Liverpool Regt, 18 April 1916, age 30 and **Lt-Col Gerald Cornock-Taylor, CBE,** Deputy Director of the Graves Registraton and Enquiries, 14 February 1919. A variety of regiments and corps are represented, including the Royal Marine Light Infantry and the ASC Canteens in the seventy-five UK and one New Zealand burials of World War I. There are also some burials from 1939-45.

Continue through Frévent to the turning to the left on the D111 at Ligny sur Canche.

By turning left here and left on Rue Claude following the green CWGC signs and then right along a narrow, winding country lane, the tiny but immaculate **Ligny sur Canche British Cemetery** may be reached. (It is a 2-mile round trip.) The beautiful wooden entrance gate is set between stone benches and inside two tightly-packed lines of headstones stretch to the Cross of Sacrifice. The cemetery, which contains 80 burials, mostly from August/September 1918, is enclosed by a fine stone wall. The care and attention lavished on this small and rarely-visited cemetery 'in the middle of nowhere',

Etaples Cemetery entrance porch and Visitors' Book/Cemetery Report

typifies the dedication of the Commonwealth War Graves Commission.

Continue into Frévent, following Toutes Directions, and take the D916, then the D925, to Doullens. Continue to the roundabout signed Arras to the left and A16 Amiens to the right. Take the second exit up a small road, Ruelle Merlin, signed Calvaire Foch. Drive uphill to the Calvary at the top.

• **Foch Memorial Cross**. Foch was familiar with Doullens, having set up his HQ here in the early days of the war. He returned again in the last year and this memorial, with bas reliefs of Foch and his *Poilus* by Albert Roze in 1921, recognises that fact, although no inscription remains.

Return to the roundabout and take the N25 signed Amiens and take the first turning to the left following the green CWGC signs to

• **Doullens Communal Cemetery Extension**. The military graves are in the local cemetery which is **Open:** 1 Feb-30 April 0830-1830, 1 May-10 Nov 0730-1900, 11 Nov-31 Jan 0830-1730.

From the summer of 1915 to March 1916 Doullens was at the junction of the French Tenth Army on the Arras Front and the British Third Army on the Somme. The Citadelle was a large military hospital and the railhead was used by

Bas reliefs, Foch Memorial Cross, Doullens

Side by side in death and killed on the same day, German and British headstones, Doullens Communal Cemetery

both armies. From March 1916 the Arras front became British and 19th Casualty Clearing Station came to Doullens, followed by the 41st, 35th, 11th CCS. At the end of 1916 they gave way to 3rd Canadian Stationary Hospital and from June 1918 the 2/1st Northumberland CCS arrived. From February 1916 to April 1918 British medical units continued to bury in French Extension No 1 of the cemetery until it contained 1,142 UK, 78 New Zealand, 69 Australian, 36 Canadian, 4 Newfoundland, 3 South African, 2 British West Indies, 1 British Civilian, 1 Guernsey, 13 German and 469 French burials. In March/April 1918 the German advance threw severe strain on the Canadian Stationary Hospital. The extension became full and Extension No 2, on new ground, had to be opened. It contains 321 UK, 27 New Zealand, 23 Canadian, 23 South African, 1 Australian, 1 Chinese Labourer and 87 German POWs. Like Etaples, another 'hospital' cemetery, the burials are in rank, according to ward. An interesting conjunction of graves has **2nd Lt James A. Donnelly** of the RFC, killed on 31 March, the last day of the RFC, and in the next-but-one grave **Lt Ronald Stonehouse,** RAF, killed on 1 April 1918, the day that the RAF was officially formed. **Brigadier H. T. Fulton, CMG, DSO**, *Croix de Guerre*, of the New Zealand Rifle Brigade who served on the Indian Front and in South Africa, died here of wounds on 29 March 1918. Side by side are the German **Paul Leine Weber** of the 8th RJP and **Pte J.T. Guille**, Royal Guernsey Light Infantry, both killed on 28 November 1917. Also side by side [I.B. 28 & 29] lie **Lt Edgar Meath Martyn**, age 25, 19th Battalion 2 Can Mounted Rifles and **Lt Francis Leopold Mond**, age 22, RFA, both of 57th Sqn RAF, who were shot down on 15 May 1918 and to whom there is a private memorial at Bouzencourt (see Itinerary Three). There is a row of French colonial troops which also contains **Muhammad Beg**, 29th Lancers (Deccan Horse), 6 November 1916 and **Kala Khan** of the RFA, 23 May 1918. There are also some British burials from World War II (mostly from 20 May 1940) and a large French World War I plot at the top of the cemetery, with a private memorial to **Georges Martelle**, 10th RIF, killed on 17 August 1916 at Belloy (qv).

Return to the N25 and turn left.

The beautifully maintained **Local War Memorial** is passed on the left.

Continue to the crossroads signed to Doullens Centre to the right. Continue following signs to Salle de Commandement Unique to the Town Hall and park behind it.

• *Unified Command Room, Doullens/RWC*

The first-floor room in the impressive town hall in which Marshal Foch was created Allied Supreme Commander on 26 March 1918, has been preserved, with the original furniture (with place names still around the table) and a stained glass window depicting the players in the drama, including Poincaré, Clemenceau, Pétain and Foch, Haig, Wilson and Milner. It is flanked on either side by magnificent paintings by Jonas showing scenes of the historic day. The conference was called at a time of extreme danger to the Allies. The German offensive had swept like an incoming high spring tide over the old 1916 battlefield and the Allies' backs were truly against the wall. 'Do you want peace today or victory tomorrow?' asked the old tiger, Clemenceau, of Haig as they arrived outside the town hall. Haig maintained that he wished to continue to fight, but desperately needed French support. He offered to put himself under command of Foch, a move since suspected by some as a clever ruse to prevent Prime Minister Lloyd George from sacking him because of the success of the German offensive, code-named 'Operation Michael'. Only Gough of Haig's Army Commanders was absent, and he was busy keeping the Fifth Army together in the face of the enemy's assault, which had started five days before. Despite an earlier February conference at Doullens, when Gough had warned Haig of the danger facing the Fifth Army, Gough was to be the scapegoat for the March Retreat. Henry Wilson, CIGS, insisted that Gough be removed and Haig concurred – perhaps another act of self-preservation.

Neither the Belgians nor the Americans were present on the 26th, but two days later General Pershing visited Foch and put '... all that I have ... at your disposal. Do what you like with them.'

Foch had been appointed Supreme Commander charged with, 'co-ordinating the action of the Allied Armies on the Western Front' whether the Belgians liked it or not. The plan worked. The entrance hall is covered in commemorative plaques of World Wars One and Two.

Open: 0800-1800, Monday to Friday. Guided tours. ☎ (03) 22 32 40 05.

Return to the crossroads and take the D938 direction Acheux, crossing the D11/D1 en route, and continue to Louvencourt. Drive through the village, past the church and the crucifix at the top of the hill and take the small road to the right.

• *Louvencourt Military Cemetery*

This unusual cemetery has a row of experimental French headstones along the wall (the area was originally a French medical centre) dating from the end of the French occupation of this sector in June/July 1915. Then the British Field Ambulance established itself here, and British burials commenced. During the 1 July 1916 battle, Louvencourt was only 6 miles behind the front line. The Somme battles carried medical units further east until in April 1918 the German offensives pushed the line back to its old position. The 1918 graves here are due to the climax of that fighting. That same year the Imperial War Graves Commission decided upon the sites of the first three permanent cemeteries to be built after the war. They were Le Tréport, Forceville and Louvencourt. It was originally intended that the Commission's three principal architects, Blomfield, Baker and Lutyens, should build one cemetery each, but in the event Blomfield designed all three and completed them by the middle of 1920. They cost more than the £10 per grave that had been allowed – the War

Stone alone cost £500 to make, move and install – and financial lessons learnt were applied to future construction, eg in small cemeteries the War Stone would be omitted.

The cemetery contains the grave of **2nd Lt Roland Leighton** of the 1/7th Worcesters who died of wounds on 23 December 1915, aged only 20. A brilliant scholar (he attended Uppingham School) and budding poet, he was engaged to Vera Brittain. In 1920 she made a pilgrimage to visit his grave and the areas where he fought. There are often violets on his grave, in tribute to the poem Roland wrote to Vera entitled *Villanelle,* whose starting lines are,

Violets from Plug Street Wood
Sweet, I send you oversea.

He enclosed four violets with the poem, which Vera still had, dry and pressed, in 1933 when she wrote her wartime story *Testament of Youth,* which charts their relationship. Later research indicates that Leighton was beginning to have doubts about their future together. Also buried here is **Brigadier General Charles Bertie Prowse, DSO** of the SLI, mortally wounded in the area

Stained glass window depicting the scene in the Unified Command Room, Doullens, on 26 March 1918

Headstone of Roland Leighton, Louvencourt Mil Cem

of the German position, the Quadrilateral (where Serre Road No 2 Cemetery is today, Map D24) on 1 July 1916, when in command of 11th Brigade. His body was moved here after the war. Prowse Point in 'Plugstreet' Wood in the Ypres Salient, now the site of a CWGC Cemetery, was named after him.

Here there are two ways in which to complete the journey to Amiens:
Option One visits Val Vion Château, Vert Galand Aerodrome, Bertangles Cemetery.
Option Two visits Warloy-Baillon CWGC Cem, Querrieu Château and CWGC Cemetery.

OPTION ONE

Via Val Vion, Vert Galand and Bertangles. Approximate driving time: 1 hour. Approximate distance: 27 miles.

Return to the crossroads with the D1/D11 and turn left on the D11 towards Beauquesne. Continue to the next crossroads and turn right signed Beauquesne on the D31.

Val Vion Château, with the famous staircase

• *Val Vion Château*

This is visible half a mile later to the left along a track bordered with chestnut trees. The view is of the back of the château where famous photographs of Haig, King George V and members of their entourages were taken, standing on the staircase in July 1916. The château was demolished by a bomb in 1940, and this is an exact post-war replica.

Continue to Beauquesne, keeping left, pass the church and turn right onto the D31. Follow signs to Candas, but at the junction with the N25 turn left. Ahead are the buildings of Vert Galand Farm.

• *Vert Galand Aerodrome Site*

This is spelt as 'Galant' on modern maps and Maurice Baring also uses the 't'. The farm buildings were used as a mess and administrative buildings by the RFC and RNAS Squadrons based at the aerodrome.

During the Somme battle of 1 July, 60 Sqn, commanded by 'Ferdy Waldron', flying Morane Bullets, was stationed there. On 3 July Maurice Baring visited Vert Galand and 'saw Ferdy Waldron go up. But this time he did not come back.' Maj Francis Fitzgerald Waldron, 11th Hussars, attd RFC, was one of the pioneers of the RFC and at one time held the height record for the Army. He was killed in aerial combat and is buried in Ecoust-St-Mein CWGC Cemetery to the north-east of Bapaume. Baring also saw Major Hubert Dunsterville Harvey-Kelly, DSO of the Irish Regiment and RFC take off for his last flight on 29 April 1917. This … gayest of all gay pilots … always took a potato and a reel of cotton with him when he went over the lines. The Germans, he said, would be sure to treat him well if he had to land on the other side and they found him provided with such useful and scarce commodities. He was the first pilot to land in France, reported Baring. Sadly the commodities did not help him — Harvey-Kelly died in captivity, having been shot down by Richthofen's six red Albatrosses. He is buried in Brown's Copse Cemetery, Roeux near Arras. His Squadron (60th) was taken over by Capt R. R. Smith-Barry, who in late 1917 went on to found the Special School of Flying at Gosport. 'The Man Who Taught the World to Fly' dramatically cut down casualties during training and his methods are still being used to this day. On 7 May 1917, Capt Albert Ball, VC, DSO and 2 Bars, MC, of 56 Sqn was posted as missing on a flight from Vert Galand. He is buried in Annoeullin Communal Cemetery German Extension near la Bassée. Baring had a room at Val Vion (see above) for his HQ during the first days of the July Somme battle.

Continue. At this point there is a sign to **Naours**, *Cité Souterraine*, to the right on the D117. These huge underground caverns and tunnels, some of which date back to the third century, were rediscovered in 1887. They were used by the Picards to shelter from the dangers of many wars, including World War I, and make a fascinating visit. British units, including the 10th Gloucesters, were billetted in the village prior to the Battle of the Somme and there is much graffiti (particularly Australian) inscribed on the walls of the caves.

Open February to September for guided visits. ☎ (03) 22 93 71 78.

Continue on the N25 and at the D97 junction after Villers-Bocage turn right to Bertangles. Continue through the village following signs to Vaux-en-A and fork right on rue du Moulin at a sign to the left to Vaux-en-A. Continue to the cemetery on the left.

• *Bertangles Cemetery (Map Side 1/5)*

To the right of the entrance is a **CGS/H Signboard** and a brief acount of the Red Baron's burial. Other signboards in the Red Baron series are at Fricourt, Vaux-sur-Somme and Cappy.

Manfred von Richthofen, the top German Ace (with eighty kills), was buried here on 22 April 1917, by the Australians, with full military honours. In 1925 his remains were moved to the German Cemetery at Fricourt, and later transported to his family home in Schweidnitz. P. J. Carisella in his book *Who Killed the Red Baron* claims that only the skull was moved and that he unearthed the rest of the Red Baron's skeleton in Bertangles in 1969 and presented it to the German Military Air Attaché in Paris. Pictures published in magazines like *I Was There* show the edge of a brick entrance post and a hedge behind the grave. The hedge and gate post are still there, so the grave site, not marked in any way, can roughly be identified as being about fifteen paces into the cemetery and fifteen paces to the right. There is one CWGC headstone in the cemetery – that of **2nd Lt J. A. Miller, RFC**, killed on 28 March 1918, age 24.

Return to the N25 and continue to Amiens.

OPTION TWO

Via Warloy-Baillon and Querrieu. Approximate driving time: 1 hour. Approximate distance: 25 miles

From Louvencourt, continue on the D938 to Acheux, then take the D47 to Varennes and then the D179 to Warloy Baillon. Follow green CWGC signs to the cemetery.

• *Warloy-Baillon Communal Cemetery & Extension.*

Graves of Lt Col P. Machell & Maj Gen E. C. Ingouville-Williams. These two exceptional officers are buried in a cemetery of particular beauty — especially in the late spring/early summer. The main cemetery was used between October 1915 and 1 July 1916, and contains forty-six graves. It adjoins the local cemetery. The extension, in what was originally an apple orchard, was used from July to November 1916 and contains 1,347 graves.

Lt Col Percy Wilfrid Machell, CMG, DSO, served with the Nile Expeditionary Force 1884-5, joined the Egyptian Army in 1886, was Inspector-General of the Egyptian Coastguard, Adviser to the Egyptian Minister of the Interior, 1898-1908, received countless Egyptian Decorations and when World War I broke out, helped the 5th Earl of Lonsdale (known as the 'Yellow' Earl, and of Lonsdale Belt fame) to raise and train his own battalion (the 11th, Service) of the Border Regiment. He was killed on 1 July 1916, leading his battalion's attack on the Leipzig Salient at the age of 54. Machell had married into a distinguished and talented family. His wife, Lady Valda, was the daughter of Admiral HSH Prince Victor of Hohenlohe Langenburg, GCB, RN, nephew of Queen Victoria. Her sisters, Lady Feodora and Lady Helena were both accomplished artists/sculptresses. Lady Helena, who served during the war with the British X-ray Section in France and on the Italian front and who was awarded the Italian Medal for Military Valour, designed the beautiful 37th Division Memorial at Monchy (depicting three soldiers back to back) a replica of which stands in the grounds at Sandhurst. Their brother was Major General

Lord Albert Edward Wilfred Gleichen KCVO, who commanded the 37th Division 1915-16, then commanded the Intelligence Bureau and Department of Information. The bronze plaque which for many years stood at the foot of Machell's grave was stolen in the early 1990s.

Maj General E. C. Ingouville-Williams ('Inky Bill') who commanded 34th Division (which suffered such heavy casualties around la Boisselle on 1 July) was killed by a shell at the Queens Nullah near Mametz Wood on 22 July 1916, after reconnoitring the area and while walking back to his car at Montauban. He too was 54 and had served with the Buffs. His funeral here was held with considerable pomp for a war-time burial.

Continue on the D919 to Vadencourt and then turn left on the D23 to

General view of Warloy-Baillon Communal Cemetery and 'Inky Bill's' (Maj Gen E. C. Ingouville-Williams) headstone

Franvillers to the crossing with the D929. Turn right on the D929 signed to Amiens and continue to Querrieu.

As the road descends to the River Hallue at Pont-Noyelles there are signs (on each side of the road) to memorials commemorating General Faidherbe's victory in the Franco-Prussian War action that took place here on 23 December 1870.

Continue over the river to the château entrance.

• *Querrieu: Château & British CWGC Cemetery Map Side 1/4*

Here Rawlinson had his Fourth Army Headquarters from the beginning of 1916. From here he organized the 'Great Push' of 1 July 1916, and watched the progress of the battle from the heights above the village that he called 'The Grandstand' and to where he took Haig to observe the barrage on 27 June. The King visited the château with Balfour in August and there are many well-known pictures of him presenting decorations to soldiers, British and French, in the grounds. The Prince of Wales installed his HQ here in 1918 and was an occasional visitor after the war. During World War II the château was again used as a headquarters – this time by the Germans and Guderian, Goering and Rommel all passed through it. The château is owned by the Count and Countess of Alcantara and they have many photographs and other

Private memorial to Driver J. P. Farrell, Querrieu British CWGC Cemetery

Querrieu Château

mementoes of their home during World War I. The elegant château, dating from the eighteenth century, was rebuilt after being burnt down in the Siege of Corbie in 1636 and extensively redesigned under Louis-Philippe in the nineteenth century. It has always played host to a string of glittering personalities, from the aristocracy and the world of the arts. Today it is used for prestigious art exhibitions and musical events. The stable block has been converted into comfortable *chambre d'hôte* rooms. ☎ (03) 22 48 24 48.

Henry Williamson, in his novel, *The Golden Virgin*, describes what must have been a typical occurrence in many towns and villages behind the lines – a 'bioscope' showing of a Charlie Chaplin film and a concert party, both housed in barns at Querrieu. 'Some of the actors dressed up as girls, with varied types of wigs' and garish makeup. 'Each herded man in the audience was fascinated, filled with longing ....' But the star turn was the actor, Basil Hallam Radford of the Kite Balloon branch of the RFC, 'famous before the war for his song *Gilbert the Filbert*'. In it Radford, known simply as 'Basil Hallam', created the comic figure of 'the Knut' – a languorous upper class twit. Sadly he was killed when the balloon in which he was observing broke away, and, having thrown all the papers overboard, he tried to descend by his parachute. It failed to open, however, and he received fatal injuries. He died on 28 August 1916, and is buried in Couin British CWGC Cemetery near Gommecourt. Ironically, balloonists were the only members of the RFC then to be issued with parachutes. Initially it was thought that if pilots had them they would be too eager to abandon their expensive, and hard-to-replace, machines.

Continue and immediately turn left following green CWGC signs to the Cemetery.

• *Querrieu British CWGC Cemetery*

This cemetery was started in 1918 by the divisions taking part in the defence of Amiens in March 1918. It contains 102 UK, 84 Australian, 1 Chinese and 12 German burials. Here is buried **Lt Col Christopher Bushell, DSO, VC,** commanding the 7th (S) Battalion, the Queen's Royal West Surrey Regiment. His VC was won on 23 March 1918, west of the St Quentin Canal when he personally led C Company of his battalion, in a counter-attack, in the course of which he was severely wounded in the head but continued to carry on, walking in front, not only of his own men, but those of another regiment as well, encouraging them and visiting every portion of the lines in the face of terrific machine-gun fire. He refused to go to the rear until he had to be removed to the dressing station in a fainting condition. There is also a most unusual private memorial in the cemetery which bears the inscription, 'Well done. Pray for 31691 **Dr [Driver] J. P. Farrell**, 9th Battery FA, AIF, killed in action May 28th 1918, age 20 years'. Around the broken column that surmounts his grave is the legend, 'For God and Australia'.

Continue to Amiens on the D929.

ITINERARY ONE

• **Itinerary One** starts at the Town Hall Square in Albert, heads directly towards the German front line along the main axis of the 1916 British attack and then swings north to follow the front line across the River Ancre and ends in Arras.
• **The Route:** Albert – Town Hall, Golden Madonna, Musée des Abris, station; Bapaume Post CWGC Cemetery; Tara-Usna Line; Tyneside memorial seat; La Boisselle – Lochnagar Crater and memorials, 34th Div Memorial, 19th (Western) Div Memorial; Ovillers – CWGC Cemetery, Breton Calvary; Pozières – British CWGC Cemetery, Fourth, Fifth Armies Memorial, KRRC Memorial, Australian 1st Div Memorial, Gibraltar Blockhouse; Thiépval – Visitor Centre Project, memorial and cemetery, 18th Div Memorial; Connaught and Mill Road CWGC Cemeteries; Ulster Tower, memorials and visitors' centre; Newfoundland Memorial Park, Visitor's Centre, trenches and memorials, Beaumont-Hamel; Argyll & Sutherland Highlanders Memorial; Beaumont-Hamel CWGC Cemetery; Hawthorn Crater; 51st Highland Div flagpole; Beaumont-Hamel church; Redan Ridge No 3 & Redan Ridge No 1 CWGC Cemeteries; Serre Road No 2 CWGC Cemetery; Braithwaite Cross; Wilfred Owen's Dugout; French Memorial Chapel; French National Cemetery; Serre Road No 1 CWGC Cemetery; Serre Road No 3 CWGC Cemetery; Sheffield Memorial Park and memorials; Queen's CWGC Cemetery; Luke Copse CWGC Cemetery; 12th Bn York & Lancs Memorial, Serre; Ayette Indian & Chinese Cemetery.
• **Extra Visits** are suggested to Ancre CWGC Cemetery; RND Memorial, SOA Lt Col Freyburg,VC, Beaucourt; Pte Amos private memorial; Salford Pals memorial, 15th, 16th, 17th Bns, HLI Memorial, Authuille; SOA Sgt Turnbull; Lonsdale CWGC Cemetery; Sucrerie Military and Euston Road CWGC Cemeteries; the Gommecourt Salient – Owl Trench, Rossignol Wood CWGC Cemeteries; Rossignol Wood bunker; SOA Rev T. Bayley Hardy VC; Gommecourt Wood New CWGC Cemetery; SOA Capt L. Green VC; CWGC HQ, Beaurains; Point du Jour CWGC Cemetery.
• **Planned duration**, without stops for refreshment or extra visits: 8 hours.
• **Total distance: 35 miles.**

• *Albert Town Hall Square/0 miles/10 minutes/RWC/Map J14/15*

The town takes its name from Albert, Duke of Lynes, whose property it became some time after 1619. Noble links remain to this day and the current pretender to the French throne, the Comte de Paris, can still count 'Marquis

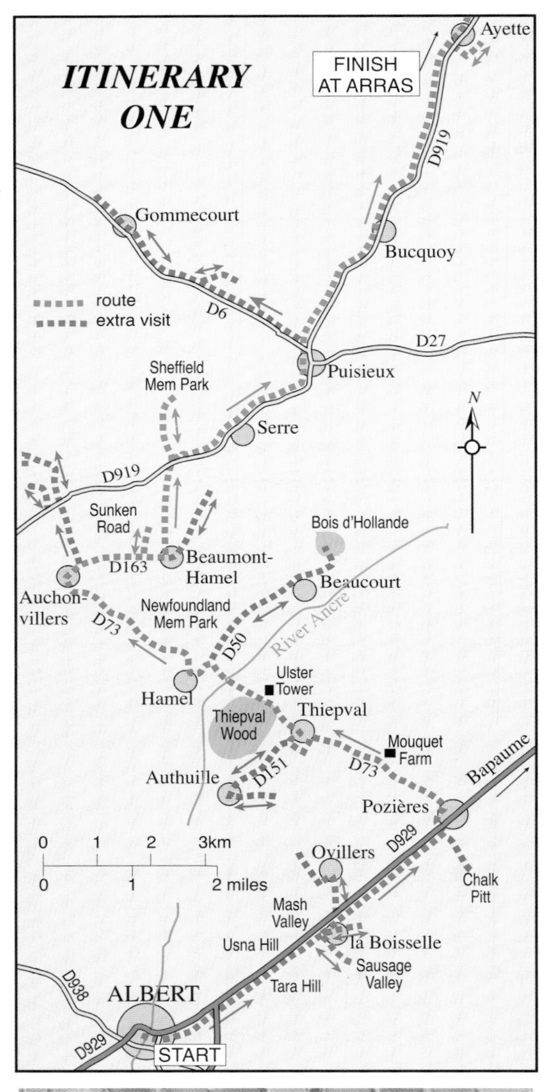

The glittering Golden Madonna, Albert

Machine Gun Corps Plaque, Albert Town Hall

Albert Station and the 'Circuit du Souvenir' tiled picture at the entrance

Entrance to the Musée des Abris and painting by Frederick Cambray inside

d'Albert' among his titles. The town's motto is *Vis Mea Ferrum* (my strength is in iron), reflecting the iron works that once gave it its prosperity. Previously it had been called Ancre (even Encre before 1610) after the river which flowed through it (right below the Basilique). The original station was built in 1846 and Albert became an important rail link, vital to the growing metallurgy industry and the burgeoning pilgrim tourist business (20,000 pilgrims arrived on 27 April 1862 alone). In 1914 Albert had 7,343 inhabitants. By 1919 it had 120.

Fierce fighting around Albert began in the early months of the war, the first enemy shelling being on 29 September 1914. Albert was a major administration and control centre for the Somme offensive in 1916, and it was from there that the first press message was sent announcing the start of the 'Big Push'. By October 1916, when the Somme offensive had pushed the German guns out of range, the town was a pile of red rubble. Yet it still offered some attractions to the troops fresh from the front line as a place of rest and rough entertainment. The YMCA Club charged 15 francs a day (for four meals and a bed), which Masefield said was 'just 5 francs a day less than the mess at Amiens'. He was dismayed when the club was forced to close on 31 March 1917 to make way either for a hospital or another HQ. The 'Bonza' Theatre operated near the old station. Some civilians drifted back in 1917 and attempted to salvage their homes and businesses. General Byng made the town his HQ while planning the November 1917 attack on Cambrai. Then, in a rude awakening on 26 March 1918, during their final offensive, Albert was taken by the Germans. It was re-taken by the British on 22 August, the East Surreys entering the town at bayonet point.

After the Armistice, the Imperial War Graves Commission established its Somme headquarters in a collection of huts joined by duck-boards along the Bapaume road. There were architects, stone masons and carpenters, landscapers, gardeners and wardens or 'caretakers' as the cemetery guardians were originally called. They were recruited from the willing ranks of ex-servicemen who undertook the often dangerous, always harrowing work of re-interring their 'pals' from isolated graves and reburying them in the beautiful garden cemeteries that were being created with help of experts from Kew and the services of the country's best architects. Mobile teams of workers, with a cook and the inevitable dog, would be driven out each Monday with basic camping equipment to the isolated, ravaged areas of the old front line. Affectionately known as 'travelling circuses', they completed their work with extraordinary despatch and cheerfulness.

The plan to declare the area a *Zone Rouge* (too dangerous to rebuild, like some of the battlefields around Verdun) was strongly resisted by the inhabitants of Albert. Its reconstruction was helped by the city of Birmingham (hence the street name, rue de Birmingham) which funded a ward in the new hospital, and Bordeaux, and it also became a centre for pilgrims – it was claimed that over 160 small cafés existed to serve them. The conducting of battlefield tours by motor vehicle became a thriving industry.

As early as 1917, John Masefield in his classic description, *The Old Front Line*, prophesied,

> "To most of the British soldiers who took part in the Battle of the Somme, the town of Albert must be a central point in a reckoning of distances. It lies, roughly speaking, behind the middle of the line of that battle. It is on the main road, and on the direct railway line from Amiens. It is by much the most important town within an easy march of the battlefield. It will be, quite certainly, the centre from which, in time to come, travellers will start to see the battlefield where such deeds were done by men of our race."

That still holds today, and the town's modest traditional hotels – the Hôtel de la Paix, for instance, is now run by Isabelle Daudigny Duthoit with her chef husband, Fréderic, continuing in the warm tradition of hospitality set by her uncle and patron for many years, Monsieur Duthoit. They have completely refurbished and modernised the premises and now offer 12 bedrooms, 8 with en-suite facilities, and it is the base for the Friends of Lochnagar. It still has a superb restaurant with the best Ficelle Picarde in the world. ☎ (03) 22 75 01 64. The Hôtel de la Basilique, ☎ (03) 22 75 04 71, opposite the Basilique as its name implies, also has its faithful regulars. They have now been joined by the smart, modern, twenty-three-bedroom Royal Picardie on the D929 Amiens road, which offers superb cuisine, ☎ (03) 22 75 37 00, so that more tourists can stay in this, the heart of the British sector.

Park in the Square. Walk to the town hall steps and face the building.

The town hall, in splendid Flemish Renaissance style, with an Art Deco interior and stained glass windows that show the town's economic activities, was opened by President Lebrun in 1932. Inside is a plaque commemorating the reconstruction of the devastated war area. To the left of the steps, on the external wall, is a **plaque to Resistance fighters, the Armies of Liberation and Gen de Gaulle**. At the bottom of the step to the left is a **bust to Emile Leturq,** 1870-1930, mayor during the reconstruction. To the right is a **plaque** commemorating the more than 60,000 casualties suffered by the **Machine Gun Corps** during 1914-18. It was unveiled at Easter 1939 by **Lt Col Graham Seton Hutchison, DSO, MC**, author of *Pilgrimage*. The colonel had been with 100 MG Coy during the attack on High Wood on 15 July 1916. Another memorial to the Corps, formed in October 1915, is the figure known as The Boy David (designed by Derwent Wood) at Hyde Park Corner in London.

Return to your car. Drive down rue Jeanne d'Harcourt and park in the square outside the Basilica.

• *The Golden Madonna, Basilique, Albert/0.2 miles/10minutes/Map J11*

The golden figure of the Virgin Mary holding aloft the baby Jesus stands on top of the church, known as la Basilique, of Notre-Dame de Brebières (Our Lady of the Ewes). Before the war thousands of pilgrims came to see another statue in the church which gave the basilica its name. Legend has it that this statue was found in the Middle Ages by a shepherd looking after his flock in a meadow. It was credited with miraculous properties and attracted large numbers of pilgrims. In 1834 Pope Gregory XVI accorded an indulgence to pilgrims who visited the statue and successively grander churches were built to house it, culminating in the 1890s basilica. This was surmounted by the 5-metre high Golden Madonna (reached by climbing 238 steps) which was coated with 40,000 sheets of gold leaf. The numbers of pilgrims continued to increase and in 1898 Pope Leo XIII dubbed Albert 'The Lourdes of the North'. In January 1915 German shelling toppled the statue to a perilous-looking angle below the horizontal, but it did not fall. Visible to soldiers of both sides for many miles around, and giving the bizarre impression that the Virgin was about to hurl the baby Jesus into the rubble below, the statue gave rise to two legends. The British and French believed that the war would end on the day that the statue fell (and it is said that the Allied staff sent engineers up the steeple at night to shore up the statue to prevent raising false hopes). The Germans believed that whoever knocked down the statue would lose the war. Neither prediction came to pass. During the German occupation from March to August 1918 the British shelled Albert and sent the leaning Virgin hurtling to the ground. The figure was never found (perhaps it was despatched to Germany in the salvage effort to make new weapons).

Today's basilica is built to the original 1897 designs, with a splendid gilt replica of the Madonna and Child on its 70-metre high spire that glints in the sun for miles around. The inhabitants of Albert vetoed the idea that she should be replaced in her famous war-time pose (the subject of many postcards, silk and board, embroidered handkerchiefs, painted plates and statues). It contains a magnificent marble pulpit, mosaics, paintings and statues by the sculptor Albert Roze. Beneath it, with its well-marked entrance to the side, is a museum.

• *Musée des Abris (Museum of the Shelters)/30 minutes/Map J13*

This interesting and well-presented museum, officially reopened on 8 October 1994, has been made in the subterranean tunnels under the basilica and other parts of the town. To either side of the main corridor are realistic scenes of 1914-18 trench and dugout life – British, French and German. Visitors emerge, through a souvenir/book shop, into the pleasant arboretum public gardens. **Open:** every day 1 Feb-15 Dec 0930-1200 and 1400-1800. June-Sept 0930-1800. Entrance fee payable. ☎ (03) 22 75 16 17.

Note at the bottom of the road Albert Station, rebuilt in Art Deco style. To each side of the main entrance are charming tiled pictures of the surrounding countryside. The picture to the right is captioned, *Circuit du Souvenir* and shows sites on the battlefield such as the Thiépval Memorial and the *Historial* at Péronne. The main hall in the station houses a Potez 36 FHZN aeroplane in commemoration of Henry Potez, born in Albert, who founded the aircraft factory at Méaulte which became Aerospatiale. The plane, restored in 1957, had been flown by notables such as Saint-Exupéry, the French World War I ace and writer of *Vol de Nuit*, and was last flown on the hundredth anniversary of Henri Potez's birth in 1991.

On the outskirts of the town to the left on the D929 as it crosses the railway, is a well-preserved **demarcation stone** (Map J28).

At a superficial glance the rebuilt red-brick town may appear unlovely, but a quiet, observant stroll around its streets is rewarding in its glimpses of a certain Art Deco charm, revealing delightful tiled pictures and patterned brickworks in its varied façades .

Drive up the rue de Birmingham, turn left and leave Albert on the D929, signed Bapaume/A1 Lille/Cambrai.

The D929 heads north east, straight as an arrow, as befits a Roman road, for Bapaume, 19km away. Barely 3.5km away along the road is the village of la Boisselle, which marked the German front line in 1916. The road passes Bapaume Post Cemetery and rises to a crest just before the village, a crest from which the 34th Division set off at 0730 on 1 July 1916 to attack la Boisselle. The ground to the left of the road was in 8th Division's area and the ground to the right in 34th Division's. Behind was Albert, under

Bapaume Post CWGC Cem and Headstone of Lt Col C.C.A. Sillery

constant German bombardment, teeming with supplies, its cellars full of troops who emerged at night into the streets with their transport and moved up to and over the crest along deep communication trenches and then fanned out into assault trenches in the valley below to await the whistle to go over the top. On their way,

'Here and there, in recesses in the trench, under roofs of corrugated iron covered with sandbags, they passed the offices and the stores of war, telephonists, battalion headquarters, dumps of bombs, barbed wire, rockets, lights, machine-gun ammunition, tins, jars and cases. Many men, passing these things as they went 'in' for the first time, felt with a sinking of the heart, that they were leaving all ordered and arranged things, perhaps forever,' reported Masefield. In some sectors men even passed rows of coffins.

Drive to the large roundabout and follow signs to Cambrai/Lille on the D929. Stop at the cemetery on the right.

• Bapaume Post CWGC Cemetery/1.3 miles/5 minutes/Map J16

This cemetery, one of the first to be completed in the sector in 1924, lies on the western slope of Tara Hill, and here the divisional boundary crosses the road and swings well left to include the hill known as Usna, 1,000m away to the northeast. Both hills were in the 34th Division area. In the cemetery, which was begun in July 1916, lie more than a hundred Northumberland Fusiliers of 34th Division, two battalion commanders of the Tyneside Scottish Brigade (**Lt Cols William Lyle**, age 40 and **Charles Sillery**, age 54, both killed on 1 July 1916) and soldiers of 38th (Welsh) Division, which recaptured the position on 23 August 1918. In Plot I Row G there is an interesting group of burials: **2nd Lt C. Edwards**, E Yorks, 29 January 1917, age 28, has the personal message, 'He responded to Lord Kitchener's appeal, August 1914'and **2nd Lt J.E.F.T. Bennett**, R Warwicks, 24 July 1916, has the soldier's decoration the MM. He lies near **Maj Sir Foster H.E. Cunliffe, Bart,** Rifle Bde, 10 July 1916, age 43. Altogether there are 327 burials, including Canadians, Australians and a South African.

Continue to the top of the crest.

• Tara-Usna Line/1.7 miles/Map J16-17

The crest, which runs from Tara Hill on the right-hand side to Usna Hill on the left-hand side, overlooks the village of la Boisselle, 900m straight ahead. It may be possible to spot Ovillers CWGC 2,500m away at 11 o'clock and the Lochnagar mine crater 1,500m away at 1 o'clock. Moving in the direction in which you are travelling, four battalions of Northumberland Fusiliers – all Tyneside Scottish, part of 102nd (Tyneside Scottish) Brigade, itself part of 34th Division – advanced towards the German lines at la Boisselle on 1 July. On the left-hand side of the road the 1st and 4th battalions moved forward, side by side in extended line, and two minutes after them, in column of platoons, to the right-hand side of the road, came the 2nd and 3rd battalions.

They had climbed out of their assault trenches in the valley ahead of you moments after the explosion of huge mines at la Boisselle. But although the men had been promised that the opposition would be disorganised by the artillery bombardment and the mines, it was not so. The Germans emerged from deep dug outs, set up their machine guns and mowed down the British infantry advancing as if on parade across the open ground. On the left-hand side no advance was made, the German trenches were not reached and casualties were around 60%. On the right-hand side, where casualties were marginally less, around 50%, a small part of the German line was captured some 700m south-east of the village.

Continue to bottom of hill. On the right is the handy, good value Poppy Restaurant, ☎ (03) 22 75 45 45. Fork right on the D20 and immediately park.

• *Tyneside Memorial Seat, la Boisselle/2.1 miles/5 minutes/Map J17 RWC*

The curved seat is on the left. Situated close to where the opposing front line trenches crossed the D929, it was unveiled by Marshal Foch, and was the first permanent regimental memorial to be erected along the road. It commemorates the attack of the 102nd (Tyneside Scottish) Brigade and their follow-up brigade, the 103rd Tyneside Irish. The latter, storming through the remnants of the 102nd, penetrated beyond the German lines in small parties to the east of the village, but no permanent gains were made astride the road. Their losses matched those of the 102nd.

Opposite, across the D929, after about 100m, is the site of what was the best-known crater in la Boisselle of the mine in Y Sap, blown at the same time as Lochnagar, but now filled in. In his novel, *The Golden Virgin*, based on his personal war-time experiences, Henry Williamson describes a visit to the 1,300ft-long gallery that led under the German fort of the same name, whose charges were to be blown at Zero Hour on 1 July. It left a crater 165ft in diameter, throwing up a high lip which afforded protection under which the infantry were able to reform. It caused little damage to the enemy as the area had been evacuated prior to the explosion. After the war, locals erected a hut by the great hole from which they sold postcards of the two craters at la Boisselle and on the other side of the road, not far from today's Poppy Café, was the Café de la Grande Mine.

Continue along the Rue de la 34ième Division, signed to La Grande Mine, for some 100m.

On the right-hand side can be seen a small fenced-off area of craters known as the Glory Hole (Map J18), which was immediately behind the German forward trenches. Williamson paints a word picture of it as a place of dread, 'a boneyard without graves' of British and German corpses, and unexploded British shells. At that time it made 'a gap of five hundred yards in the British lines, an abandoned no-man's-land of choked shaft and subsided gallery held by a series of Lewis-gun posts'.

Tyneside Memorial seat, la Boisselle, and detail of bas relief

There was much aerial activity over the area on 1 July. Cecil Lewis, serving with the RFC, describes in his book *Sagittarius Rising*, 'We were to watch the opening of the attack, co-ordinate the infantry flares (the job we had been rehearsing for months) and stay over the lines for two and a half hours.' Continuous, overlapping patrols were due to run throughout the day. The patrol was ordered to 'keep clear of La Boisselle' because of the mines that were to be blown. From above Thiépval he watched as,

> "At Boisselle the earth heaved and flashed, a tremendous and magnificent column rose up into the sky. There was an ear-splitting roar, drowning all the guns, flinging the machine sideways in the repercussing air. The earthy column rose, higher and higher to almost four thousand feet."

Turn right on the C9 signed La Grande Mine and 100m later fork left on C102. Park at the crater.

• *La Boisselle/Lochnagar Crater/2.7 miles/20 mins/Map J19-24 OP*

The land containing the crater was purchased in 1978, and is maintained privately, by Englishman Richard Dunning (☎ 01483 810651 for enquiries about the 'Friends of Lochnagar' and their connection with Landmine Action)

Left: Pte George Nugent Cross Above: Grimsby Chums seat

Tom Easton plaque

Plaque to Gunner W.G. Noon

Young Friends on 1 July at the Cross

The Lochnagar Crater

as a personal memorial to all those, of both sides, who fought in the Battle of the Somme. Thus the fate of the other large craters at la Boisselle – of being filled in and built upon – was averted. When standing at the rim and peering down into its vast depth it is difficult to grasp quite how large this crater is. **Note that as the crater is subject to increasing erosion it is strictly forbidden to clamber down into it.** Please also remember that the area still contains the remains of many of those killed by the explosion and it is therefore a burial ground. Indeed wooden crosses at the bottom of the crater stood out starkly against the white chalk for many years after the war. Several memorials have progressively been erected in the area. One is a **stone** in memory of **Tom Easton**, a private in the 2nd Battalion of the Tyneside Scottish. Below it is a **plaque to 129364 Gnr Noon, W.G.**, B/160 RF 34th Div 1916-1919, 1895-1963. To its left is a **memorial seat** on which a plaque simply states, 'Donated by Friends who visit in memory of friends who remain'. A further **plaque to John Giles**, founder of the WFA, has been added. A brick shelter has been erected to house the **Lochnagar Crater Memorial Visitors' Book** (which please sign). It is estimated that there are now over 400,000 visitors to the crater each year (and, encouragingly for future remembrance, many of them are schoolchildren). A simple **12ft-high cross** made from church timber originating on Tyneside, with the inscription, 'Lochnagar Crater Memorial 1914-1918 In Remembrance – *A la Mémoire*' is the focal point of the well-attended annual ceremony of remembrance that takes place here every 1 July at 0730 hours. On the far side of the impressive gaping hole of the crater is a **memorial seat to Harry Fellows,** 1896-1987, ex-12th Northumberland Fusiliers, who fought on the Somme, erected by his son, Mick. The seat was bought from the proceeds of Harry's moving poetry. To the left of it is a **seat to the Grimsby Chums**, Saturday 1 July 1916, erected in July 1999. From this seat you have the best OP vantage point from the crater's rim

Stand with your back to it.

Take the Memorial Cross as 12 o'clock. Just to the left and beyond is the spire of la Boisselle Church and just to its left on the skyline is the Thiépval memorial, 4,000m away. On a clear day its flags can be seen. A further 4,000m away beyond Thiépval is Beaumont Hamel. At 11 o'clock is the road up which you have driven which runs roughly parallel to, and beside, the German front line trench. At 2 o'clock on the horizon is a long line of poplars. At their left hand end is the wireless mast at Pozières, 4,200m away, which stands on the D929 opposite the Australian Memorial at Pozières Windmill, always a useful reference point around the battlefield and visited on Itinerary 2. In front of the trees, 900m away, is Gordon Dump Cemetery at the north-eastern end of Sausage Valley. The valley curves around from behind you 500m away, and from there to your right-hand side up to the cemetery, which is positioned close to a battlefield track junction once known as Gordon Post. The valley was named 'Sausage' after a German spotter balloon which was flown in the area and the christening of the opposite valley across the D929 as 'Mash' was inevitable.

Thus the general shape of the German front line to the north may be seen: i.e. Beaumont Hamel to Thiépval, Thiépval to the Glory Hole (by the poplars at 10 o'clock) and from there up the road to where you are now standing. At 7 o'clock the Golden Madonna at Albert should be visible on an average clear day, at 10 o'clock in the dip is the Poppy Café and the crest, 1,000m away, running to behind the Glory Hole, is the Tara-Usna line, from which the Tynesiders advanced towards la Boisselle and where you now stand.

Continue round the crater to the cross to the right of the path.

This simple **wooden cross is in Memory of 22/1306 Pte George Nugent**, Tyneside Scottish, Northumberland Fusiliers. His remains were found at this spot by Friends clearing the area on 31 October 1998. George Nugent was reinterred in Ovillers CWGC Cemetery (qv) on 1 July 2000.

Mine warfare had been carried on in this area well before July 1916 and there were many craters in No Man's Land. In June, along the Western Front as a whole, the British had blown 101 mines and the Germans 126. In this area some of the shafts dug, from which tunnels then reached out to the enemy line, were over 100ft deep with tunnels at up to four levels. When dug, the mine here was called Lochnagar, and it was started by 185th Tunnelling Company and packed with two charges of 24,000lb and 36,000lb of ammonal. It was exploded, along with sixteen other British mines along the Somme front, at 0728 on 1 July, and the circular crater measured 300ft across and was 90ft deep. Debris rose 4,000ft into the air and, as it settled, the Tyneside attack from Tara-Usna began.

Following the failure of that attack, the 10th Worcesters were ordered to move up from beside Albert to make an assault at dawn on 2 July. So chaotic were conditions in the communication trenches, that the battalion got lost, and the attack did not go in until 3 July. The Worcesters took the crater area and the village, **Private Thomas George Turrall** winning a **VC** in the process, (a Gilbert Holiday drawing commemorates the action) but the battalion lost a third of its fighting strength and the Commanding Officer was killed.

Return to the Rue du 34th Division and turn right on what is now Rue Georges Cuvillier (Mort pour la France) towards the church, passing a splendid Poilu memorial on the left. Stop beside the octagonal remains of a water tower as the buildings stop and walk up the path to the left.

• *34th Division Memorial/3.3 miles/10 minutes/Map J7*

This handsome memorial, comprising a figure of Victory (who, a few years ago, lost the laurel wreath she was brandishing) on a stone base, which commemorates the Division's deeds in the area on 1 July 1916, the first battle in which it was engaged, also incorporates the Division's striking chequerboard emblem. Below the statue the composition of the Divisional Units is inscribed. There is an identical memorial (but with its laurel wreath complete) at Mont Noir in the Ypres Salient (Ypres Map K1). Ovillers CWGC Cemetery may be seen on the slope behind the statue.

34th Div Memorial

19th (Western) Div Memorial

Return to the church. Stop at memorial in front of it.

• 19th (Western) Division 'Butterfly' Memorial/3.4 miles/5 minutes/Map J6

This memorial, whose divisonal emblem of a butterfly is engraved at the top, commemorates their casualties of 2 July-20 November in la Boisselle, Bazentin le Petit and Grandcourt. The Divisional Units are inscribed on the base. It was the 19th that finally took the village on 4 July.

Return to the D929 by turning right behind the Poilu. Turn right on the D929 and after 200m, turn left and follow signs to Ovillers CWGC Cemetery.

• Ovillers CWGC Cemetery/4.3 miles/15 minutes/Map J4/5

This cemetery contains 3,265 burials of soldiers (and sailors of the Royal Naval Division) from the UK, Canada, Australia, South Africa, New Zealand and France (there are about 120 French graves), of which 2,477 are unidentified. It was started as a battle cemetery behind a Dressing Station and was in use until March 1917. After the Armistice, graves from Mash Valley and Red Dragon Cemeteries, as well as many temporary graves from the surrounding battlefields, were concentrated here. There is a special memorial inside the

Headstone of Sgt C.C. Castleton, VC, Ovillers CWGC Cem

Breton Calvary with detail of bas relief, Ovillers

Special Memorial in Ovillers CWGC Cemetery to soldiers originally buried in Mash Valley, whose graves were subsequently lost

Sir Harry Lauder, whose son is buried in Ovillers CWGC Cemetery

front wall to thirty-five soldiers originally buried in Mash Valley whose graves were subsequently lost. It also contains the grave of **Capt John C. Lauder** of the Argyll & Sutherland Highlanders, killed by a sniper (a Scottish newspaper in the 1980s hinted that it may have been a British one – young Lauder was not a universally popular officer) on 28 December 1916. His distraught father, Sir Harry Lauder, visited the 'brown mound' of his son's grave, with its temporary wooden cross, in June 1917. At that time there were 500 graves in the cemetery. Sir Harry was on a strenuous tour, which took him from Folkestone via Boulogne, to Vimy Ridge, Aubigny, Tramecourt, Arras, Athies, le Quesnoy, Doullens, Albert (where he commented on the Leaning Virgin, still clinging to her perilous position) and thence to Ovillers. He gave concerts to entertain the troops at each stop, often coming under fire. Lauder called it the 'Rev Harry Lauder, MP Tour', and it was a tremendous morale-raiser. It is chronicled in his book *A Minstrel in France* published in 1918, which describes his love of, and pride in, 'My boy, John', which parallels Rudyard Kipling's feelings for 'My Boy, Jack', his son Lt John Kipling, killed at Loos in September 1915. It was as a result of the shattering blow of his son's death that Lauder wrote *Keep Right on to the End of the Road.*

Pte George Nugent (qv) whose remains were found at the Lochnagar Crater in 1998, was reinterred here, with full military honours and in the presence of members of his family, on 1 July 2000. His personal message reads, 'Lost, found, but never forgotten.' In the French plot are several of the Breton soldiers who were killed in the actions of December 1914, when the French held the sector.

In October 1916 the 2nd/5th Gloucesters moved from their reserve position on Aubers Ridge to the Somme, serving at Grandcourt, Aveluy and Ovillers. With them was the poet and musician, Ivor Gurney and here he wrote one of his most disquieting poems, *Ballad of the Three Spectres:*

As I went up by Ovillers
In mud and water cold to the knee,
There went three jeering, fleering spectres,
That walked abreast and talked of me.

One prophesied a 'Blighty one' for him – correct, as in September 1917 he was gassed at St Julien and sent home. The second predicted that he would die in 'Picardie', which he did not do. The third, and most fearsome prediction, was:

He'll stay untouched till the war's last dawning
Then live one hour of agony.

It could be said that the mental turmoil in which Gurney lived for the last fifteen or so years of his disturbed life were indeed one long hour of agony.

In the village of Ovillers after the war a Nissen hut stood on the site of the church, proclaiming 'This was Ovillers Church'. At one time a memorial to the miners whose tunnels riddled the slope leading up the village stood in Ovillers. The rebuilt village sits on the site of the old light railway, the bath house and the encampment known as Wolfe Huts. Gurney would have been pleased to know that after the war, Gloucester paid for two wells in Ovillers.

Turn round and return to the junction with the road that leads to the D929 to the right (up which you drove).

To the left here is a cart track (which may be driven up if the ground is extremely dry, otherwise it is a 10-minute return walk) signed **Calvaire Breton.**

It leads to an imposing memorial **Calvary** (Map J5a) with an imaginative bas relief of crosses with an inscription around the base to *'les braves du 19 RIF, 7 dec 1914'* and the words *'Je n'abandonne pas mes bretons'*. It is also in memory of **Capt Henby Baillard** and **Lt Augustin de Boisanger** who fell here and **André Pitel**, the Regiment's Adjutant. In the first year of the war this sector was mostly manned by men from the west of France - la Vendée and Brittany.

Return to the D929, turn left signed Bapaume.

As you drive to the crest of the Pozières Ridge it may be possible to see the Thiépval memorial 2,800m away to the left.

Continue to a large cemetery enclosure beside the road on the left. Stop.

To the right is a brown lozenge-shaped sign to Pozières and Gibraltar.

• *Pozières British Cemetery & Memorial/6.2 miles/15 minutes/Map J8/9*

The memorial is the wall that surrounds the cemetery. It is to men of the Fifth and Fourth Armies who have no known grave, and was designed by W. H. Cowlishaw of the (then) Imperial War Graves Commission. It relates to the period of the final German assault of March 1918 and over 14,600 names are inscribed on the wall. Among these the Rifle Brigade, the Durham Light Infantry and the Machine Gun Corps each have over 500. The Manchesters have almost 500, including **Lt Col Wilfrith Elstob**, CO of their 16th Bn who won the **VC** at Manchester Hill Redoubt near St Quentin on 21 March 1918. The cemetery contains over 2,700 burials, from the UK, Australia and Canada, including **Sgt Claude Charles Castleton**, 5th MGC, AIF, who won the **VC** on 28 July 1916 in this area.

Continue about 300m. Park near a memorial cross on the right.

• *KRRC Memorial/6.6 miles/5 minutes/MapH10*

The Kings Royal Rifle Corps had two battalions in the original BEF and raised twenty more during the war. There is a similar memorial in the Ypres Salient at Hooge (Holts' Ypres Map I31) and another in Winchester.

Continue to small road to the right.

This was known as **Dead Man's Road. Note** that at the end of this narrow track (negotiable by car only if dry) is the **Chalk Pit** where on 15 July 1916 the 8th East Lancs with the remnants of the 11th R Warwicks gathered as they were repulsed by the enemy in their drive from Contalmaison towards Pozières. Battalion HQs were established in the pit under heavy artillery fire and at 1400

Pozières 5th & 4th Div Memorial and CWGC Cem

Australian 1st Div Memorial and 'iron harvest', Pozières

Ross Bastiaan Plaque, Mouquet Farm, Thiépval

hours Major-General Ingouville-Williams (qv), commanding 34th Division, made a visit to assess the situation. He ordered a further bombardment and assault to take place at 1700 hours. This was met by heavy machine gun fire but the East Lancs managed to dig in some 300 yards short of the village. The following day the weary men were relieved and their wounded evacuated to a dressing station in Contalmaison. During the attack the 112th Brigade sustained 1,034 casualties, of which the 8th East Lancs had 365. It was the Kitchener Battalion's first battle of the war.

Turn left almost immediately, signed up a small road to the Australian 1st Division Memorial.

There is another brown lozenge-shaped sign to *Site de Pozières* here.

• *Australian 1st Division Memorial/1993 RB Plaque & Gibraltar Blockhouse/6.7 miles/15 minutes/Map G47/48*

The obelisk memorial sits on the forward slope of Pozières Ridge, the ground rising to its crest 500m away as the D929 continues on through the village towards Bapaume. At the memorial entrance is a low bronze, **Ross Bastiaan** (qv) *bas relief* plaque, unveiled by the Australian Minister for Veterans' Affairs on 30 August 1993 and sponsored by AMPSOC. Beyond the obelisk the Thiépval Memorial can be seen on the horizon.

The ridge was a major feature, furiously contested by both sides and, with Thiépval towards its northern end, it sits like a barricade across the D929. It was a formidable obstacle, with its fortified cellars, network of defensive trenches and twin OP blockhouses. One, called Gibraltar, is in the bank to your right as you drive up to the memorial and it has recently been cleared by the CGS/H to make its entrance easily visible. The other was at The Windmill, see Itinerary Two. There are informative signboards, a large car park and a wooden viewing platform (which gives the German viewpoint and indicates points of interest). The entrance to the blockhouse has been protected and entry is forbidden.

Following the collapse of the night attack offensive which began Part 3 of the Somme Battle on 14 July, four unsuccessful assaults were made on Pozières. The first attack was made by the British 48th Division on the left (Pozières Memorial) side of the D929 and the 1st Australian Division on the right (KRRC Memorial) side, the Australians having moved up from Albert and then through Sausage Valley. The attack went in thirty minutes after midnight on 23/24 July. The main trench of the German garrison, the 117th Division, ran parallel to and on the left beside the small road you have just driven up. The trench and the village were taken on 24 July, but the Germans still held the crest of the ridge (marked by the tall wireless mast) and counter-attacked. Although the Australians held on, after three days the division had lost over 5,200 casualties and had to be relieved. The subsequent actions are summarised in Itinerary Two, Pozières Windmill entry.

Continue to the T junction by the village war memorial. It is surmounted by the cockerel emblem of France. Opposite is the school and *Mairie*.

Turn left. After approx 100m, shells and other battlefield relics are piled in the garden against the house on the right owned by private collectors.

Continue along the D73 road.

This road roughly follows the route of the German Second Line to Thiépval, which can be seen ahead. Ovillers is to the left, 2,500m away and roughly half way between Pozières and Thiépval is the site of Mouquet Farm (known to Tommy as Mucky Farm and to the Aussies as Moo Cow Farm) on the right. A farm has been rebuilt close to the original site. On 10 September 1997 a **Ross Bastiaan memorial plaque (Map H15)** was unveiled here by the Australian Deputy Prime Minister, Mr Tim Fisher. It commemorates the Australians who fell in August/September 1916 in the struggles for Thiépval and is sited close to the line of the German 'Constance' Trench.

Continue to Thiépval village. The village was virtually wiped out in the war and the present small cluster of church, houses, school/*Mairie* and farm is far smaller than the original thriving village. Turn left before the church (occasionally used as an exhibition hall), and follow signs to the memorial.

To the right is

• *The Thiépval Visitor Centre Project/9 miles/Map G44a*

The project is the brainchild of Sir Frank Sanderson who, on visiting Lutyens' great Memorial in 1998, felt that modern-day visitors should have some background information about it, what happened at this historic site and what the Memorial represented. The natural progression was to propose a Visitor Centre that would provide some basic educational information and refreshment facilities. He has worked tirelessly to gain support for the project and now has the backing of the British Embassy in Paris, the IWM, the CWGC, the Lutyens Trust, the RBL, Madame Potié the Mayor of Thiépval and several well-known military historians. The Duke of Kent became patron of the project and the *Conseil Général de la Somme (CGS)* then agreed to match any funds raised in the UK, to supervise the building of the Centre and to run and maintain it in conjunction with the *Historial*. The target fund has now been set at £485,000 and several major donations have been made. Forty architects applied to design the Centre and a jury was set up (which included Paul Lutyens, great-nephew of Sir Edwin) to choose the successful applicant - a French architectural practice, KOZ. The design is modern in character, but care has been taken not to intrude on Lutyen's classical and dominating memorial (from which the Centre cannot be seen) by keeping it low and by making much use of glass to show the wooded canopy beyond.

The exhibition space inside it will be designed by Graham Simpson Design Consultants. There will be a reception area with shop, tea-room, toilet and first-aid facilities, a rest room for guides and drivers and a fully-equipped seminar room. It is planned to have computer access to the CWGC and other nationality websites to research the names of soldiers killed in the vicinity.

Perhaps, only naturally, the concept of the Project has encountered some opposition, especially from the many faithful regular visitors to the Somme who remember the tranquillity of the area in years gone by. Then visitors tended to be 'pilgrims' or serious military historians, who came armed with Masefield's *Old Front Line* and other classic and modern accounts of the battle and who were perfectly aware of the significance of the site and what happened there. They fear the onset of a battlefield theme park effect of too many interpretative and visitors' centres, now that the area is also served by the *Historial, the Musée des Abris,* Delville Wood, the Ulster Tower Visitor Centre, the Beaumont-Hamel Visitor Centre and private organisations like Avril Williams and the Tommy Café. It has to be recognised, however, that the bulk of today's visitors have moved from 'pilgrims' to 'tourists', with student groups far outnumbering adult visitors and many adult groups having only a very general interest. The sheer volume of such visitors may well be justification for facilities such as the Thiépval Visitor Centre project.

Donations are still actively being sought and should be made to The Thiépval Project, Charities Aid Foundation, Trust Department, Kings Hill, West Malling, Kent ME19 4TA.

The estimated completion, as with many such major projects, has somewhat slipped from the original date to a target of 1 July 2004.

Continue to the entrance to the Memorial and park.

The house opposite the entrance was built in the 1980s by the mayor, Madame Potié, on the site of the cottage of the old guardian for many years, Monsieur Poprawa, and serves as a staging and command post for ceremonies. To the left of the entrance to the memorial are the gardeners' huts and garages for the CWGC section, for many years supervised by now-retired Arthur Leach. Arthur is the son of Serre Road No 2 gardener, Ben Leach, who during World War II hid and then sent on their way to the Spanish border, several Allied airmen.

• *Thiépval Memorial & Cemetery/9.1 miles/25 minutes/Map G46/45 OP*

Outside the entrance is a **CGS/H Signboard**. The structure is both a battle memorial and a memorial. As the former it commemorates the 1916 Anglo-French offensive on the Somme and as the latter it carries the names of over 73,000 British and South African men who have no known grave and who fell on the Somme between July 1916 and 20 March 1918. The Australian Missing are commemorated on the Villers Bretonneux Memorial, the Canadians on the Vimy Ridge Memorial, the Indians at Neuve Chapelle, the Newfoundlanders at Beaumont Hamel and the New Zealanders at Longueval. The memorial, 150ft high, which dominates the surrounding area, was designed by Sir Edwin

The Thiépval Visitor Centre Project

Name of Lt George Butterworth MC on the Thiépval Memorial with a private tribute

The Thiépval Memorial and Anglo-French Cemetery

Lutyens and has sixteen piers on whose faces the names of the Missing are inscribed. It stands on a concrete raft 10ft thick, built 19ft below ground – the solution of surveyor Major Macfarlane to the problems of building over the warren of tunnels and dugouts that formed part of the German second line. It is the largest British war memorial in the world and was unveiled on 31 July 1932, by HRH the Prince of Wales in the presence of the President of the French Republic. The event was not without controversy. At the time ex-servicemen were suffering from the mass unemployment that was to lead to the general depression. Where was the land 'fit for heroes to live in', promised by Lloyd George? **Bruce Bairnsfather**, the creator of Old Bill, used his popular folk hero to express his views in an article in the *Daily Herald*. Would not the money used to create this splendid edifice not have been better spent in caring for the men without limbs, without minds, living a twilight existence in the Star and Garter Home? Yet posterity might feel that it is appropriate to have an enduring focal point for remembrance for those who gave their lives for their beliefs – to remind us that they were fighting for our peaceful future. 'The Thiépval Arch will stand as firmly as the Empire whose sons it commemorates', wrote **H. A. Taylor** hopefully in his enduringly interesting *Good-bye to the Battlefields,* in 1928. The war correspondent, **Sir Philip Gibbs**, wrote of Thiépval in a 1916 despatch, 'It is historic ground. A hundred years hence men of our blood will come here with reverence as to sacred soil.' His prophecy would seem to be accurate.

During the mid-1980s the memorial underwent some drastic changes. It had to be refaced with sturdy Manchester red house brick stock, owing to the deterioration of the original attractive, but soft, rust-coloured bricks selected by Lutyens, and the handsome semi-circular hedge, which was such a striking feature around the lawns in front of the memorial, was killed in the winter frosts of 1984/5 and had to be removed.

Walk through the entrance into the 40-acre park.

The path heads directly towards the tip of the Leipzig Salient, marked by an isolated copse of tall trees, 1,000m away and from which one can walk to the Lonsdale CWGC Cemetery (see Extra Visit below). The path points almost exactly at the Golden Madonna in Albert, 6.4km away.

Walk to the War Stone.

Among the names commemorated on the memorial – each important to those who mourn it – are the brilliant musician **Lt George Butterworth MC**, of the 13th Bn, DLI (qv), killed on 1 August 1916; **Major Cedric Charles Dickens** (qv), descendant of the great novelist, killed on 9 September 1916; **Pte Watcyn Griffith**, killed in Mametz Wood on 10 July 1916, while carrying a message from his famous brother, author Wyn Griffith; **Lt William Ker** of Hawke Bn, RND, mentioned in A. P. Herbert's moving tribute to his fallen comrades, *Beaucourt Revisited;* **Lt Thomas Kettle**, Royal Dublin Fusiliers, the Irish poet and former MP; **Lce Sgt Hector Hugh Munro** (qv) of the 22nd Royal Fusiliers, the author Saki, killed by a sniper on 14 November 1916, at the age of 46, in the area of what is now Munich Trench Cemetery; **Cpl Alexander Robertson** of the 12th Yorks & Lancs, the same battalion as fellow poet, John William Streets (qv) and, like him, killed on 1 July 1916; some unfortunate men 'shot at dawn' – **Pte Cairnie** of the 1st Scots Fusiliers, **Pte Farr** of the 1st W Yorks, **Pte Skilton** of the 22nd Royal Fusiliers; **Victoria Cross winners T/Capt Eric Frankland Bell** of the 9th RIF, **Pte William Buckingham** of the 2nd Leicesters, **T/Lt Geoffrey Cather** of the 9th RIF, **Pte 'Billy' McFadzean** of the 14th RIR, **Rifleman William Mariner** of the 2nd KRRC, **T/Lt Thomas Wilkinson** of the 7th LNL and **Sgt Maj Alexander Young** of the Cape Police, SAF. **Pte Reginald Giles,** 1st Gloucesters was **only 14 years old.**

Behind the memorial is a **small Anglo-French cemetery**, which symbolizes the joint nature of the war. Its construction was paid for equally by both Governments and 300 dead of each nation are buried there. On the base of the Cross of Sacrifice in the cemetery is the inscription 'That the world may remember the common sacrifice of two and a half million dead there have been laid side by side soldiers of France and of the British Empire in eternal comradeship'.

How To Find An Individual Name On The Thiépval Memorial

First look up the regiment of the name that you are searching for. These are listed in alphabetical order. Within each regiment, ranks are listed in order of seniority. Within each rank, names appear in alphabetical order. Regiments are not broken down by battalion, with the sole exception of the London Regiment. The number of the pier and the letter of the face on which the names of casualties from each regiment appear, are shown on pages 14-18 of the Cemetery Report Introduction.

The memorial has sixteen piers, or columns, on which all the names are inscribed. Each pier is numbered and each face is lettered. The number allocated to each pier and the letter allocated to each face of the piers are shown on the plan on page 13 of the Memorial Report Introduction. The reports are vital to this operation. Ideally, you should ascertain the pier number and face letter of the name you are looking for in advance of your visit by visiting the CWGC Debt of Honour website (qv).

Stand beside the War Stone with your back both to it and the cemetery. Look straight ahead over the far wall and between the avenue of trees. That is 12 o'clock.

At 9 o'clock through the arch is the obelisk of the 18th Division memorial and behind it on the crest is the area of the Schwaben Redoubt. At 12 o'clock in the middle ground is Mouquet ('Mucky') Farm and behind it, running right to left across your front, is the Albert-Bapaume road. On that road, but just concealed behind the right-hand avenue of trees, is the **Pozières Wireless Mast**, probably the most useful refrence feature on the battlefield. The Pozières

Ridge/Thiépval Plateau feature running towards you from beyond Mucky Farm and the area up to and including Thiépval were not finally cleared until September. On the 15th, Part 4 of the Somme battle had opened with the tank attack from right to left along the horizon at 12 o'clock, that area having been taken by the Australians in August. Mucky Farm fell on 26 September and Thiépval to the Essex, Middlesex and Suffolk county regiments of 18th Division on the 27th. Throughout the whole period of German occupation to 1916, the village was garrisoned by the 180th Württemberg Regiment. It fell again to the Germans on 25 March 1918 and was recaptured by the 17th and 38th (Welsh) Divisions on 24 August 1918.

Return to your car. Continue round to a T junction 100m further on and park.

• *18th Division Memorial/9.3 miles/5 minutes/Map G44*

This obelisk to the victors of Thiépval is a replica of the one in Trones Wood (Itinerary 2) and bears the same exhortation: 'This is my command, that ye love one another'. It gives the order of battle of the brigades which made up the division and the division's battle honours. In 1995 the trees flanking the obelisk were cut down, completely changing the aspect of the memorial. Now there are open views behind it of Thiépval Wood, the Connaught Cemetery, Mill Road Cemetery and the Ulster Tower.

Extra Visit to the Salford Pals Memorial & 15th, 16th and 17th Battalions Highland Light Infantry Memorial at Authuille, SOA of Sgt Turnbull VC (Map G49), Lonsdale CWGC Cemetery (Map G43) Round-trip: 3-6 miles. Approximate time: 25 minutes.

Turn left on the D151 and follow the road down into the village of Authuille and stop at the plaque, next to the Poilu local memorial on the right.

The Salford Pals Memorial was unveiled on 1 July 1995, by members of the Lancashire Fusiliers Association, the Lancashire & Cheshire Branch of the WFA and the Mayor of Authuille in a simple and moving ceremony. The site was chosen as, of the four Pals Battalions raised in Salford during 1914 and 1915, three of them (the 15th, 16th and 19th Lancashire Fusiliers) fought in this area against fortress Thiépval in the opening days of the Battle of the Somme from 1 July 1916. Their initial attack was met by a determined defence

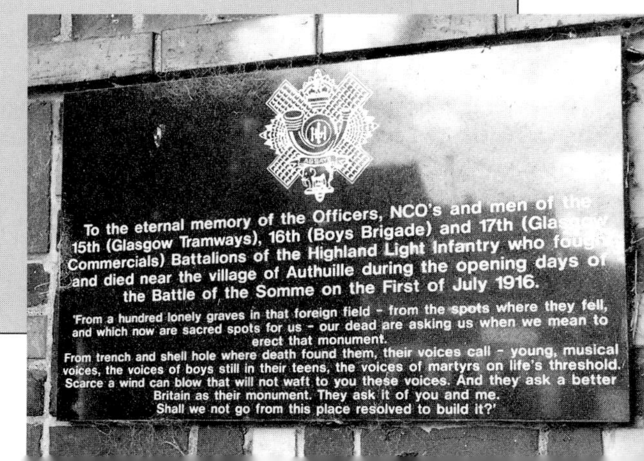

Memorial plaque to 15th, 16th and 17th Glasgow Bns, HLI, Authuille Church

18th Division Memorial with the Ulster Tower and Mill Road CWGC Cemetery on the skyline

Extra Visit continued

from twenty-five machine guns and soon the lanes around Authuille were filled with the dead and dying men from the dockyards, coal mines, textile mills and engineering works of Salford. Many are buried in the nearby cemeteries of Aveluy Wood (Lancashire Dump)(Map G41) – where **2nd Lt Francis Kennard Bliss**, brother of the composer Arthur Bliss, is also buried – and Authuille (Map G42). Many more are commemorated on the Thiépval Memorial.

Salford Pals Memorial, Authuille

Continue to the Church on the right.

1 July 1996, the 80th Anniversary of the opening day of the Battle of the Somme, saw the unveiling of a long overdue **memorial to three Battalions of the Highland Light Infantry** – the 15th (Glasgow Tramways), 16th (Boys' Brigade) and 17th (Glasgow Commercials – which included men from Strathclyde University

Extra Visit continued

and affiliated schools). At a memorial service to the 17th Bn held in Glasgow Cathedral on 8 July 1917, the Bn Padre, Rev A. H. Gray ended his address by asking for a special memorial for the fallen and with the words;

"From a hundred lonely graves in that foreign land – from the spots where they fell and which now are sacred spots for us – our dead are asking us when we mean to erect that monument. From trench and shell hole where death found them, their voices call – young, musical voices, the voices of boys still in their teens, the voices of martyrs on life's threshold. Scarce a wind can blow that will not waft to you these voices. And they ask a better Britain as their monument. They ask it of you and me. Shall we not go from this place resolved to build it?"

On coming across this account three-quarters of a century later, Glaswegian Charles McDonald, of the Thistle and Poppy Society, was so moved that he resolved to take the appeal for a monument literally and started to raise funds. His original idea was to erect a female figure representing 'Mother Glasgow', with three children representing the three battalions. When it became clear that this would not be achieved in time for the eightieth anniversary, Charles decided on a simple black marble plaque engraved with the regimental crest, a tribute to the three battalions and the poignant words of the Rev Gray. The memorial is on the church at Authuille, from where the battalions made their assault on Thiépval Ridge on 1 July 1916. The figure of the mother and her three children will be erected in another site in the area where the battalions fought and fell as soon as sufficient funds have been raised.

Turn round and return to the sharp left turn on the 'C' road, signed to Ovillers and the Londsale Cemetery.

This is the route the Salford Pals took in their attack on the Thiépval fortress. The road runs round the tip of the Leipzig Salient to the left and there are superb views

Unveiling the new Salford Pals Memorial, Authuille, 1 July 1995, with the Honour Guard in World War I uniform

Extra Visit continued

on reaching the crest. This area was the **SOA of Sgt James Youll Turnbull VC** of the Highland Light Infantry. On 1 July 1916 his party captured an important enemy post which was then bombarded by the enemy throughout the day. Turnbull held on as several parties were wiped out and replaced around him, but was himself killed later in the day in a 'bombing' counter-attack.

Continue to the path to the cemetery to the right.

Lonsdale Cemetery was named after the Earl of Lonsdale, who recruited a 'Pals' unit, the 11th Bn, the Border Regiment, which attacked the Leipzig Salient from this point on 1 July. It contains the grave of **Sgt Turnbull VC** (see above). The battalion's CO, **Lt Col Percy Machell** (qv), was killed here on 1 July 1916. This interesting officer served in Egypt and the Sudan and had been Military Adviser to the Egyptian Ministry of the Interior during 1898-1908 (Simkins, Kitchener's Army). Machell is buried in Warloy-Baillon Communal Cemetery Extension (Map S1/4).

The cemetery makes an excellent vantage point from which to study the attack on the Leipzig Salient.

Return to the 18th Div Memorial and pick up the main itinerary.

Turn right.

Thiépval Château, once an imposing building with an elegant façade containing twenty-four windows, used to stand on the left of this road. Before the war it gave employment to the majority of the villagers living in its shadow, but it was never rebuilt.

Continue. After 200m turn left at the crossroads onto the D73, signed to Beaumont Hamel Memorial Park. Continue.

On 1 July this road was in No Man's Land, running parallel with the British front line about 150m to your left and the German line up to 300m to your right.

• Connaught & Mill Road CWGC Cemeteries/10 miles/20 minutes/Map G29/36

Connaught Cemetery was begun in the autumn of 1916, and after the Armistice the burials from ten or so other cemeteries nearby were concentrated here. Of the more than 1,200 soldiers, sailors and Royal Naval Division Marines in the cemetery, the majority fell in the 1916 Somme offensive – many of them Ulstermen – and over half are unknown. A further measure of the chaos and destruction on the battlefield, in which men simply disappeared, is that for one-third of those buried not even their units are known.

Behind the cemetery is Thiépval Wood, known today to the locals as

Authuille Wood, and not to be confused with the wood of the same name just south-east of the village of Authuille. The Somme Association (qv) are negotiating to acquire this area which is of such historic interest to the Irish as well as to the British Regiments which also occupied it.

Opposite the cemetery is a track leading to Mill Road Cemetery which was begun in Spring 1917. It sits just forward of the main German position (1 July 1916) on the crest. The area is so riddled with tunnels that subsidence still occurs and many of the headstones in the cemetery are laid flat. There are some 1,300 burials, including Ulstermen from 1 July and 18th and 39th Division men from later attacks. The notorious Schwaben Redoubt extended beyond the same ridge. Monsieur Poprawa (see above) recalled his team of horses falling into the great chasms of the underground chambers as he ploughed the area when the land was restored to agriculture between the wars.

Continue and park by the entrance to the memorial on the right.

• *Ulster Tower Memorials & Visitors' Centre/10.1 miles/35 minutes/RWC /Map G31/33/34/35/37/OP*

Outside the entrance gate is a **CGS/H Signboard** about the 36th Ulster Division. Stand with your back to the gates. Straight ahead at 12 o'clock is Thiépval Wood (now shown on modern French maps as Authuille Wood). At 7 o'clock is Mill Road Cemetery. At 9 o'clock is Connaught Cemetery and beyond it the Thiépval Memorial. At 2 o'clock on the horizon is Beaumont Hamel Memorial Park. At 3 o'clock is a small track leading down to St Pierre Divion village in the Ancre Valley. 200 yards down the track, on the right, are the remains of a German machine-gun post (Map G32). At 1 o'clock on the far slope beyond the Ancre is Hamel Church and between 2 and 3 o'clock above the first horizon is the church at Beaumont Hamel.

On 1 July the Ulsters walked, and then charged, from the forward edge of Thiépval Wood, across the road, up past where the tower stands and on via Mill Road to the crest and beyond. They were the only soldiers north of the Albert-Bapaume road to pierce the German lines. Some say that their achievement was due to a mixture of Irish individualism, alcoholic bravura and religious fervour. Whatever the reason, it was a magnificent feat of arms. Within 1½ hours five lines of German trenches had been overwhelmed. Some small parties of 8th and 9th Royal Irish Rifles penetrated into and beyond the Schwaben Redoubt itself but unsupported by advances on their left or right, shelled by their own artillery, exposed to enemy machine guns on their flanks and subject to fierce counter-attacks, they were forced to withdraw at the end of the day. Fourteen hours after the assault began the lines finished virtually where they started but the Irish, unlike most, had won the race at 0730. If the rest of the Fourth Army had advanced at the same speed it is certain that the outcome on 1 July would have been totally different. An eye witness of the

The Ulster Tower

The Orange Order Memorial

The Memorial Chapel

Irish action wrote:

> "Then I saw them attack, beginning at a slow walk over No Man's Land and then suddenly let loose as they charged over the two front lines of the enemy's trenches shouting, 'No Surrender, boys' ... perhaps the Ulstermen, who were commemorating the anniversary of the Boyne, would not be denied."

This is an ideal viewpoint for several literary connections.

Edmund Blunden, serving with the 11th Royal Sussex Regiment, established an ammunition dump near Hamel, the village seen due west over the River Ancre and the railway line. Armed with a copy of his realistic and vivid account of his war experiences, *Undertones of War*, with its supplement of the best of Blunden's war poems, one can identify Jacob's Ladder, Kentish Caves and Brock's Benefit, described in 'Trench Nomenclature' –

Genius named them, as I live! What but genius could compress
In a title what man's humour said to man's supreme distress?

In *The Ancre at Hamel: Afterwards* he describes, on a subsequent visit to the area, the river and his searing memories of the comrades who fell around it,

The struggling Ancre had no part
In these new hours of mine,
And yet its stream ran through my heart;
I heard it grieve and pine,
As if its rainy tortured blood
Had swirled into my own,
When by its battered bank I stood
And shared its wounded moan.

The beautiful cemetery seen on the upward slope of the valley is the Ancre Cemetery. It is on the site of the RND's successful but costly attack of 13 November 1916, and in it lie some casualties of the operation. A. P. Herbert, of Hawke Battalion, lost some well-loved comrades. His grief for them is expressed in the haunting poem *Beaucourt Revisited,* written when the battalion returned to the Ancre in 1917 and very similar in feeling to Blunden's poetic reminiscences,

And here the lads went over and there was Harmsworth shot,
And here was William lying – but the new men knew them not.
And I said, 'There is still the river and still the stiff, stark trees;
To treasure here our story, but there are only these;'
But under the white wood crosses the dead men answered low,
'The new men know not Beaucourt, but we are here, we know'.

Harmsworth is **Lt the Hon Vere Harmsworth** of Hawke Bn, son of the newspaper magnate, Lord Rothermere, who was killed on 13 November 1916, and is buried in Ancre CWGC Cemetery. William is **Lt W. Ker**, also of Hawke Bn, and who died on the same day, but who is commemorated on the Thiépval Memorial. To read the poem while overlooking the scene of its action is an extremely emotional experience.

Visit the memorial and Visitors' Centre.

This is a replica of the tower known as Helen's Tower on the estate of the Marquis of Dufferin and Ava at Clandeboye in County Down, where the 36th (Ulster) Division trained before coming to France. The tower has had an interesting and checkered existence since it was built in 1921. In the late 1920s and '30s when the cemeteries and the memorials (other than Thiépval) were completed, visitors averaged about 300-400 per day. A former Ulster Division Sgt-Major, William MacMaster, and his wife lived in the one-room-per-floor apartment in the tower and acted as guardians. At that stage, there were preserved trenches behind the tower, around which MacMaster guided his visitors. One is reminded of Philip Johnstone's marvellously satirical 1918 poem *High Wood*, in which a guide conducts a group of tourists around the battlefield:

... this trench
For months inhabited, twelve times changed hands;
(They soon fall in) used later as a grave.
... Madame , please,
You are requested kindly not to touch
Or take away the Company's property
As souvenirs; you'll find we have on sale
A large variety, all guaranteed.

Macmasters, it is said, however, guided his pilgrims with genuine feeling. After World War II a succession of guardians came from Ireland, but the loneliness of the job often seemed to induce a desire to over-party with the local community, resulting in subsequent recall. After many years with no resident in the tower, Ulster started to take an active interest in this focal point of their sacrifice in the Great War and in 1991, the 75th Anniversary of the 1 July battle, **Princess Alice** re-dedicated the tower. A **plaque commemorates the occasion**, and a splendid cake representing the tower was made for the event by the women of Ulster. Another **memorial to the 36th (Ulster) Division Victoria Cross winners, Capt Bell (1 July 1916), 2nd Lt Emerson, Lce Cpl Seaman, Fusilier Harvey, 2nd Lt de Wind, Rifleman McFadzean (1 July 1916), Rifleman Quigg (1 July 1916), Lt Cather (1 July 1916) and 2nd Lt Knox** was also erected. **The flagpole** was donated by the women of Ulster. A striking, but somewhat controversial, black marble memorial obelisk with gold lettering to the 36th (Ulster) Division was erected outside the tower grounds on 12 September 1993 (Map G30). It is known as the '**Orange Order Memorial**'. On 1 July 1999 it was moved to an enclosed area to the right rear of the Tower and re-dedicated. Beside it is a **bench dedicated to the VCs of the Orange Order** from the Orange Brethren.

By 1994 the Somme Association (qv), based in Craigavon House in Belfast, was established under Royal Patronage, and undertook to 'co-ordinate research into Ireland's part in the First World War and provide a basis for the two traditions in Northern Ireland to come together and learn of their common heritage'. It took over care of the tower, declaring it to be Northern Ireland's National Memorial.

On 1 July 1994 a smart new Visitors' Centre was opened behind the tower, offering refreshments, books, maps and souvenirs for sale, some interesting displays charting Ireland's part in the Somme Battle, and a 12-minute video. It has excellent, clean toilets and welcoming custodians from the Somme Association.

Open every day except Monday, February - end November. ☎ (03) 22 74 87 14, Fax: (03) 3 22 74 80 68.

Behind the centre is a small copse which has preserved its 1916-18 contours, with trench lines and shell holes.

In the tower itself, the memorial chapel is full of commemorative plaques, pictures of Irish actions, flags and standards, a Visitors' Book and a **private memorial to Lt W. J. Wright**, 14th RIR, killed 2 July 1916, which was removed from Thiépval Wood the better to preserve it. The memorial details do not tie up with CWGC records which list **Lt M. J. Wright**, 14th RIR who was killed on 1 July 1916. He is commemorated on the Thiépval memorial. Of particular interest is a reproduction in oils by Carol Graham RVA of the painting which shows survivors of the Ulster Division's attack on the Schwaben Redoubt on 1 July repulsing a counter-attack on a trench outside Grandcourt. Its title is the Royal Irish Rifles' motto, *Quis separabit?* The painting was donated by the artist's father, Mr A. N. Graham. On the wall are the lines,

Helen's Tower Here I Stand
Dominant Over Sea and Land
Sons' Love Built Me and I Hold
Ulster's Love in Letter'd Gold.

Return to your car and continue downhill.

You are driving down Mill Road which descends into the Ancre Valley. Ahead on the skyline is the Beaumont Hamel Newfoundland Memorial Park, which at a distance looks like a wood. *Cross the river.* To the right is the site of the mill which gave the road its name.

Cross the railway.

Extra Visit to the Ancre British Cemetery (Map G21), the RND Memorial at Beaucourt (Map G24), SOA Lt Col B. C. Freyburg VC (Map G24) and Pte Amos's Private Memorial (Map G11)
Round-trip: 4 miles. Approximate time: 40 minutes

Turn right and continue to the cemetery on the left.

Ancre British Cemetery was constructed on the site of No Man's Land at the time of the RND 13 November 1916 attack. It is a concentration

Extra Visit continued

cemetery and also has burials from the 1 July 1916 attack by the Ulster Division and the 3 September attack by 39th Division. There is a bronze laurel wreath plaque on **Vere Harmsworth's** grave (Map G22), presented by Hungarian Scouts in gratitude for the stand by the *Daily Mail* on the restitution of Hungarian territory after the war. Here, too, is buried **Capt E. S. Ayre**, one of four Newfoundland cousins killed on 1 July (qv). A track to the right of the cemetery gives an excellent overview of the cemetery and the area of the RND attack of 13 November. This attack was launched at 0545 in thick mist behind a creeping barrage on a 1,200yd-front running north from the Ancre. The final objective line lay just beyond Beaucourt village, the first German trench line being roughly along the high ground on the track to the right of the cemetery. The RND start line was approximately where the road from the Ulster Tower meets the railway line. The right-hand battalion, the Hood, commanded by Lt Col B. C. Freyburg, (who had single-handedly created a dummy diversionary attack on the Turkish lines at Bulair during the Gallipoli campaign) moved quickly forward and cleared the entrances along the Ancre to the enemy tunnels that ran to Beaumont Hamel. In the centre, casualties were heavy, the Hawke Battalion having almost 400 within 30 minutes and the fighting became confused both there and alongside the 51st Highland Division to the north. It was decided that the attack should be renewed the following day. At dawn on 14 November the final assault on Beaucourt was personally led by Freyburg. The garrison of 800 surrendered but Freyburg was wounded for the third time, and this time seriously. 'For his conspicuous bravery and brilliant leadership as Battalion Commander' he was awarded the VC. Although the attack was eventually successful, the price was high – the Naval Brigades had almost 3,000 casualties. Also taking part in what was known as 'The Battle of the Ancre', was the 22nd Bn, Royal Fusiliers. Serving with them was the 46-year-old **Lce Sgt Hector Hugh Munro**, better known as the author **Saki**. Despite his age and history of ill-health, Munro had enlisted in the ranks on 25 August 1914, refusing a commission. After a year's service in France, he was hospitalized with malaria, but discharged himself on 11 November 1916, when he heard that a 'show' was soon to take place. Saki was hit by a sniper on 14 November, just after uttering the words, 'Put that bloody cigarette out' to a man who had just lit up.

In August 1928 the British Legion and the British Empire Service League organised a massive pilgrimage to Flanders and the Somme. Earl Haig was to have led the mourners, but died on 29 January, so Lady Haig was at their head. The Prince of Wales, Patron of the Legion, joined the throng in Béthune. After visiting Flanders, the party travelled to the Somme via Notre Dame de Lorette and Vimy Ridge, being billeted with local people (a

Extra Visit continued

logistic nightmare to arrange in itself) and travelling by train. They were lubricated by 31,500 bottles of beer and mineral water and by 26,000 quarts of tea, brewed by French Army Field Kitchens, and devoured 23,500 slices of both ham and cake. The women in the party upset the calculations – that they would drink three bottles of mineral water to one of beer, by consuming half and half! On 6-7 August 10,000 pilgrims arrived at Beaucourt Station by train-loads of 500 at intervals of 10-15 minutes and then wandered off in groups by foot, charabanc and 'excellent Citroen cars' to the Ancre Cemetery, the Ulster Tower and the Newfoundland Park. The cemetery already looked much as it does today, the Ulster Tower stood out bare and granite on the crest, but the Thiépval Memorial was not to be unveiled for another four years. Among the sadness was the unfailing humour of the Tommy. 'I wonder if my blinkin' leg is still up there?' mused a one-legged veteran, looking up to Beaumont Hamel. 'Well, I dunno; Somebody's bin muckin' abaht 'ere since I was 'ere larst', commented another.

Continue along the road. Gare de Beaucourt was the station at which the pilgrims arrived, and some sheds from that period still remain. The travellers were lured back to catch their return trains by the promise of tea, which they took in a field adjoining the station. The Legion report on the Pilgrimage claimed that several times during the two days 1,500 pilgrims were entrained and despatched on three different trains in the space of 10 minutes! A supremely evocative picture of this area just before the war and during the Somme Battle of 1 July 1916 is given in the fictional account by Sebastian Faulks in *Birdsong*.

Continue into Beaucourt-sur-Ancre. The **RND Memorial** may be seen on a bank to the left on entering the village. In this area is the SOA where Lt Col B. C. Freyburg (later **Lt Gen Freyburg, GCMG, KCB, KBE, DSO, 3 bars, GOC New Zealand Forces 1939-45, Governor General of New Zealand 1946-52) won the Victoria Cross** while commanding Hood Battalion on 13 November 1916.

Continue through the village on the D50. After about half a mile, a track to the left skirts a small wood (Bois d'Hollande). Approximately two-thirds of the way up the wood and some 10m inside is a small wooden cross on a large tree. It bears a brass **plaque to Pte D. Amos**, 15258, 9th Bn NSR who died on 21 November 1916 at this location. Be warned – it is not easy to find.

Turn round, return to the railway crossing and pick up the main itinerary.

Turn left and follow the signs to the Newfoundland Memorial Park up the D73 to the right.

To the left at this point, through the village of Hamel and to its right, is the site of the bottom of **Jacob's Ladder** (Map G28) and at its top, just short of Mesnil village and to the left of the road, the site of the fortified position known as **Brock's Benefit**.

Continue to the park entrance and park in the large car park on the left.

Here there is a signboard of welcome and a reminder to respect the site.

In the distance in a field to the left (but approached from a track from Mesnil) is **Knightsbridge Cemetery** (Map G26) in which is buried **2nd Lt W. D. Ayre**, another of the family of four Newfoundlanders killed on 1 July 1916 (qv).

• *Newfoundland Memorial Park/Visitor's Centre/12 miles/50 minutes/OP/Map G20/19/18/17/17a/16/15/14/13/12*

The park covers 84 acres and was purchased by the then Government of Newfoundland as a memorial to the soldiers and sailors of Newfoundland. It was officially opened by Earl Haig on 7 June 1925. There are a number of memorials and cemeteries in the park, as well as preserved trench lines which have been maintained in their original shape, the Visitor's Centre and the Director's house. In the late 1920s, the 'warden', Billy Brown, a Newfoundland veteran, lived in a log cabin. At that stage the preserved trenches in the park contained duckboards, and the wreckage of an aeroplane, boxes of hand grenades and many other relics littered the battlefield. The great Pilgrimage of August 1928 visited here too, and members were photographed holding rifles and shell cases and wearing tin hats. They were much impressed by the 'defiant' Caribou and the 'indomitable' Highlander memorials (see below) that were already well-established in the Park.

Walk into the park.

The regular visitor of many years will have noticed that since the opening of the Visitor's Centre and the increase in visitors, especially of students, the nature and atmosphere of the park has changed - from a true battlefield to a memorial park. This has been necessary to protect the precious and vulnerable trench lines and craters from the erosion caused by the sheer volume of feet walking on them. Therefore areas which were freely visitable are now protected by strong wire fences, some electric. Duckboards and wooden bridges have also been constructed in and over the trenches while the Canadian authorities search for the most sympathetic way to preserve the site. Archeological explorations are being undertaken by members of the Durand Group (qv)

At each side of the entrance are **plaques** erected in 1997 confirming that the Park, initiated in 1922, is now a Canadian Historic Site and Monument. Plaques describe how the idea was conceived by Padre Thomas Nagle and the construction was under the direction of R. H. K. Cochus, landscape artist, from funds raised by the Government and the women of Newfoundland. There is a dispenser to the left for self-guided tour leaflets. A path to the right leads to the **Visitor's Centre**.

This typical Newfoundland wooden building was opened in July 2000. It contains a recreated living room, complete with working stove and contemporary artefacts. The exhibits are imaginatively and sensitively mounted (some on a large board in the shape of a ship), with many personal photographs, letters and other ephemera. A continuing story follows a dwindling band of 32 Newfoundland soldiers through the Great War on the Western Front and in Gallipoli. There are excellent toilet facilities and a small sales stall. In the same way as at Vimy the Centre is manned by knowledgeable Canadian students (often actual Newfoundlanders) who compete for the honour and who give guided tours of the Park. Coaches should book ahead. ☎ (03) 22 76 70 86. The Centre is **open every day**: April-December 1000-1800 and January-March 0900-1700. Closed Christmas and New Year's Day. Guides are available from January to mid-December. The Park is open 24 hours a day, 365 days a year.

The attack on 1 July was in the direction in which you are walking. The assault division was the 29th, which had done so well in Gallipoli, and whose previous General, Hunter-Weston, was now its Corps (VIII) Commander. Some 1,350m ahead of you, beyond Y Ravine at the bottom of the park, on a curve in the German lines, a massive mine of 40,600lb of ammonal was placed by 252nd Tunnelling Company, 75ft under a German redoubt known as **Hawthorn**. Believing that it would be to his soldiers' advantage, Hunter-Weston had the mine blown at 0720, ten minutes before the infantry went over the top. It was not to their advantage. On the contrary, it only served to give the Germans a warning of imminent attack. The first brigade that went in, the 87th, was cut down and the 88th was ordered up. One assault formation of the 88th was the 1st Battalion of the Royal Newfoundland Regiment. They made their attack across the area of the park you are now entering. It lasted less than half an hour. The Newfoundlanders had done all they could, wrote the divisional commander later, 'because dead men can advance no further.' Every officer who went forward was either killed or wounded. Of the 801 men who went into action, some authorities say that only 68 members of the battalion were not wounded, one of the the highest casualty counts for any regimental unit on 1 July. Among those killed here were three members of the Ayre family (qv). **2nd Lt Gerald W. Ayre** is commemorated on the Newfoundland Memorial below the Caribou – see below.

The Durand Group (qv), under Lt Col Phillip Robinson, have undertaken much archaeological and historical research here at Beaumont Hamel Park and in unit records, which offers alternative figures for the wounded and missing. Confusion is simply one of the states of war and this is particularly true of casualty figures, e.g. Are the 'attached personnel' accounted for?; Was the recent draft allowed for?; Did more survivors turn up after the roll call?; Did everyone actually take part in the fighting? Whatever the precise number of casualties the Newfoundlanders suffered greatly on 1 July. The 29th Division had an overall casualty percentage on 1 July of about 26%. The Newfoundlanders had a rate of about 65% but Robinson believes that the 10th

Private memorial to Pte Amos in the Bois d'Hollande

Preserved trenches at the Beaumont Hamel Newfoundland Memorial Park

The Visitor's Centre, Newfoundland Memorial Park

The grieving Newfoundland Caribou

A Canadian student guide

51st Highland Division Memorial

Hunters CWGC Cemetery

Battalion of the West Yorkshire Regiment at Fricourt had an equivalent rate of about 70%. Nevertheless the achievements of the Newfoundlanders were recognised by King George V in December 1917 when he gave the regiment the title 'Royal.'

The first **memorial** to be seen is that to **29th Division**, its distinctive red badge displayed on a stone cairn, which is on the left of the path a few metres from the entrance. Then almost immediately on the left is the bronze box containing the Visitors' Book and registers and a plaque on the right carrying a **verse by John Oxenham**.

Continue on the path to the Caribou and climb to the top.

The Caribou was the emblem of the Newfoundland Regiment and there are three more identical bronzes in France commemorating other regimental actions – at Gueudecourt (Itinerary Three), Masnières (Cambrai 20 November 1917) and Monchy le Preux (Arras 14 April 1917). It is a most poignant memorial – the animal appears to be baying for her lost young – as well as a striking piece of sculpture. On the parapet around the Caribou are orientation arrows which identify various parts of the battlefield, including the **three British cemeteries** in the park. On the left is **Hawthorn Ridge No 2** (containing 214 burials from 1 July 1916), and the attractive, circular **Hunters** (containing forty-six men buried in what had been a large shell hole), on the right **Y Ravine** (containing 366 burials, including Newfoundlanders from 1 July and RND from November 1916). At the base of the mound on which the Caribou stands are **three bronze plaques** on which are named **591 officers and men of the Royal Newfoundland Regiment** (including **2nd Lt W. D. Ayre**), 114 of the Newfoundland Naval Reserve and 115 of the Newfoundland Mercantile Marine who lost their lives during the war and have no known grave. To the right of this group is a separate **bronze plaque** to the **staff of the Imperial Tobacco Company of the 1st Newfoundland Regiment**. To the left a plaque to commemorate the 200th anniversary of the Royal Newfoundland Regiment was unveiled on 1 July 1995. Also visible are the **'Danger Tree'**, a twisted skeleton of an original trunk which marks the spot where casualties were heaviest on 1 July (about a third of the way to Y Ravine) and in the distance at the bottom of the slope, the handsome kilted **Highlander of the 51st Highland Division**, standing on a platform of Aberdeen granite. The bronze figure commemorates the action of the Division in taking Beaumont Hamel and the natural feature of Y Ravine on 13 November during Part 5 of the Somme Battle. In his book *The 51st Division War Sketches*, published in 1920, divisional artist Fred Farrell shows a splendid drawing of '7th Gordons Clearing 'Y' Ravine'. The Germans took advantage of this natural shelter and riddled the banks of the ravine with tunnels and deep, comfortably furnished, well-provisioned dugouts. Booty from these and other strong German defensive positions taken during the attack, included 'tinned beef from Monte Video, Norwegian sardines, cigarettes (including Wills' Gold Flake), cigars and many thousand bottles of excellent soda and of beer' (Regimental History). More mysterious were the 'piano, some ladies' dancing slippers, silk stockings, and petticoats'. The Jocks deserved their perks. Casualties sustained represented 45% of those who took part in the attack. In the days that followed, the remnants of the division were detailed to clear the battlefield, which still bore the skeletons (picked clean by the thousands of rats which swarmed over the area) of casualties from the 1 July 1916 attack. 152nd Brigade alone buried 669 bodies in the cemeteries at Mailly Maillet and Auchonvillers. It was an unnerving task even to these hardened soldiers.

Between the Highlander and the Ravine (about 20m deep) is a **Celtic memorial cross** commemorating the Division's casualties at High Wood in July 1916.

Keeping to the authorised pathways, examine the trench lines (marked as 'British Front Line' and 'German Front Line') and craters, which still contain some battlefield debris. Walking briskly it takes 10 minutes to get to Y Ravine.

Return to your car and continue past a CWGC sign right.

This is to **Hawthorn Ridge Cemetery No 1. (Map G2)** and contains 152 UK burials (including many public schoolboys of the 16th Middlesex) and a Newfoundland burial. It was made by V Corps after the 1916 Somme battles.

At the first road junction go right on the D73 signed Mailly Maillet and enter Auchonvillers. Auchonvillers (obviously 'Ocean Villas' to Tommy) was described by Blunden as 'a good example of the miscellaneous, picturesque, pitiable, pleasing, appalling, intensely intimate village ruin close to the line …' 'The French', he felt, had modelled it 'comprehensively as a large redoubt, complete with a searchlight. There were many dugouts under houses and in the gardens, but of a flimsy, rotted and stagnant kind; the Somme battle had evidently swamped all old defence schemes.' The cemetery used by the 51st Highlanders in November 1916 is known today as **Auchonvillers Military Cemetery** (Map G1), with just over 500 burials. It was started by the French in 1915. **Auchonvillers Communal Cemetery** contains fifteen burials with red sandstone headstones, mostly of 1st Borders from April 1916.

On the left on entering the village is the welcoming guest house run by Avril Williams, who bought this attractive but originally derelict site and has been progressively improving the facilities over the years until it now offers 4 en-suite twin rooms, and a self-catering apartment. The tea room caters for groups (who must book in advance) and individuals and can serve breakfasts, lunches, teas and dinners. ☎ (03) 22 76 23 66.

An original trench line has been excavated at the rear and other investigative work (with the help of the Durand Group) is in progress. Its well-preserved cellar was used as a dressing station. A dividing wall was built in 1914 by the French, and half was used as a ward, and still shows the marks where bunks were attached to the wall, the other half being used as a surgery/makeshift operating theatre. There are many scratched or carved names from 1916, mostly of members of the RIR, both patients and stretcher bearers. A tunnel, now bricked up, led into the cellar, the entrance to which

A wartime occupant of the dressing station

Excavated trench line, Avril Williams' garden, Auchonvillers

was protected by a gas curtain. Avril has many interesting personal items and artefacts found in the cellar or in the garden and sells books and maps relating to the Somme battles.

250m later at the crossroads before the church in Auchonvillers turn right on the D174 signed to Beaumont Hamel. 350m later the road forks.

Extra Visit to Sucrerie Military Cemetery & Euston Road Cemetery/Map D7/6. Round-trip: 4.0 miles. Approximate time: 30 minutes.

Take the left fork to Hébuterne and continue to the crossroads with the D919 (N319). Turn left and immediately right along a rough, tree-lined track (you are advised to leave your car and walk to the cemetery or risk getting stuck if it is at all damp) following CWGC signs.

Sucrerie Military Cemetery is situated on what was one of the routes from Colincamps to the front line on 1 July and later Somme battles and where

Extra Visit continued

mass graves were prepared for the casualties. In it, in a row of officers, is **Lt Col the Hon L. C. W. Palk, DSO**, CO of the 1st Hampshires, who lost all twenty-six of their officers and 559 of their men on 1 July. Lt Col Palk, obviously a fan of the cartoonist, Bruce Bairnsfather, exhorted his battalion that this was the greatest day the British army had ever had, dressed himself in his best uniform, donned white gloves and led his battalion HQ across No Man's Land. Lying mortally wounded in a shell hole, he turned to another man lying near him and said, 'If you know of a better 'ole, go to it'.

Return to the crossroads, and immediately turn left. At the next fork take the left hand road, the D129E, and stop at the cemetery on the left.

The Bairnsfather cartoon that inspired Col Palk's last words

Euston Road Cemetery, like Sucrerie Military Cemetery, was constructed on one of the main routes from the rear areas to the front line. Many of the burials are from 1 July 1916, notably that of the exceptional war poet, **Sgt John William Streets** of the 12th 'Sheffield Pals' Battalion of the York and Lancs.

Streets broke the mould of the perceived image of the 'golden' poet from a public school and of the officer class. He was born, the eldest of twelve children, to a Derbyshire miner, whose profession he followed from the age of 14. A sensitive boy, he loved the countryside, literature and art. Indeed his main dilemma, on deciding to quit the mine, was whether he should become a writer or an artist. With the encouragement of a perceptive teacher Streets taught himself Latin, Greek and French and from an early age wrote poems of exceptional literary ability. The outbreak of war solved his dilemma. He enlisted on 6 September 1914 at the age of 29. Throughout his training in the UK, Will continued to write poetry and send snippets home in the regular letters he wrote to his mother. The poetry and letters showed signs of the malaise common to many poets – intimations of mortality. In the case of the poets from World War I, however, the premonition was based on the growing casualty figures. In December 1915 the battalion moved to Egypt for training, but arrived too late to participate in the action at their ultimate destination – Gallipoli. In March 1916 the

Extra Visit continued

12th Battalion arrived on the Somme and the poetry continued, still, despite worsening conditions, in an heroic and patriotic mode. Recognition was just beginning for this self-taught bard (he had been published in *The Poetry Review* and a compilation called *Made in the Trenches*) when the carnage of 1 July cut short his life. The battalion had moved into assembly trenches behind John Copse (see below) and Streets was wounded soon after their attack began. He was seen going to the assistance of another seriously wounded man and then disappeared. At first there was some hope that he was simply missing, as his body was not immediately found. It was later identified, and he is buried here in Euston Road Cemetery. Coincidentally, Streets' twin brothers were serving with the RAMC at the dressing station in the Basilica at Albert. One of them sent home Will's 'worn, red-covered pocket-books' with 'jottings in it of stray ideas or phrases that occurred to him for stories or for verses'. Adcock included a chapter on Streets in his book of soldier poets, *For Remembrance*, and his slim collected works were published in May 1917 by Erskine Macdonald as *The Undying Splendour*. His posterity was assured. The inscription on his headstone, 'I fell, but yielded not my English soul; that lives out here beneath the battle's roll', is a quotation from his own work. Another soldier poet of the 12th Battalion Yorks & Lancs, Corporal Alexander Robertson, was killed in the same attack as Will Streets. He is commemorated on the Thiépval Memorial.

Return to the fork and follow the main itinerary.

Fork right on the D163 signed to Beaumont.

To the left of the road was the British position known as 'The Bowery'.

After 800m stop at the memorial on the bank on the left.

• *Argyll & Sutherland Highlanders Memorial/14 miles/10 minutes/Map G4*

Unveiled in 1923 by the Duke of Argyll, this imposing Celtic cross commemorates and gives details of the war service of the 8th Argyllshire Bn, Princess Louise's Argyll & Sutherland Highlanders, the 51st Highland Division, the 61st Division, and the 15th Scottish Division: 'Mobilised Service from 4 August 1914 to 12 November 1919. Service in the field from 1 May 1915 to 11 November 1918: 3 years and 195 days. Killed in Action: officers 51, NCOs and men 831. Wounded: officers 105, NCOs and men 2,527'. The Gaelic inscription translates as 'The complete heroes of the Great War, the braves who went before us'. 'Cruachan' is the war cry of the Campbells. The memorial stands at the entrance to the Sunken Road, where the cine-cameraman, **Geoffrey Malins**, attached to Maj Gen H. de B. de Lisle's 29th Division (part of Hunter-Weston's VIII Corps) from 28 June to film *The Battle*, filmed men of the 1st Lancashire Fusiliers on 1 July. At the top of this road was a trench called Jacob's Ladder (not to be confused with the trench of the same name at Hamel, frequently mentioned by Edmund Blunden) and a chalk feature known as White City. From this vantage point he filmed, 'with shaking hand, as ... for all the world like a gigantic sponge, the earth rose in the air to the height of hundreds of feet. Higher and higher it rose, and with a horrible, grinding roar the earth fell back upon itself, leaving in its place a mountain of smoke.'

His historic, and much-shown, sequence of the great Hawthorn mine going up at 0720 hours on 1 July, was the high point of his film *The Battle of the Somme*, first shown to an invited audience in London on 10 August and seen by thousands when it was put on general release at the end of the month. Prior to *The Battle of the Somme*, front-line pictures were rarely published. In 1916, however, the Press Bureau asked for tenders for the exclusive right to reproduce, as postcards, pictures taken by official photographers at the front. *The Daily Mail* tender was accepted, half the profits to go to military charities, with a minimum payment of £5,000. On 6 September seven sets of six postcards were put on sale. Card No 13 in Series II shows the Hawthorn explosion.

The filled-in entrances to underground tunnels and dugouts can be discerned by the eagle-eyed to the right of the bank in the Sunken Road. Other entrances have also been filled in in the steep chalk cliffs to the left of the road as one leaves the village towards Beaucourt.

Standing at the memorial and looking due south across the D163, a copse can be seen on the skyline. This is the Hawthorn Crater. To the left is a path leading to a cemetery.

• *Beaumont-Hamel British CWGC Cemetery/5 minutes/Map G3*

There are two long lines of graves, many unknown, others from 1 July 1916 and early 1917. There is one German grave.

Continue on the D163. To the right is a sign leading to Hawthorn Crater up a steep path through the fields. Park and walk up the path between fields.

• *Hawthorn Crater/14.1 miles/15 minutes/Map G6*

The double crater, which appears as a figure-of-eight from the air, is now enclosed by wire, and filled with hawthorn and other thick undergrowth. A sergeant who had worked on the tunnel described the 'exploding chamber' as 'as big as a picture palace, and the gallery was an awful length. It took seven months to build, and we were working under some of the crack Lancashire miners'. The tunnel leading to the mine prepared for 1 July was 75ft deep and 1,000ft long, with a charge of 40,600lb of ammonal. It had been prepared by 252nd Tunnelling Company. It was fired 10 minutes early and formed a crater 40ft deep and over 300ft wide at its largest diameter. Although the German

Returned WW1 stained glass fragment, Beaumont Hamel Church

Argyll & Sutherland Highlanders Memorial, Beaumont Hamel

redoubt here was totally destroyed, no advance was made and another attack was launched on 13 November when a 30,000lb charge was blown under the old crater which the Germans had fortified. The mine was successfully blown at 0545 (the figure-of-eight shape of the crater is due to the two explosions) and the 51st Division advanced steadily along its whole front.

Continue into Beaumont Hamel.

At the crossroads in the village, on the left, is a flagpole. Stop.

• *51st Highland Division Flagpole/14.4 miles/5 minutes/Map G8*

The flagpole bears a plaque recording its presentation by the officers, NCO's and men of the 51st Highland Division to the inhabitants of Beaumont Hamel to commemorate the recapture of the village by the division on 13 November 1916. In their regimental history it is reported that the village was 'famous for its manufacture of powder-puffs' before the war!

Continue. Turn right to the church and park.

• *Beaumont-Hamel Church Stained Glass Fragment/14.5 miles/5 minutes/Map G7*

A small fragment of stained glass with the head of a sweet Virgin Mary is incorporated in the plain coloured glass window of the church to the left of the entrance. A plaque records that it was found in the ruins of the original church in 1914 and returned in 1962 by **Lt Georg Muller** of the German 99th Infantry Regiment and re-installed by villagers Monsieur and Madame Welferinger-Letesse, who worked with devotion for *Souvenir Français* for many years.

Return to the D163.

Extra Visit to Waggon Road (Map D27)/OP & Munich Trench/(Map D28) CWGC Cemeteries on Redan Ridge/OP Round-trip: 1.6 miles. Approximate time: 25 minutes

The vantage point from the crest of the ridge gives such a good overall view of the 1 July 1916 battle, that this diversion is highly recommended. Binoculars are essential. The extraordinary feeling of remoteness, of peace and of beauty experienced in these cemeteries also make the journey rewarding.

Drive straight over and continue uphill on the narrow road, following green CWGC signs to the cemeteries.

To the right on the crest is **Waggon Road, V Corps Cemetery No 10**, which contains 195 UK burials, 36 unidentified. Forty-nine of the burials are of men from 11th (Lonsdale) Battalion, the Border Regt, which attacked on the Ancre in July (qv) and also in November 1916. Waggon Road was the name given to the road running north to the village of Serre from Beaumont Hamel Station. *Go to the cross and stand facing the entrance gate.* That is 12 o'clock. The skyline to the front, left to right, gives the axis of the British attack on 1 July. To the left at 11 o'clock is the church spire at Auchonvillers on the British start line. The shape of the battle can now be followed by finding these points: at 12 o'clock is the Cross of Sacrifice of Serre Road No 2 Cemetery. This is the site of the German front line defensive position known as The Quadrilateral. At 9 o'clock is the Newfoundland Memorial Park and both the Caribou and the Kilted Highlander Memorials can be seen. At 7 o'clock is the copse at the end of the Leipzig Salient and the Thiépval Memorial. At 2 o'clock is the Memorial to the Sheffield Pals on the Serre Road. The road up which you have driven runs

Waggon Road CWGC Cem

Extra Visit continued

due north along the German front line of 1 July, with the British line about 600m to the left.

Continue. To the left is **Munich Trench, V Corps Cemetery No 8**, with the legend 'Beaumont Hamel' inscribed on the gatepost. The 126 burials, of which 28 are unknown, are arranged in three lines of graves, enclosed by a hedge. The grass path leading to this isolated cemetery is immaculate, witness to the dedication of the CWGC in that little-visited sites are as lovingly cared for as are those that are more accessible. Indeed, in October 1995 the visitors' books for these two cemeteries dated back to 1975.

Turn round and return to the D163. Rejoin the main itinerary.

Turn left and return to the flagpole. Take the small road uphill to the right (Rue de la Montagne).

Redan Ridge Cemetery No 2 is signed to the left (Map G5a). It is on the site of 'Watling Street', 100m west of the old German front line and has 279 burials of 2nd, 4th and 29th Divs.

Continue to the first cemetery on the left.

• *Redan Ridge CWGC Cemetery No 3/15.1 miles/5 minutes/Map D26*

This lovely little cemetery contains only fifty-four graves, mostly of 2nd Div from 1 July and 13 November 1916 and thirteen special memorials. It is on the site of German front line trenches.

Continue to the D919. Turn left and continue to the large British cemetery on the left.

• *Serre Road CWGC Cemetery No 2/Val Braithwaite Memorial/ 16.1 miles/20 minutes/Map D24/23*

Designed by Sir Edwin Lutyens, this is one of three Serre Road cemeteries. They were begun by V Corps in the spring of 1917, over-run by the Germans in March 1918 and re-taken in August. There are over 7,100 burials in this concentration cemetery, making it the largest British cemetery on the Somme battlefield. It contains some German graves and that of **Private A. E. Bull**, 12th Yorks & Lancs, who has a private memorial in Sheffield Park (qv). It was in the gardener's hut in this cemetery that CWGC worker Ben Leach hid two RAF pilots when visited by Germans inspecting German graves during World War II. At the roadside outside the cemetery wall is a **private memorial to Lt V. A. Braithwaite, MC**, a regular officer of the SLI, son of Gen Sir Walter Braithwaite, KCB, Chief of the General Staff in Gallipoli, where his son served as his ADC. Besides winning one of the first MC's of the war at Mons, Braithwaite had twice been mentioned in Despatches. In his *Gallipoli Memories*

Compton Mackenzie remembers with affection the unsophisticated, 'tall, sunburnt young Wykehamist'. He was killed on the first day of the Somme battle, (though on the Thiépval memorial the date is given as 2 July) along with his commanding officer, adjutant and fourteen other officers in the battalion. Their attack had been made along the line of the road towards you, and to its left, against the German stronghold known as Quadrilateral Redoubt, which was on the site of the cemetery.

Turn round and continue back up the D919 towards the chapel on the right.

• *Probable Site of Wilfred Owen's 1917 Dugout/16.2 miles*

Beyond Braithwaite's Cross, before the French Chapel, and to the right of the road, is the probable site (located by researcher Philip Guest) of 'the advanced post, that is a "dugout" in the middle of No Man's Land' described by the poet **Lt Wilfred Edward Salter Owen** of the 2nd Bn, the Manchester Regt, in a letter to his mother of 16 January 1917, where he suffered 'seventh hell'. Here one of Owen's most powerful poems, *The Sentry*, was inspired by an incident when a sentry was blown down the dugout steps by the force of a shell blast and blinded. The man's terror and distress: 'O sir, my eyes – I'm blind – I'm blind, I'm blind', would haunt Owen. A few days later the battalion moved to billets in Courcelles (a village slightly further behind the lines than Colincamps) from where Owen wrote home on the 19th, describing his close encounter with a gas shell. This incident was probably the inspiration for the episode in one of his best-known poems, *Dulce et Decorum Est:*

Gas! GAS! Quick, boys! – An ecstasy of fumbling,
Fitting the clumsy helmets just in time ...

But they were not in time for one poor lad who virtually drowned 'under a green sea'. Like the blind sentry, Owen saw the gas victim 'In all my dreams'. Owen was killed a week before the Armistice and is buried in Ors CWGC cemetery.

• *French Memorial Chapel & German Memorial/16.4 miles/5 minutes/Map D21/22*

In the porch of this sadly neglected chapel there are two interesting memorials. One is to a remarkable man, Maistre Joseph de la Rue, who founded the memorial. He seems to have been the French equivalent of 'Woodbine Willie' (the Padre, Geoffrey Studdert-Kennedy). A professor of history before the war, he became Chaplain to the 243rd and 233rd RI during 1914-18, was Chaplain to the Army in 1939-45, and Chaplain to the Galliéni Group in 1940-3, *Chevalier de la Légion d'Honneur, Médaille Militaire* and *Croix de Guerre*. Below his imposing plaque is a small, modern plaque, one of the few German memorials on the Somme, to the memory of comrades of the Bavarian Reserve Infantry Regiment 1 who were killed at Serre.

Walk over the road.

V. A. L. Braithwaite private memorial, with a sea of headstones from the Serre Road CWGC Cemetery No 2 in the background

The French National Cemetery at Serre-Hebuterne

The French Memorial Chapel and signs to the Redan Ridge, Waggon Road and Munich Trench Cemeteries

Bavarian Res Inf Regt No 1 memorial, Serre Chapel

The Register Box at the French Cemetery

Sheffield Memorial Park: Accrington Pals Memorial (above)

Barnsley Pals Memorial

Chorley Pals Plaques

Barnsley Pals Plaques

• *French National Cemetery Serre-Hébuterne/10 minutes/Map D17/20*

Created in 1919 for the dead of the 243rd RI of the 10-13 June battles of 1915 it was enlarged in 1923 for other dead of the 243rd and 327th RI. It contains 834 burials, of which 240 are in the mass grave. At the top of the cemetery is an impressive memorial, with a bronze *bas relief*, to the men of 233rd, 243rd and 327th RI from Lille.

Continue to the next cemetery on the same side of the road.

• *Serre Road CWGC Cemetery No 1/16.5 miles/5 minutes/Map D18*

This was begun in May 1917 by V Corps but was enlarged after the Armistice by the concentration of over 2,000 graves from other parts of the Somme battlefield. There are some 2,100 burials, including 71 French soldiers. On 1 July it was the Leeds and Bradford Pals who attacked here, i.e. the 15th, 16th and 18th West Yorks.

Continue 100m. Park off the road by the beginning of the track, Chemin des Cimetières, leading to the left signed Luke Copse, Railway Hollow, Queen's and Serre Road No 3 Cemeteries. Walk along it. If it is very dry you may consider driving up it as far as the first cemetery on the right.

• *Serre Road No 3 CWGC Cemetery/16.7 miles/5 minutes/Map D15*

This tiny cemetery contains eighty-one burials (mostly of W Yorks from 1 July) and four special memorials.

Continue. As the path curves to the right, an enclosed wooded area is on the left. Walk in.

• *Sheffield Memorial Park & Memorials/Railway Hollow CWGC Cemetery 15 minutes/Map D12/31a/13b/13c/13d/13e/16*

Originally there were four small copses in this area, named after the Apostles, Matthew, Mark, Luke and John. The remnants of them now merge into one wooded area, in which is the park, where, as at Beaumont Hamel, craters and trench lines have remained undisturbed by agriculture and have been allowed to grass over naturally.

'I am the grass; I cover all', wrote the American poet Carl Sandburg and graphically described the potent work of that benign plant which covered bodies from Austerlitz, Waterloo, Gettysburg, Ypres and Verdun. Here it covers some of the trenches from which the Pals from the northern towns received their baptism of fire as part of Kitchener's New Army. The **Accrington Pals** (Map D13b, a symbolic broken brick wall), the **Chorley Pals** Y Co (Map D13a, a plaque on a tree), the 13th/14th York & Lancaster, **Barnsley Pals** (Map D13e, a smart black marble monument with coloured badges and on the tree a small black plaque naming the sponsors, including Sir Nicholas Hewitt and the *Barnsley Chronicle*) and the **Sheffield Pals** (Map D3d, a brick memorial gateway with commemorative plaques) have all placed memorials here to their sacrifice. On a tree to the left is a small plaque to **Alister Sturrock**, I July 1994. A wooden cross bears a plaque in memory of **Pte A. E. Bull** of the 12th York & Lancs, killed here on 1 July 1916, whose body was found on 13 April 1928 and who is now buried in Serre Road No 2 CWGC Cemetery. At the foot of the slope at the rear of the park is **Railway Hollow CWGC Cemetery** (Map D12) containing 107 UK burials (mostly York & Lancs of 1 July, plus 2 French graves). It is situated on the line of the old military railway which ran through here.

Emerge from the park and walk to the cemetery straight ahead.

• *Queen's CWGC Cemetery/5 minutes/Map D14*

This cemetery contains 311 burials, mostly from July and Nov 1916, with a large number of Accrington Pals who attacked from their trench, now within the park, on 1 July.

Return to the entrance to the park, turn right.

• *Luke Copse CWGC Cemetery/5 minutes/Map D11*

This small cemetery (seventy-two burials) contains men of the Sheffield City Battalion who attacked here on 1 July, including **brothers L Cpl F. and Pte W. Gunstone**, and has a memorial to men of the 2nd Suffolks who fell here on 13 November 1916.

The three cemeteries, Serre Road No 3, Queens and Luke Copse, all lie just on the No Man's Land side of the British line of 1 July. At 0720 the assault troops of 31st Division climbed out of their trenches to file through the passages cut in their own wire, intending to lie in No Man's Land before advancing together to capture the village of Serre. It was their first time in battle. They were immediately subjected to heavy machine-gun fire from Serre village and bombarded by both field and heavy artillery. At 0730 when the leading waves stood up in order to advance, the fire increased and hardly any troops reached the German front trench, barely 400m away. Those that did were either killed or taken prisoner. The 31st Division contained four Rifle Battalions from Hull, one from Leeds, two from Bradford, one from Accrington, one from Sheffield, two from Barnsley and one from Durham. These were 'Pals' battalions, made up of volunteer soldiers hailing from a single town or village, or even a single factory or football team. They worked together, lived together, joined up together and frequently died together, devastating whole communities back home at a stroke.

Return to the main D919 road. Continue towards Serre. Park by the memorial on the left

• *12th Bn York & Lancs Memorial/Serre Village 17.5 miles/5 minutes/Map D19*

This was raised by Sheffield to her Pals, known as the Sheffield City Battalion. Sheffield adopted Serre after the war. A glance at the 140m contour lines on the

Holts' map shows the predominating position held by the Germans in this village, which they had prepared as a fortress. At this northern end of the Fourth Army sector there were no significant gains at all during the Somme fighting. Following the July failures by the 4th and 31st Divisions, the 3rd and 31st tried again on 13 November to no avail. The memorial is located here because during the unsuccessful assault on Serre on 13 November 1916, some British troops briefly entered the village and found bodies of men of the 12th Bn still lying where they had fallen in July. Eventually on 24 February 1917 the Germans withdrew from Serre and the 22nd Manchesters moved in the following morning.

Continue on the N919 signed to Arras, to Puisieux.

Like Serre, this was abandoned by the Germans on 24 February 1917 in their retreat to the Hindenburg Line.

Continue to the junction left in Puisieux with the D6.

Extra Visit to Owl Trench CWGC Cemetery, Rossignol Wood CWGC Cemetery & Rossignol Wood Bunker. Round trip: 7.6 miles. Approximate time: 45 minutes

Turn left up the D6 following green CWGC signs.

The British attack of 1 July had included a diversionary assault (from your left) by Sir Edward Allenby's Third Army on a German salient at Gommecourt. Its object was to divert attention away from the main thrust astride the Albert-Bapaume Road. The task was given to 56th Division, a London and Middlesex territorial force under General Hull and 46th Division from the Midlands. Beginning early in May, great pioneer works were begun behind the British lines. Headquarters were built, roads, railways and pipe lines laid and even a new front line dug some 400m in front of the old one. These preparations so caught the Germans' attention that on 1 July three divisions-worth of artillery hammered the British attack. Many Tommies believed that the enemy knew exactly when to expect them. 56th Division took the German front line (roughly the road you are driving along) and more, but lost it all by the end of the day. 46th Division to the north was unable to advance at all, and was thus incapable of supporting its neighbour. General Stuart-Wortley was relieved of command less than a week later. In this area the D6 runs roughly parallel with the German line, which from

Three Unknowns, one headstone, Owl Trench CWGC Cem

Extra Visit continued

Rossignol Wood CWGC Cemetery onwards was about 400m to your left and was in 56th Division's area. The line bent sharply to the right 400m beyond Gommecourt village, this northern part being in 46th Division's area, with the assault being down the D6 from Foncquevillers directly towards the village.

Continue to **Owl Trench** (Map D10), the first cemetery you reach on the left. This tiny cemetery contains only fifty-three burials, from 31st Division's attack on the German rearguard in February 1917 during their retreat to the Hindenburg Line. The burials, many of W Yorks, are mostly three to a grave, therefore the cemetery looks even smaller than it actually is.

Continue a few hundred yards further. On the left is **Rossignol Wood Cemetery** (Map D9). This was begun on 14 March 1917 by the N and S Staffs and used again in August 1918 by the New Zealanders. It has thirty-four UK, seven New Zealand and seventy German graves, i.e., considerably more German than British graves.

Continue to the next junction and turn right towards the wood. Stop at the first corner of the wood and walk south some 100m along the edge to an obvious indentation.

A few metres inside **Rossignol Wood** is a German bunker (Map D30). Near it one of the most exceptional Padres of World War I won the Victoria Cross.

The **Rev Theodore Bayley Hardy** spent the day of 5 April 1918 there comforting a badly wounded man injured in the 8th Lincolnshires' attack on the wood. At dusk he returned to ask for a volunteer to help him bring back the wounded man, and a sergeant, G. Radford, helped him to bring the man to safety. The Padre then continued to tend the wounded under fire and later in the month at Bucquoy, on 25, 26 and 27 April, again acted

Memorial to 46 North Midlands Division in Gommecourt Wood New Cemetery

Extra Visit continued

with such self-sacrificing heroism to save others' lives that he was nominated three more times for the Victoria Cross. Radford was awarded the DCM, and Hardy went on to add the DSO, MC and DCM to his VC. That month he was also appointed Chaplain to King George V, who presented him with his VC in 1918 (an event immortalised by the artist Terence Cuneo). Despite pleas to accept a safe appointment at Base, Hardy – who had almost refused to accept his VC, but agreed when it was pointed out by Col Hardyman, CO of the Somersets, that if he did refuse it would only 'be advertising yourself all the more' – continued in the front line. On 11 October 1918 the 8th Lincolns and the 8th Somersets were crossing the River Selle at Briastres when the Padre was shot through the thigh. Evacuated to No 2 Red Cross Hospital at Rouen, he died on 18 October, less than a month before the end of the war. He was 55 years old and the most decorated non-combatant of the conflict.

Return to the main road and turn right. On the right, opposite Gommecourt Park, was the fortified position known as Kern Redoubt, or the Maze.

Continue through the village to the final cemetery on the road.

Gommecourt Wood New Cemetery (Map D2) contains 682 UK burials, 56 New Zealanders and 1 Australian. There are ten special memorials. On the right-hand wall inside the cemetery is a memorial **plaque to 46th N Midlands Division** (Map D1).

Immediately to the S of the cemetery is the **SOA** of Capt John Leslie Green VC (Map D3). On 1 July 1916, **Captain John Leslie Green of the RAMC**, attd 1/5th Battalion the Sherwood Foresters, although himself wounded, rescued an officer who had been wounded and was caught up in the enemy wire, with grenades constantly being thrown at him. He dragged him to a shell hole where he dressed his wounds, and had almost succeeded in bringing the man to safety when he was killed. Capt Green is buried in Foncquevillers Military Cemetery (Map A4)

Return to the N919 at Puisieux, turn left and pick up the main itinerary.

Note that if further itineraries are to be followed, you may wish to finish Itinerary One here and return to your base on the Somme. If returning to one of the Channel Ports, the remainder of Itinerary One is directly en route.

Continue in the direction of Arras through Bucquoy, whose church is an interesting example of Art Deco architecture (qv), *to the fork with the D7 at the edge of the village of Ayette. Take the fork to the right and immediately turn left up a small track.*

• *Ayette Indian & Chinese Cemetery/23.7 miles/10 minutes/Map B2*

This unusual cemetery, which has a pagoda-shaped shelter but no Cross of Sacrifice, contains ten soldiers of the Indian Army, forty-two men of the Indian

Labour Corps and twenty-seven of the Chinese Labour Corps (British), one German prisoner and six Chinese Labour Corps (French). The Indian and Chinese headstones bear inscriptions in their own languages.

Continue on the D919 to Beaurains.

Extra Visit to the Commonwealth War Graves Headquarters at Beaurains/Round trip: 2 miles. Approximate time: 15 minutes

At the outskirts to the town turn right, following the green CWGC signs to the imposing low brick building on the right (Rue Angèle Richard, 62217 Beaurains).

This is the administrative headquarters for the Commission in France, and cemetery registers are held for all the cemeteries in the area. Behind are workshops from which carpentry, masonry, engraving, ironwork and gardening repairs and maintenance are organised.

The offices are open during normal working hours, Monday to Friday, with a break for lunch. Telephone ahead if you wish to consult a register or enquire about a burial ☎ (03) 21 71 03 24 or use the CWGC Debt of Honour website (qv) in advance of your visit to find the information you are seeking.

• *Arras/33.2 miles/RWC*

Arras is a possible base for touring the Somme (you can also visit Vimy, Neuve Chapelle, le Cateau and Cambrai from it) Certainly it is an agreeable and historic town, with some picturesque areas of interest. Known by the Romans as Nemetacum, the town, where Julius Caesar wintered in 51BC, was renowned in the Middle Ages for its drapers and bankers. Then came a reputation for tapestry making and indeed the word 'arras' became synonymous with tapestry in Tudor times (Shakespeare often used the word: Polonius was slain by Hamlet when hiding behind the 'arras', for example). In the eighteenth century the prosperous corn trade gave rise to the elegant, tall, narrow houses of the merchants, with their elaborate gables, that can still be seen around the *Places* or squares. Arras abounds with hostelries. All around the station square is a variety of restaurants and cafés – from quick snack to a gourmet restaurant at the station (which also has a modest buffet). The Astoria is a good compromise. A new conference centre has been built in the square, with a three-star Mercure Hotel ☎ (03) 21 23 88 88. The Hotel Moderne, Bvd Faidherbe ☎ (03) 21 23 39 57, is fine too. The *Places*, also offer a variety of eating possibilities. Beneath the *Grand' Place* is a huge car park and under the Gothic-style town hall and Belfry Tower (Arras's pride and joy, erected between 1463 and 1551 to house the city bells and the watchman who kept an eye out for fires) are the *boves* – underground tunnels and chambers much-utilized in World War I. Inside is a Tourist Office where guided visits can be booked ☎ (03) 21 51 26 95.

Faubourg d'Amiens Cemetery and Memorial at Arras

On the town ring road, just south of the junction with the N25 to Doullens, and near the Citadel (designed by Vauban to protect Arras from the Spanish and Dutch and still a working garrison), is the impressive **Faubourg d'Amiens CWGC Cemetery and Memorials to the Missing.**

The Arras Memorial wall carries the names of 36,000 missing in the battles around Arras, including the poet **Capt T. P. Cameron Wilson.** Also on the wall is the name of **Private John William Griffin** of the 6th KOYLI who died on 12 October 1916 and whose death plaque, medals and photo are shown here. A circular 4.5″ diameter bronze plaque carrying the deceased's name was issued for all those who died in the war and families often framed this with the loved one's medals and photo as a constant reminder of their loss. The cemetery contains 2,700 burials and just within the wall is the **Royal Flying Corps Memorial** bearing the names of all RNAS, RFC and RAF missing on the Western Front, including **Major Lanoe Hawker VC** and **Major E. ('Mick') Mannock VC, and Lt Robin Cuttle, MC (qv) who gave his name to the Austalian town of Robinvale.**

Pte John Griffin, his Death Plaque and, l to r, 14-15 Star, and War and Victory Medals

A path beside the cemetery leads to the *Mur des Fusillés*, where French World War II resistance workers were shot.

• ***End of Itinerary One***

OR

Extra Visit to Point-du-Jour Military Cemetery. Round trip: 10 miles. Approximate time: 20 minutes

Continue north on the ring road and follow signs to Douai onto the N50 dual carriageway. The cemetery is on the right about three miles from the centre of Arras with a small parking area beyond.

The cemetery, designed by Sir Reginald Blomfield, is in the village of Athie, in the Valley of the Scarpe, which was captured by the 9th (Scottish) Division (including the S African Brigade) on 9 April 1917 and remained in Allied hands for the remainder of the war (the **9th Scottish memorial** is less than half a mile ahead towards Douai, in the centre of the road and well signed).Point-du-Jour ('Daybreak') was the name of a house on the St Laurent-Blangy-Gavrelle road which had been strongly fortified by the Germans and which was captured by 34th Division on 9 April. Two cemeteries were made on the right of the road between St Laurent-Blangy and Point-du-Jour and one of them (No 1) developed into the present cemetery. Used from April to November 1917 and again in 1918 it contained 82 graves at the Armistice (now part of Plot I). It was then enlarged as remains were brought in from the surrounding battlefields. It now contains 786 WW1 burials, 52 UK Navy, 264 UK Army, 2 Airforce and 378 UK Unknown, 5 Canadian and 9 Unknown, 2 New Zealand, 66 S African and 8 Unknown and 3 UK 1940. There are 3 French plus 3 Unknown burials. There are 22 Special Memorials and 6 Memorials to casualties buried in other cemeteries but whose graves have been destroyed.

Here are buried **Lt Colonel F.S.N. Savage**, DSO and twice MiD, age 36, who commanded the 11th Battalion, the R Warwicks, had served in the S African Campaign as a boy, fought at Ypres in 1914, at Neuve-Chapelle, Fromelles and Festubert in 1915, Arras in 1917, was wounded at Festubert and killed on 23 April 1917 and **Lt Colonel C.J. Burke**, DSO, age 35, of the RIR, who went to France in 1914 as commander of No 2 Squadron RFC, and served with the 1st East Lancs, killed on 9 April 1917.

More recently the cemetery has been used for the burials, in June 2002, of the 23 soldiers of the Lincolnshire Regiment (the Grimsby Chums) found in January 2001 in St Laurent-Blangy (through which you have just driven). They lie together in a row in front of which are the graves of the five soldiers of the 15th Royal Scots found in June 2001 and reinterred later in the month, including Pte Archie McMillan (see pages 261,2 for more details).

Reverential Firing Party, reinterment of Pte Archie McMillan, R Scots, in Point du Jour CWGC Cem, June 2002

Itinerary Two

• **Itinerary Two** starts at the Town Hall Square in Albert, turns east along the old 1916 front line of the British right flank, then heads north through the woods – Mametz, Bernafay, Trones, Delville and High – to the Albert-Bapaume Road at Courcelette. It ends in Pozières.

• **The Route:** Albert – Communal Cemetery Extension, French National Cemetery; Dartmoor CWGC Cemetery; Fricourt – CWGC British Cemetery, Church Memorials, New Military CWGC Cemetery, German Cemetery; 38th (Welsh) Div Memorial, Mametz Church; 38th (Welsh) Div Dragon Memorial; 12th Manchesters Memorial; Donald Bell, VC Memorial; Harry Fellows' Grave; Flat Iron Copse CWGC Cemetery; site of the 14 July 1916 cavalry charge; Caterpillar Valley CWGC Cemetery; New Zealand Memorial to the Missing; Bristol's Own Cross; Longueval Road CWGC Cemetery; Bernafay Wood CWGC Cemetery; Liverpool & Manchester Pals Memorial; Capt Monclin Private Memorial; Pommiers Redoubt; Dantzig Alley CWGC Cemetery and Memorials; Manchester Regt Memorial; Shrine Corner; Devonshire CWGC Cemetery; Gordon CWGC Cemetery; Carnoy CWGC Cemetery; 18th Div Memorial; SOA Capt Chavasse VC+Bar; Guillemont Rd CWGC Cemetery; 16th Irish Div Memorial; French 265th Inf Memorial; 20th Light Div Memorial; Private Memorials to Capt Dickens and Lt Irwin; Private Memorial Lejoindre and Pfister; Delville Wood – CWGC Cemetery, Memorials, Museum and Visitors' Centre; Pipers' Memorial, Longueval; SOA 'Billy' Congreve VC; New Zealand Memorial; Cameron Highlanders/Black Watch Memorial; 47th (London) Div Memorial; 20th Bn RF Tree; Glasgow Highlanders Cairn; London Cemetery and Extension; Martinpuich – 47th Div/German Memorials, Bunker; Courcelette – German Headstone, Adanac Military CWGC Cemetery, Canadian Memorial; Pozières – Tank Corps Memorial, Australian Windmill Memorials, Butterworth Trench, Sunken Road and 2nd Canadian Cemeteries, Tommy Café.

• **Extra Visits** are suggested to: Méaulte Bunker; Grove Town CWGC Cemetery; Capt Dodgson Private Memorial; Contalmaison Château CWGC Cemetery; 'Nine Brave Men' Private Memorial; Capt Wallace Private Memorial; Pte Tomasin Private Memorial; Point 110 Old and New Military Cemeteries; area of Sassoon's Raid; Maltkorn Farm; Private Memorials to Capt Cochin and Boucher & Lapage; Private Memorial Lt Marsden-Smedley; Dickens Cross.

- **Planned duration**, without stops for refreshments: 8 hours 40 minutes.
- **Total distance**: 49.7 miles.

- ***Albert Town Hall Square/0 miles/RWC/Map J14***

Leave the Square on rue Jean Guyon signed to Bray and A1 Paris. En route keep to the left of the town war memorial, signed Péronne.

Extra Visit to the Méaulte Bunker (Map J36) and Grove Town CWGC British Cemetery (Map M3) Round-trip: 8.6 miles. Approximate time: 35 minutes.

Fork right, following signs to Méaulte and Aérospatiale on the D329 and continue under the motorway to Méaulte. At the crossroads near the Aérospatiale factory turn right on the D64 signed to Morlancourt onto Rue de l'Aviation.

In the garden of house No 36 on the left is an enormous World War I (although some local experts feel it may be of a later date) bunker in excellent condition, currently used as a duck coop!

Return to the D329. Turn right and continue to an airfield to the left and turn right on the C6, signed Etineham, and follow the green CWGC signs to the cemetery up a long track that is often muddy.

Grove Town CWGC Cemetery. Among the interesting burials here is that of **Maj Edmund Rochfort Street**, DSO, 2nd Battalion the Sherwood Foresters who died of wounds on 15 October 1916. Age 40, born in London, Ontario, he was gazetted in 1898 as a Lieutenant in the Hampshire Regiment, served in India and the South African campaign, resigned 1906, gazetted Capt in the Sherwood Foresters October 1914. Also buried here is **Sgt Leslie Coulson** of the 2/2nd Londons (known as the 'Two and Twopennies'), 8 October 1916. This unusual war poet, a professional journalist before the war, and whose collected poems (including the bitter *Who Made the Law?*) were published by his father as *From an Outpost*, was wounded near Lesboeufs in the same attack that killed Maj C. C. Dickens (qv). His family chose the closing words of Manoah's elegy for his son Samson from Milton's *Samson Agonistes* – '... nothing but well and fair, and what may quiet us in a death so noble'.

An unusual rank on a headstone here is that of **Shoeing Smith Ernest** Arthur Smither of the 21st (E of I) Lancers, 25 March 1917, age 30. The register records the fact that in September 1916 the 34th and 2/2nd Londons established a clearing station here (called locally 'demi-lieue') to deal with casualties from the Somme battlefields. It was moved in April and except for a few burials in August and September 1918 the cemetery was closed. It contains 1,366 burials from the UK, 14 Australians, 11

The Méaulte Bunker

Newfoundlanders, 1 New Zealander, 1 French and, originally, 34 German prisoners who were removed in 1923. It was here, at 20th Inf Bde HQ, that Capt Martin's 'plasticine' model (qv) of the ground threatened by the crucifix machine gun overlooking Mansel Copse was displayed.

Return to Albert and pick up the main itinerary.

Fork left on the D938 direction A1/Historial on rue 11 Novembre.

• *Albert Communal Cemetery Extension/0.5 miles/10 minutes/Map J29*

This is on the right and was established during the first part of the Somme fighting, known as the Battle of Albert. It was used by fighting units and field ambulances from August 1915. In August 1918 5th CCS was established here. Plot II was made by 18th Div. There are 618 UK graves, 202 Canadian and 39 Australian, 12 unknown and 2 BWI. There are many interesting burials here, including communal graves for thirteen 10th Essex soldiers blown up by a German mine at la Boisselle in November 1915 and eleven soldiers of the 41st Siege Battery killed by a shell when unloading ammunition in July 1916. There are also two **Brigadier-Generals – Henry Frederick Hugh Clifford DSO**, CO of 149th Bde, 50th Division, killed on 11 September 1916 by a sniper from Delville Wood while inspecting advanced assembly trenches, age 49, son of Maj Gen the Hon H. H. Clifford VC, KCMG, CB, and **Randle Barnett-Barker DSO and Bar**, CO of 99th Bde, 47th (London) Division killed at Gueudecourt on 24 March 1918. Next to the British military plot is a sad plot with what appears to be CWGC headstones. This is a local paupers' graveyard and the headstones are damaged stones discarded by the Commission. The area was over-run by the Germans in the March 1918 offensive and re-taken by the 8th East Surreys on 26 April.

In the civilian cemetery there is a plot at the back enclosed by a high hedge. It contains crosses marking the graves of the **Breton soldiers** killed in

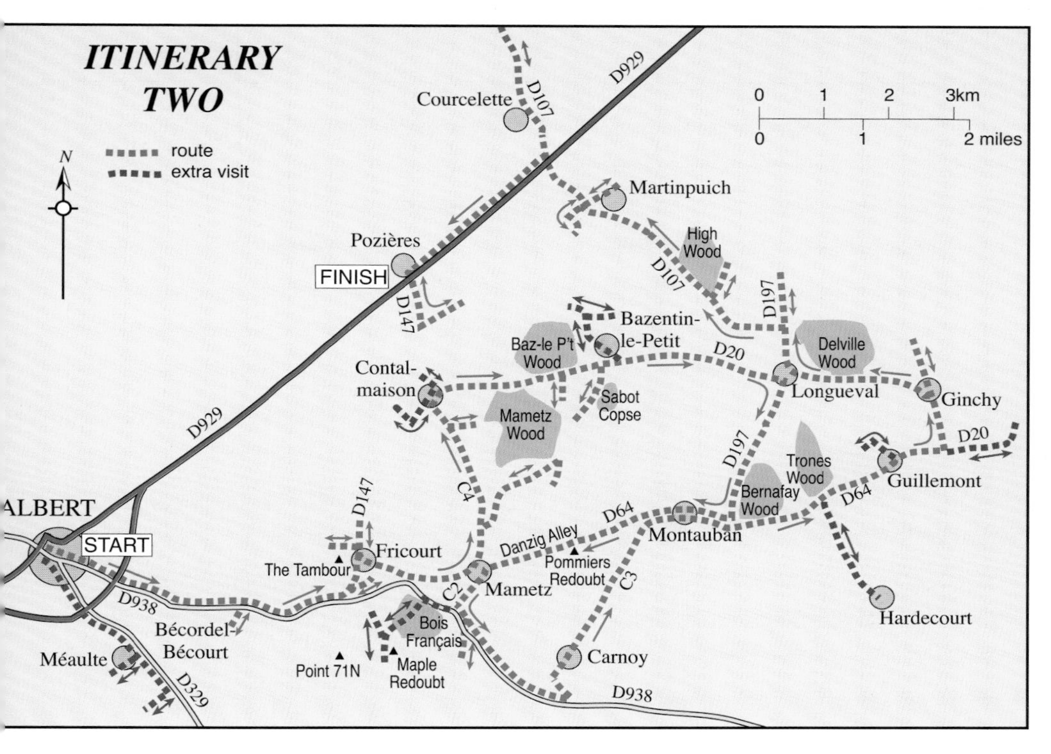

Breton Plot, Albert Comm Cem.

1914/15/16. Among them is the **Adjutant of the 19th RIF, Jules Boccard**, 7 February 1915, who was the probable successor to André Pitel, commemorated on the Breton Calvary at Ovillers (qv). Outside the plot is a grey marble stone inscribed *A Nos Soldats Bretons.*

Continue on the D938.

• *French National Cemetery, Albert/0.9 miles/15 minutes/Map J30*

On the left is this large concentration cemetery from the Somme battlefield with 6,290 burials (including three British, one of whom is a Chinese Labourer, 5 December 1918, who only has a number (33295) not a name inscribed on his headstone and two Polish). 2,879 of them are in four mass graves (including two of the British).

Continue over the roundabout, following signs to Péronne/Historial and A1 and continue past the junction with the C2. Take the first small road to the right to Dartmoor, Cemetery.

• *Dartmoor CWGC Cemetery/2.2 miles/15 minutes/Map J37*

Originally Bécordel-Bécourt cemetery, this was begun in August 1915 and its name was changed in May 1916 at the request of the Devonshire Regiment. Behind the British lines of July 1916, the area nearby was used by XV Corps Main Dressing Station from September 1916. A notable burial among the total of 768 (632 UK, 71 Australian, 59 NZ, 4 Canadian, an Indian and an unknown) is **Lieutenant Henry Webber** who, aged 68, is believed to be the oldest soldier killed in action during the war. Born on 3 June 1849, he graduated from Oxford and then entered the Stock Exchange. He was a well-known figure in his home town of Horley, having served both as a Justice of the Peace and Chairman of the District Council. After the war broke out, Webber put much effort into helping the recruiting drive and pestered the War Office to allow him to join up, despite his age. In May 1916 he was appointed a Temporary Lieutenant in the 7th Bn, the S Lancs Regt and joined the regiment in France. Webber, who had been a member of the Surrey Stag Hunt, and therefore a good horseman, became the First Line Transport Officer to the Battalion, and it was after taking rations to the battalion in Mametz Wood on 21 July, that he was killed by a shell while talking to his CO. Three of his sons served in the army as officers and all survived. This exceptional old gentleman was honoured by being mentioned in Despatches and his family received messages of condolence from the king. Also buried here is **Pte J. Miller**. Pte Miller, who, despite being shot clean

Headstone of Lt Henry Webber, age 68, Dartmoor CWGC Cem

through the stomach from behind, delivered an important message, falling dead at the feet of the officer to whom he delivered it. He won a posthumous **VC** and the citation is in the cemetery report. Also buried next to each other are **father and son Sgt George and Cpl Robert Frederick Lee,** of 156th Bde RFA, killed on 5 September 1916. This area, too, was taken by the Germans in March 1918 but was retaken by 12th Division on 24 August.

Return to the D938, turn right and continue in the direction of Fricourt.

The British attack on 1 July was made in the direction you are travelling, by a brigade of the 17th (Northern) Division, led by the 7th Battalion Green Howards. Due to a misunderstanding, they attacked 15 minutes or more after the zero hour of 0730, and were cut down by the German machine guns.

On entering the village, turn left at the crossroads onto the D147 direction Pozières. Stop 200m later on the left.

• Fricourt CWGC British Cemetery (Bray Road)/Green Howards Memorial/3.5 miles/10 minutes/Map J38/39

The 1 July front line crossed the D938 road at about where you turned left, and Fricourt village was just inside the German lines. The village had been fortified by the Germans, using the cellars in the houses to provide shelters up to 45ft deep. 'One at Fricourt had nine rooms and five bolt-holes', wrote John Buchan, 'it had iron doors, gas curtains, linoleum on the floors, wallpaper and pictures on the walls, and boasted a good bath-room, electric light and electric bells. The staff which occupied it must have lived in luxury'. But according to John Masefield, 'although the ... stairs with wired treads, the bolting holes, the air and escape shafts, the living rooms with electric light, the panelled walls, covered with cretonnes of the smartest Berlin patterns, the neat bunks and the signs of female visitors, were written of in the press, ... it was not better fitted than other places on the line.'

There were also machine-gun positions and redoubts on the crest behind the cemetery. Mine warfare had been initiated in this area by the French in 1915 and this was taken over by 178th Tunnelling Company who had shafts up to 115ft deep leading to the crest – an area known as the **Tambour**. Three mines were placed there for the 1 July offensive and one failed to explode. The plan was to pinch the Fricourt salient out of the line by taking la Boisselle on its left and Mametz to its right. The village was carried after 36 hours of fighting and 1,500 German prisoners were taken. The area was lost to the Germans in March 1918 and re-taken on 26 August.

The cemetery was used by the 7th Yorkshires (Green Howards) between 5 and 11 July and, at the end of an avenue of twenty headstones of men who died on 1 July, a **memorial Celtic cross** to the regiment has been placed in the far right-hand corner of the cemetery which names all those of the Regiment who fell in the area on 1 July 1916. Two-thirds of the 130 or so burials belong to the 7th Green Howards, the Alexandra Princess of Wales' Own Yorkshire Regiment, and fifty-nine of them are believed to be in a mass grave in the centre of the cemetery, originally a shell-hole. One grave of note is that of **Major R. G. Raper** of the 8th S Staffs, who was killed on 2 July 1916. He was originally buried in a private grave, marked by his family after the war. The village of Fricourt, perhaps because his body was singled out in this way, made a cult of Roper, naming after him the road that leads from the attractive village *Poilu* war memorial to the village church.

Continue to the Poilu. Take the fork to the right along rue du Major Raper to the church and park.

If the church is locked, ask at the café opposite. This is closed on Wednesdays, in which case enquire at houses around the square for the keyholder.

• *Fricourt Church Memorials/3.8 miles/10 minutes/Map J41*

The Raper family gave funds to the church, which was rebuilt during 1928-31, and the Stations of the Cross are dedicated to **Major Raper**. There is also a **plaque to the 494 officers, 8,421 WO's and soldiers of the 17th (Northern) Division** who gave their lives in France and Belgium during the 1914-18 war, and a plaque to **Sgt Pierre Louis Viget** of the French 156th Régiment d'Infanterie who died in Fricourt on 3 October 1914, decorated with the *Médaille Militaire, Croix de Guerre* and Gold Star.

Return to the Poilu. Turn right on the D147 towards Contalmaison. Some half a mile to the left is a sign to Fricourt New Military Cemetery. Turn up the track and drive, with extreme caution, as far as you can, according to weather conditions. Walk the final few metres.

• *Fricourt New Military Cemetery/4.6 miles/15 minutes/Map J40*

This cemetery was made by the 10th Bn, the W Yorkshire Regiment in No Man's Land between the British and German front lines of 1 July. The cratered feature of the Tambour, where the poet **Lt Alfred Victor Ratcliffe** of the battalion, which had one of the highest casualty rates of 1 July, was killed, lies between the cemetery and the village. Behind the Tambour on the skyline is the Bois Français. Ratcliffe is buried in the cemetery with 207 other UK burials and a New Zealander.

Return to the D147. Turn left and continue to the cemetery on the right.

• *Fricourt German Cemetery/4.9 miles/10 minutes/Map J34*

There are 5,056 marked burials, plus 11,970 in mass graves at the rear of the cemetery. The black metal crosses mark up to four burials, the names

Headstone of Lt A.V. Ratcliffe, poet, with private memoral, Fricourt New Mil Cem

Memorial to Green Howards, Fricourt Brit Cem

Station of the Cross dedicated to Maj Raper, Fricourt Church

Entrance to German Cem, Fricourt

being inscribed on both sides of the arms of the crosses. The headstones mark Jewish graves. The remains of Baron Manfred von Richthofen were removed to this cemetery from his original burial place at Bertangles (qv). In 1925 they were moved again to the family home at Schweidnitz in eastern Germany by his brother Bolko. He was buried in Section 4, grave 1177, now occupied by Sebastian Paustian, in the ninth grave in the second row in the right hand corner.

The discrepancy of one between the total number of burials given above and the figures given at the entrance to the cemetery may well be because of the removal of von Richthofen's remains.

Turn around and take the first left towards Mametz and turn left at the T junction on the D64 signed to Mametz.

Between Fricourt and Mametz the British line for 1 July ran roughly parallel to the road you are taking and some 750m away to the right. The assault troops were a mixture of New Army and regulars of 7th Division and within the first hour they had taken the German front line trenches, which ran some 250m to your right,watched by **Siegfried Sassoon,** a 2nd Lt in the RWF. The village of Mametz held out until mid-afternoon and then fell.

Continue to the church on the left.

• *38th (Welsh) Division Memorial, Mametz Church/5.3 miles/10 minutes*

If the church is locked, continue through the village to the last group of buildings on the left as you leave the village towards Dantzig Alley Cemetery. Go through the archway into the courtyard and apply to Madame Roger in the house in the right-hand corner, driving up to the house so that she can clearly see you. This special lady lost her husband in 1944, shot by the retreating Germans as he came to the roadside to welcome the advancing Americans and was left a widow with three young children. She will be delighted to give you the key, but if she is not available, apply at the *Mairie*. **Note that driving here will alter your running total mileage.**

The handsome marble memorial, emblazoned with a magnificent red dragon, is on the left-hand wall just before the altar. The inscription is in Welsh, French and English. It reads, 'Dedicated to the Glory of God this tablet in memory of the 38th (Welsh) Division of the British Army is committed to the pious care of the sons of France in whose land they repose in everlasting alliance.' The villagers of Mametz feel very involved with their Welsh Allies and there are always fresh flowers below the memorial. The Welsh reciprocate the feeling. Mametz was 'adopted' by Llandudno after the war.

Continue to the crossroads in the village.

In the green opposite is a **CGS/H Signboard** about the Welsh memorial.

Turn left on the C4 following signs to the Mémorial Gallois/38th (Welsh) Division Memorial on the C4, direction Contalmaison.

After half a mile turn right, following green CWGC signs to the Welsh Memorial. Continue to the fork and go right to Mémorial Gallois.

You are now passing the area of the **Queen's Nullah**. Here the author of *Up to Mametz*, **Lt Llewelyn Wyn Griffith**, who served with the 15th RWF, but was attached to the staff during the attack on Mametz Wood, saw walking wounded streaming to the ADS sited in a dugout in the bank in the nullah after the Division's first attack on the wood on 5 July. Here too **Major General E. C. Ingouville-Williams**, commanding 34th Div, was killed by a shell on 22 July after reconnoitring the area and while walking back to his car at Montauban. He is buried in Warloy-Baillon Communal Cemetery (see Approach Two).

Fork left, following signs to Mémorial Gallois.

Note soon the sharpness of the cliff to your right. To the left is Death Valley.

Continue and park at the foot of the magnificent Welsh Dragon.

Walk up the steps.

• *38th (Welsh) Division Red Dragon Memorial/7.9 miles/10 minutes/Map K39*

This most emotional of all the Western Front memorials was designed by sculptor-in-iron, David Petersen. It was erected mostly through the tireless fund-raising and organizational efforts of the **Cardiff Western Front Association** led by member **Harry Evans and his Welsh historian wife Pat**. The exuberant, winged red dragon spits fire and grasps the enemy's barbed wire in its powerful claws. The Welsh inscription means, 'Let us respect their endeavours. Let our memories live on.' It was unveiled at a grand ceremony on 11 July 1987 and, although not an official national memorial, is the focus of Welsh remembrance on the Western Front. Beside it is a bronze tablet with the ORBAT of the 38th Division, a sketch map and summary of the two attacks on the Wood in July 1916. In 1994 the site was cleared through the initiative of Major Tony Swift of UK Movements and Liaison Staff who found clear traces of the World War I light railway system between the memorial and the Hammerhead (part of Mametz Wood and so-called because of its shape). Behind the dragon is a **memorial seat placed by Major Huw Rodge**, Retd, of the RWF. It is a perfect site from which to contemplate the sacrifice of the Welsh, overlooking as it does the notorious Hammerhead feature of the wood. One can almost hear the strains of *Jesu lover of my soul* … to *Aberystwyth* sung by the 'genuine Taffies' on the right of the line wafting over as they waited to go in to the attack, as did the poet **David Jones** who (like Wyn Griffith) served here with the London Battalion of the RWF. To a first approximation, the dragon faces the wood, as did the attacking Welsh.

On the morning of 7 July 1916, one week after the first day of the Battle of the Somme, two British divisions began a pincer attack on Mametz Wood, a German stronghold held by the Prussian Guard. The two divisions were the

38th (Welsh) Div Memorial, Mametz Church

38th (Welsh) Div Memorial sign, Mametz, one of few – or the only – Welsh language road signs in France

17th (Northern), attacking from the west, and the 115th Brigade of the 38th (Welsh), commanded by Brigadier-General H. J. Evans, attacking from the east. The attack, in bald military terms, was a failure. German machine guns, sited in Acid Drop Copse (which the 17th Division attacked), Flat Iron and Sabot Copses and in the Hammerhead (attacked by the 16th Welsh Cardiff City Battalion and the Gwent Battalions of the SWB) apparently unaffected by the preparatory artillery bombardment, inflicted heavy casualties upon the attackers approaching across the open ground. Battlefield communications broke down and a covering smokescreen failed to appear. At the end of the day neither division had even reached the wood, let alone captured it. The divisional commander, Maj-Gen Ivor Philipps, a peace-time MP and Lloyd George appointee, who was 'ignorant, lacked experience and failed to inspire confidence' (Maj Drake-Brockman, quoted by Colin Hughes in his definitive account of the action *Mametz*) was finally relieved of his inappropriate position.

Three days later, at 0415 hours on 10 July, the two divisions were ordered in again. The main thrust this time was towards the southern face of the wood by the Welsh – a frontal assault. The leading battalions were the 13th Welsh (2nd Rhonddas), the 14th Welsh (Swansea Battalion) and the 16th RWF (Caernarvon and Anglesey Battalion), reinforced by the 15th. Despite the hail of German small arms fire they made it to the wood. The struggle became increasingly bitter in the thick undergrowth beneath the splintered trunks. More and more battalions of the small men from South Wales were committed to the struggle until almost the whole division was in among the trees and the brambles. According to David Jones 'General Picton was of the opinion that the ideal

38th (Welsh) Div Dragon Memorial, overlooking Mametz Wood

infantryman was a south Welshman, five feet four inches in height'. Siegfried Sassoon, however, handing over Quadrangle Trench to them, had called them a 'jostling company of exclamatory Welshmen ... panicky rabble ... mostly undersized men' and felt that 'As I watched them arriving at the first stage of their battle experience I had a sense of their victimisation.' Ideal soldiers or victims, they fought with determination. The bloody contest, often bitter hand-to-hand fighting, continued for two days until, on the night of 11 July, the Germans withdrew, driven out from the north of the wood. At one stage 'friendly' artillery rained down on the desperate Welshmen. Wyn Griffith was commanded by Brig-Gen Evans to send messengers to the Queen's Nullah to stop this 'sheer stupidity'. One of the runners he despatched was his young brother, Watcyn. Watcyn got through with his message but was hit by a shell as he tried to return. 'I had sent him to his death, bearing a message from my own hand in an endeavour to save other men's brothers', wrote the distraught Wyn Griffith. Pte W Griffith is commemorated on the Thiépval Memorial (qv).

The cost to the 38th (Welsh) Division, proudly raised by Lloyd George and inadequately officered by his cronies and protégés, was high – some 4,000 men were killed or wounded. Although they did capture the wood they came under severe criticism for having taken five days to do so, and in 1919 Lt Col J. H. Boraston, co-author of *Sir Douglas Haig's Command,* effectively accused them of a lack of determination which prevented a significant Fourth Army advance on the Somme. It was a stigma not expiated until their successful attack on the Pilckem Ridge of 31 July 1917. This Haig called 'the highest level of soldierly achievement' in the Preface to the Division's History.

The epic struggle is described in what is most probably the war's most original work of literature, David Jones's *In Parenthesis.* Like Philip Johnstone in the poem *High Wood* (qv), Jones anticipates future battlefield tours. Wounded and encumbered by his rifle he decides to 'leave it for a Cook's tour to the Devastated Areas and crawl as far as you can and wait for the bearers'. Officer Robert Graves and Private soldier Frank Richards, both serving with the 2nd Bn the RWF, describe the horror of mopping up in the wood on 15 July, a few days after the attack. 'Not a single tree in the wood remained unbroken', wrote Graves in *Goodbye to All That* as he charged through 'the wreckage of green branches', past 'bloated and stinking' corpses. Richards recalled in *Old Soldiers Never Die,* 'We rested in shell holes, the ground all around us being thick with dead of the troops who had been attacking Mametz Wood.'

(At this point you have the option to walk, or if it is exceptionally dry, drive to Flat Iron Copse CWGC Cemetery some 800m further along the track. Otherwise it will be covered later in the Itinerary.)

Return to the C4 and turn right. To your right is Death Valley, followed shortly by the small Quadrangle Wood. To your left is Bottom Wood. Continue to the village of Contalmaison, park by the civilian cemetery on the right and walk through it to the rear wall.

• *Memorial to 12th Manchesters/10.3 miles/10 minutes/Map K21*

This impressive memorial is to the 1,039 Officers, NCOs and men of the 12th Bn, the Manchester Regt who fell in World War I. It was erected by relatives and the Old Comrades Association. Beyond the cemetery is Acid Drop Copse (see the account of the attack on Mametz Wood above). From the front of the cemetery **Peake Wood CWGC Cemetery** (see page 262) may be seen in the valley below.

Continue to the memorial on the bank to the right.

• *Memorial to 2nd Lieutenant Donald Simpson Bell VC/10.4 miles/10 minutes/Map K20a*

On 9 July 2000 this handsome memorial was unveiled to Donald Bell, the first professional footballer to enlist in November 1914, by members of his family and the present Green Howards Regiment. Bell worked his way through the ranks and was commissioned into the 9th Battalion Princess of Wales's Own Yorkshire Regiment (now the Green Howards). On 5 July the 8th and 9th Battalions were ordered to take a 1,500m long position known as Horse Shoe Trench between la Boiselle and Mametz Wood. The attack started at 1800 hours and the trench, with 146 prisoners and two machine guns, was captured. Then a German machine gun began to enfilade the 9th Battalion. Bell, supported by a Corporal and a Private, rushed the gun position. He shot the gunner and blew up the remainder with Mills bombs. He then bombed the nearby trench, killing over 50 of the enemy. Bell died five days later performing a similar act of gallantry. He is buried in **Gordon Dump CWGC Cemetery** and there is a memorial to him in St Paul's Church, Harrogate.

Continue to the junction with the D147.

Extra Visit to Private Memorial to Capt Dodgson (Map J27)& Contalmaison Château CWGC Cemetery (Map K20) Round-trip 1.0 miles. Approximate time 20 minutes

Turn left on the D147, drive downhill and after some 500m park (ahead is Peake Wood CWGC Cemetery, Map J26) and walk up a small farm track to the right.

The small stone memorial is some 250m up and to the right of the track. Capt Francis Dodgson of the 8th Yorks Regt fell at this spot on 10 July 1916. He is buried in Serre Road No 2 Cemetery. From this point the Pozières Memorial may be seen straight ahead on the horizon and to the right is Contalmaison Church tower.

Turn round and return to the junction. Continue on the D147 to a CWGC sign to the right.

Contalmaison Château CWGC Cemetery is one of the most attractive cemeteries on the Somme. Surrounded by a mellow brick-topped flint wall

Memorial to 12th Manchesters, Fricourt local cem

Memorial to footballer 2nd Lt Donald Bell, VC, Contalmaison

Headstone of Cpl Edward Dwyer, VC, Flat Iron Copse CWGC Cem

Grave of Harry Fellows, who died 1 September 1987, Mametz Wood

Extra Visit continued

and framed by trees it is approached by a well-tended grass path. It contains the grave of **Pte William Short** of the 8th Battalion, the Yorkshire Regiment, who died on 6 August 1916 in Munster Alley trench where he continued to throw grenades at the enemy despite being mortally wounded. For this gallant action he was awarded a posthumous **Victoria Cross**.

Return to the D147 and rejoin the main itinerary

Turn right on the D20 following signs to Bazentin and Longueval.

After some 500m you will be driving along the edge of Mametz Wood. The wood is owned by the Comte de Thézy who gave a plot of land for the burial of Harry Fellows.

Continue to the far, north-east corner of the wood and, if not muddy, turn right down the small track to a metal gate and stop. Park and walk 150m into the wood. The grave is on the right. Be careful not to disturb the game birds that are raised in the wood.

• *Grave of Harry Fellows/11.5 miles/10 minutes/Map K22*

The headstone is like a CWGC headstone, but with a curved top, and is in a small glade. It bears the inscription 'This tree is dedicated to the memory of 13587 L/Cpl H Fellows, 12th Battalion, Northumberland Fusiliers, 1914-1918, whose ashes are buried in this wood. Died 1st September 1987 Aged 91', followed by some lines from one of his own poems:

Where once there was war,
Now peace reigns supreme,
And the birds sing again in Mametz.

Harry is featured in the film describing the British involvement in the Battle of the Somme which is shown at the *Historial* Museum, Péronne.

Continue to the green CWGC sign pointing right to Flat Iron Copse Cemetery. Drive carefully down the track, passing Sabot Copse on the left, and park by the entrance gate.

• *Flat Iron Copse CWGC Cemetery/12.5 miles/15 minutes/Map K23*

Sir Herbert Baker designed this cemetery which contains some notable burials. It had been begun by the 3rd and 7th Divisions on 14 July 1916 as they cleared Mametz Wood (which is immediately behind the rear wall of the cemetery) after its capture by the 38th. There are over 1,500 burials, including three pairs of brothers. Two of the pairs are Welshmen, killed in the July attack on Mametz Wood – **Lts Arthur and Leonard Tregaskis** and **L/Cpl H and Cpl T.**

Hardwidge. The Tregaskis brothers were in the 16th (Cardiff City) Welsh and were killed on 7 July, the Hardwidges were in the 15th (Carmarthenshire) Welsh Regiment and were killed on 11 July. Both sets of brothers died when one attempted to help his wounded brother.

Privates Ernest and Herbert Philby served with the Middlesex Regiment and were both killed on 21 August 1916. The **Victoria Cross winner** buried here, **Sgt Edward Dwyer** of the 1st East Surreys, is particularly interesting. He won his award 'for conspicuous bravery and devotion to duty at Hill 60 [in the Ypres Salient] on 20 April 1915' and was used back in Britain to help the recruiting effort by giving talks about his experiences. In December 1918 a memorial medallion, paid for by Fulham schoolchildren, was unveiled in Fulham Library by Lt Gen Sir Francis Lloyd. Dwyer was born in Fulham. Dwyer's wife, 'Billie', continued to serve in France as a nurse after his death. In the 1980s Pavilion Records of Sussex produced a remarkable pair of records (now in cassette and CD forms) (GEMM 3033/4) which feature original recordings from the 1914-18 period. Track 2, side 2 of the first record is a monologue by Sgt Dwyer, most probably the only contemporary recording of a First World War VC in existence. To the right as one enters is a Special Memorial to the nine graves behind it (the majority of the them of the Rifle Brigade), men all killed in 1916 and originally buried in Mametz Wood Cemetery, whose graves were destroyed in later battles.

Return to the D20. Turn right. Continue some 600m to the crossroads with the D73 in Bazentin le Petit.

Extra Visit to Private Memorials: 'Nine Brave Men', (Map K6) & Capt Wallace (Map K7).
Round trip: 1.7 miles. Approx time: 15 minutes.

Turn left on the D73, passing a sign to Bazentin le Petit Communal Cemetery (Map K8) on the right and, after the church, a sign to Bazentin le Petit Military CWGC Cemetery (Map K5) to the left.

As the road bends sharply to the left there is a memorial in the corner, refurbished in 1989 by 82nd Junior Leaders Regt RE. It is to nine men of 82nd Field Coy RE who were killed on 29 July 1916. The names of the men are listed on the front of the memorial and on the rear is a somewhat faded plaque which tells their story, placed by Sgt S.R. Brooks who was part of the renovation party which also included Capt J. Dargavel, Cpl Moffat and Sgt J. Moores. The company had been formed by Captain R.F.A. Butterworth in Bulford in 1914 and went with him to France, suffering severely in the July 1916 battles. On 29 July Sections 3 and 4 went on a wiring party to Bazentin where they came under murderous H.E. and machine-gun fire. Knowing the work was vital, Lieutenant Howlett (with No 4 Section) and CSM Deyermond (with No 3 Section) carried on, though

Extra Visit continued

6 men were killed and 19 wounded out of a total of 40 men. Three men had been killed in similar circumstances the previous night and their commanding officer (to be promoted to Lt Colonel in October) christened them the 'Nine Brave Men'. 'One lived in such close touch with the lads in those days that one knew every man personally, and very often intimately', wrote this caring officer. 'Choate was a first-rate carpenter and a most lovable man, Ellison just a boy from a North Country workshop, Vernon a fitter and a fine stalwart fellow'. He personally wrote to each of the next of kin and promised that one day he would go back and raise 'a little stone to their memory'. Butterworth was then moved ('with great regret') to take up his new job as CRE of 16th Division in the Messines sector. There he had a block of granite engraved and waited for an opportunity to take it to the Somme. This he did in November 1917 when, with his Adjutant, Capt Stradling, and two Sappers, (as he later wrote in the Sapper Magazine of October 1923 when he was serving in Hong Kong) they 'constructed our small tribute of affection and respect to the memory of our nine brave comrades', using bricks collected from the debris lying around.

The nine are listed on the memorial but looking them up on the CWGC Debt of Honour website it seems that two of them are mis-spelt. Tregidgo (listed as Tredigo) is commemorated on the Thiepval Memorial, as are Choat, Joiner, Havilland, Blakeley, Robotham and Vernon. Ellisson (listed as Ellison) is buried in Caterpillar Valley and Higgins in Bécourt CWGC Cemeteries.

The story of 82 Squadron RE, from 1914-2001, has been put on a CD by Captain Simon Mann, 2i/c of the Squadron when it was disbanded in December 2001. All its property and history have been moved from Arborfield to Chatham and the Squadron will be reformed as a Bomb Disposal Unit.

Take the track to the right.

At the end of it, up the bank to the right is the cairn, (refurbished on 23 October 1994, with help from the WFA) surmounted by a calvary, to Capt Houston Stewart Hamilton Wallace of the 10th Worcester Regiment who was killed on 22 July 1916. Capt Wallace is commemorated on the Thiépval Memorial.

Behind it, on the skyline, is High Wood, which could be reached by walking along the grassy track ahead.

Return to the crossroads and rejoin the main itinerary.

*Continue on the D20 signed Longueval, to a green CWGC sign to **Thistle Dump Cemetery,** Map K10, on the left, with High Wood behind it.*

• Site of the 14 July 1916 Cavalry Charge/13.9 miles/Map K10

The small track to the cemetery continues past it, runs effectively due north

Memorial to 'Nine Brave men' of 82nd Fd Coy RE, Bazentin

Memorial to Capt Wallace and detail, Bazentin

and emerges on the D107 Longueval to Martinpuich road at the south-east corner of High Wood. The valley that it crosses is Caterpillar Valley. The attack that began at 0325 on the morning of 14 July achieved total surprise and some three miles of the German second line, from Bazentin le Grand to Longueval, were taken by the middle of the day. 7th Division, opposite High Wood, discovered to their surprise that the wood was empty and General Watts, the GOC, urged XV Corps HQ to allow him to press the attack on the wood. Corps insisted that the attack should wait until cavalry arrived. Only a small force – the Deccan Horse and one squadron of the 7th Dragoon Guards – was available and that was moving up slowly from south of Albert. Not until after 1900 hours was the attack eventually launched, by which time the Germans had re-entered the wood. Thus, when the cavalry charged, pennants flying and lances glittering in the evening sun, few survived to reach the wood. (Their route was up the slope to the left of the track.) The wood was not taken. A second, frontal, infantry assault on High Wood was planned by 100th Brigade for early on 15 July and the assault battalions – the 1st Queens, the 9th HLI (Glasgow Highlanders) and the 16th KRRC – moved up Death Valley, past Flat Iron Copse and deployed into Caterpillar Valley ready for the assault. The attack began in a heavy mist. German machine guns took a heavy toll as the troops struggled up the slope towards the wood and at 1,000 the Brigade reserve, the 2nd Worcesters, was quickly committed, their line of advance being along and then to the left of the track. Fighting in the wood became hand-to-hand and after 24 hours only the south-west corner of the wood was in British hands and the four battalions of the Brigade had over 1,300 casualties. It is possible to walk the path of the charge and the Worcesters' attack.

Continue to the large cemetery on the right. Park.

• *Caterpillar Valley CWGC Cemetery & New Zealand Memorial to the Missing/14.4 miles/15 minutes/Map K24/25/OP*

The area was captured by the 12th Royal Scots and the 9th Scottish Rifles on 14 July. Lost again in the Kaiser's March Offensive of 1918, it was recovered on 28 August 1918 by the 38th (Welsh) Division. The vast cemetery, second only to Serre Road No 2 (which, technically speaking, is not in the Département of the Somme), contains 5,197 UK burials, 214 New Zealand, 98 Australian, 19 South African, 6 Canadian and 2 Newfoundland, with 38 special memorials. The majority are unknown.

On the left-hand wall is the **New Zealand Memorial to the Missing**, following their decision to list their missing in cemeteries near where they fell. Others are in Buttes New, Polygon Wood; Cité Bonjean, Armentières; Grevillers; Marfaux; Messines Ridge and Tyne Cot. They are not listed on the Menin Gate. 1,205 are listed here. The cemetery stands on the Longueval Ridge and is an excellent vantage point. Stand with your back to the entrance. Straight ahead at 12 o'clock is the New Zealand Memorial on the skyline. At 1 o'clock is a calvary. In this area 'Billy' Congreve VC (qv) was wounded. At 2 o'clock is the church of Longueval and behind it Delville Wood. At 3 o'clock at the D107 road junction is the Bristol's Own Cross. Ahead, between the road and the New Zealand Memorial, is Caterpillar Valley. At 11 o'clock is High Wood, at the left hand edge of which is London CWGC Cemetery. At 10 o'clock in the Valley is Thistle Dump CWGC Cemetery. Just before 10 o'clock is the wireless mast at Pozières and at 9 o'clock the Bazentin Woods. From the shelter at the rear of the cemetery, Montauban Church is straight ahead at 12 o'clock and at 1 o'clock on the skyline is the memorial cross to French soldier Capt H. T. de Monclin on the D64. At 10 o'clock is Trones Wood, at 11 o'clock is Bernafay Wood and at 3 o'clock Mametz Wood.

Continue on the D20 to the junction with the D107 to the left and park.

• *Bristol's Own Cross/14.6 miles/5 minutes/Map K29*

This memorial was raised by British and French volunteers under the leadership of Dean Marks. Inspired by an old photograph showing Bristol veterans standing beside a cross on the Somme, Dean investigated and found that the cross in the picture had disappeared during World War II. He determined to replace it and helped by friends, members of the WFA, Bristol Civil Authorities and others he set to work. In the seventieth anniversary year of the Battle of the Somme, Dean, his two-year-old daughter Amy, his father Roy, the Mayor of Longueval and a party of helpers put up the new cross. It stands where the 12th Battalion Gloucestershire Regiment set off to battle and commemorates those who fell around Longueval and Guillemont between July and September 1916.

Continue to the crossroads with the D197. Turn right, signed Montauban, and continue to a cemetery on the left after some 500m.

• *Longueval Road CWGC Cemetery/15.4 miles/5 minutes/Map K28*

Cleared by the 5th Division in July 1916, the start point for the 8th Black Watch's assault of the 14th on Longueval, used as a Dressing Station from September 1916, lost in the Kaiser's spring 1918 offensive, this area was finally retaken by the 38th (Welsh) Division on 28 August 1918. The cemetery contains 182 UK, 22 Australian, 7 Canadian, 7 New Zealand, a Newfoundland and a German burial, with three special memorials. To the right of the road ahead is the distinctive shape of Montauban church spire, ahead is Bernafay Wood and to the left Trones Wood.

Continue to the next cemetery on the right.

• *Bernafay Wood CWGC Cemetery/16.1 miles/5 minutes/Map K27*

The area was taken by the 9th (Scottish) Division on 3-4 July 1916 with little loss of life. A dressing station was then set up here. This same division was driven from the wood in the Kaiser's Offensive on 25 March 1918. They recaptured it briefly but it was the 18th Division who finally regained it on 27 August 1918. It contains 793 UK burials, 122 Australian, 4 South African, 2 New Zealand, an Indian and 32 special memorials.

Continue. At the crossroads with the D64 turn right, signed Montauban. At the first crossroads in the village, stop.

• *Liverpool & Manchester Pals Memorial/17.1 miles/5 minutes/Map K40*

Graham Maddocks, author of *Liverpool Pals*, led a committee that raised funds for this memorial, designed by Derek Sheard and inaugurated on 1 July 1994 at an Anglo-French ceremony attended by bands from the RAF and 43rd RI from Lille. The Pals were part of 30th Division that took the village on 1 July 1916.

Continue through the village, past the church on the right with its distinctive spire, on the D64 to a memorial cross on the right.

• *Private Memorial to Capitaine Monclin/17.5 miles/10 minutes/Map K38/OP*

This private memorial (the cross which was visible from the back of Caterpillar Valley Cemetery) is to Capitaine Henri Thiéron de Monclin and his soldiers of the 5th Coy of the French 6th Inf Regt, who were killed on 28 September 1914. It makes an excellent observation point.

This entire ridge, of the D64 from before Montauban to the far edge of Mametz village, was taken on 1 July 1916, the biggest advance of the day. Take the Pozières wireless mast, visible straight ahead, as 12 o'clock. The Golden Madonna at Albert is at 10 o'clock, the Thiépval Memorial is at 11 o'clock, High Wood is at 1 o'clock, Caterpillar Valley Cemetery is at 2 o'clock to the left of Longueval Church and immediately to the left is the New Zealand Memorial, apparently level with it, but actually beyond the area of Caterpillar Valley which is in dead ground between them. Delville Wood is at 2 o'clock to the right of Longueval Church.

Continue along the D64. After about half a mile stop by a track leading to the right.

• *Pommiers Redoubt/18.1 miles/5 minutes/Map K between 38 and 36*

Nothing now remains of this position which was so important during the July-September 1916 battles, the objective of 54th Brigade (the 7th Bedfords and 11th Royal Fusiliers) on the opening day. The redoubt, and White Trench beyond (the start line for the 10 July attack of the 38th Division on Mametz Wood) were taken by the afternoon, as was the village of Mametz. The redoubt, named after the apple trees which grew along the ridge, was used by Brig-General Evans as his temporary 115th Brigade HQ during the 10 July attack on Mametz Wood. 'What's it like at Pommiers Redoubt?', asked Lieutenant (soon to be acting Captain and then Brigade Major as his superior officers became casualties in the Wood) Wyn Griffith of his Brigade Signalling Officer who had just returned from the HQ. 'Just like any other hole in the ground', replied Taylor. But the redoubt was a typically complicated German system of dugouts and its position commanded excellent views over the wood. It was used again by 2nd KOSBs after the attack on High Wood, and then by 10th West Yorks and the 8th KRRCs in September, by which time it had become a busy, and very muddy, camp site.

Continue. Stop at the cemetery on the right.

Bristol's Own Cross, with High Wood behind to the left

Capitaine de Monclin Private Memorial with High Wood on the right horizon

Liverpool & Manchester Pals Memorial, Montauban

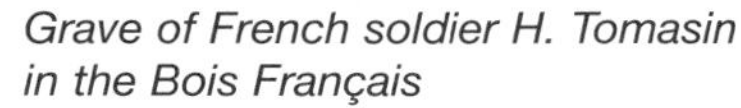

Grave of French soldier H. Tomasin in the Bois Français

14th (S)Bn, 38th (Welsh) Division Memorial and seat, Dantzig Alley CWGC Cemetery

• *Dantzig Alley CWGC Cemetery & Memorials/18.8 miles/15 minutes/Map K37, 35, 36/OP*

Danzig Alley Trench, which gave the cemetery its name (but note the different spelling), ran parallel to the D64 at this point and was part of 7th Division's (the 22nd Manchesters) objective on 1 July 1916. They achieved it at approximately 0800 hours. The large cemetery (it contains 1,923 UK, 17 New Zealand, 13 Australian, 10 Canadian, 3 South African burials and 87 special memorials, many from 1 July, was begun soon after the battle and by 11 November 1918 it contained 183 graves – all now in Plot I (see map in Cemetery report). After the Armistice, eight or more other cemeteries were concentrated here. On the left-hand wall by the box containing the Cemetery Report and Visitor's Book is a memorial **plaque to the RWF on the Somme** 1916-18. At the back of the cemetery overlooking open country, is a memorial seat erected by **14th (S) Battalion the Royal Welsh Fusiliers** of the 38th Welsh Division raised in Anglesey and North Wales who had their baptism of fire in the second attack on Mametz Wood. It bears an inscription in Welsh from one of the regiment's most famous sons, the bardic poet Pte Ellis Humphrey Evans who, although he too was a North-Walian, served in the 15th (London) Battalion (as did Wyn Griffith and David Jones). Evans, whose bardic name was Hedd Wyn, was killed on 31 July 1917 on the Pilckem Ridge. The translation reads,

Distance cannot make you forgotten,
The children of those dear hills,
Heart and heart remain together
Even when separated.

On a clear day the view from the wall which incorporates the memorial is truly remarkable and binoculars are recommended. At the extreme left is the water tower in Mametz. In front is a valley, known by the soldiers who had to cross it under enemy fire as Death Valley, which runs left to right between the cemetery and the various woods and copses ahead. The feature stretches from Fricourt, 2,000m away beyond the water tower, to High Wood, 5,000m away at 2 o'clock. Take 12 o'clock as straight ahead facing the spire of Contalmaison church which should be visible on the sky-line. The water tower is at 9 o'clock and the Golden Madonna at Albert can sometimes be seen at 10 o'clock. Just to the left of 12 o'clock on the skyline the Pozières Memorial to the Missing may be seen and further right on the skyline at the tip of the finger of wood that points left from the main wood in view, is the wireless mast at Pozières Windmill. The bulky wood with the finger is Mametz Wood, and where it disappears behind the near fold in the ground to the right is the beginning of Caterpillar Valley where, in the late afternoon of 14 July the 7th Dragoon Guards and the Indian Cavalry of the Deccan Horse gathered for their charge on High Wood (see Historical Summary, Part 3 and page 125/6). Their target is just visible to the extreme right on the skyline. About halfway between the cemetery and the wood is White Trench, from which the Welsh attacked on 10 July. The ground then drops sharply down a steep cliff to the Willow Stream. However poor visibility may be, it will be possible to appreciate how German machine guns sited in the woods beyond Death Valley dominated the open ground, and how wise a decision it was to move up at night for the attack of 14 July.

Continue to the crossroads in Mametz and stop.

• *Manchester Regiment Memorial/19.1 miles/5 minutes/Map K34*

This memorial plaque was erected by the Cheshire and Lancashire Branches of the WFA in memory of the 20th, 21st, 22nd and 24th Battalions of the Manchester Regiment who, as part of 7th Division, 'successfully freed this village on the morning of 1 July 1916'. Pointing to the right at the corner is a green CWGC sign to the Welsh Memorial (*Mémorial Gallois*).

Turn left on the C2 following signs to Carnoy, then fork right downhill towards the D938. Some 500m later pass a civilian cemetery on the right and stop by the 150m sign.

• *Shrine Corner/19.5 miles/5 minutes/Map K/OP*

You are now standing just behind the German forward trenches of 1 July and facing the British. Ahead is a valley – the Vallée St Martin – and a house with the word Mametz painted on its side which was the old railway station. Take that as 12 o'clock. At 1 o'clock is the tip of the Golden Madonna, visible along a bare skyline. At 10 o'clock (not straight ahead of you) on the forward slope the other side of the valley, is a wood with a track running up the left-hand side. In the wood is the Devonshire Cemetery on the site of a trench occupied by that Regiment prior to 1 July. To one officer in the Devons, Vallée St Martin gave off a foreboding of death. By extraordinary concidence his name was Martin too – Captain D. L. Martin. He was convinced that a German machine gun, sited just about where you are now at the base of the shrine (a crucifix), would decimate his company as they left their trench for the 'Big Push'. Martin was an artist and made a 'Plasticine' model of the 20th Brigade area, when at home on leave shortly before the attack, which reinforced the danger the machine gun presented. So good was the model that it was used in briefings by the Brigade Commander and HQ 20th Infantry Brigade circulated a secret letter to its units instructing Commanding Officers to 'arrange for all officers to inspect this model at 0900 hours on 22 June'. But the message of the danger presented by the machine gun was not heeded. Haig did not encourage questioning from his subordinates and even the most intelligent soon learned that to do so might mean being *dégommé* (literally unstuck) or *limoged*, or what was known in the Boer War as stellenbosched – that is being relieved of one's command and sent back to an unattractive dead-end post. The suppression of any hint of lack of enthusiasm for a plan spread down through all levels. Captain Martin's doubts were not passed any higher. In the event he was right. As the Devons made their way to and through the remnants of the wood, Mansel Copse, the gun opened fire and you can see how exposed they were.

Continue downhill on the road that was called Shrine Alley to the D938 junction.

Extra Visit to Private Memorial to H. Tomasin (Map J44), Point 110 New CWGC Cemetery (Map J45), Point 110 Old CWGC Cemetery (Map J43) & Siegfried Sassoon's Raid on Kiel Trench. Round-trip: 3 miles. Approximate time: 25 minutes

Turn right on the D 938 and turn left, following signs to Point 110 Old & New Military Cemeteries. Drive uphill through the woods – Bois Français to the right and Bois Allemand to the left. Stop at the top. Walk down the track to the right and 150m down is an entrance into the wood.

It leads to the large tomb, decorated with shells, of French soldier H. Tomasin of the 26th RI, Class of 1900. The well-tended site is surrounded by hawthorn trees.

Return to your car and continue straight ahead, following green CWGC signs to the cemetery on the right.

Point 110 Old Military Cemetery was begun by French troops in February

Extra Visit continued

1915 and continued by the Dorsets and other British units from August 1915 to September 1916. The French graves were later removed to the Albert French National Cemetery. Now it contains a hundred soldiers from the UK, and three unknowns.

Walk towards the further cemetery.

The cemeteries are built on what was known as King George's Hill in September 1916. 'Point 110' refers to the contour on which they stand. Approximately half way between the two is a track which leads to the right down to the D147 road in the valley. At this point Siegfried Sassoon's raid may be studied. A copy of his *Memoirs of an Infantry Officer*, Part One, Section III to hand will help to follow the precise course of the raid. It started from Point 71N, where the track to the right meets the road. The objective was 'to enter the enemy loop on the edge of the crater; to enter Kiel Trench at two points; to examine the portions of the trench thus isolated, capture prisoners, bomb dug-outs, and kill Germans.' At 1030 on the night of 25 May 1916 Siegfried accompanied the raiders to his CO's HQ at Maple Redoubt. The redoubt was on the approximate site of the two CWGC Cemeteries. Kiel Trench lay over the ridge, approximately half way between Maple Redoubt and the old railway house from which you started the diversion. The raid did not achieve its objectives and Sassoon's favourite Corporal, O'Brien, was mortally wounded. (He is buried in **Citadel New Military CWGC** Cemetery, Map M4.) 'I would have given a lot if he could have been alive', wrote Sassoon, 'but it was a hopeless case .... But when I go out on patrol his ghost will surely be with me.' For his part in the raid Sassoon was awarded the MC. 'He remained for 1½ hours under rifle and bomb fire, collecting and bringing in our wounded. Owing to his courage and determination all killed and wounded were brought in', reads his citation.

Point 110 New Military Cemetery. Here is buried **2nd Lt David Cuthbert Thomas** of the 3rd Bn RWF, friend of both Sassoon and Graves, killed on 18 March 1916, age 20. Graves dedicated a poem, *Goliath and David: For D.C.T. killed at Fricourt, March 1916*, to him. The cemetery was begun by 403rd RI in May-July 1915. It was continued by British units in February-July 1916. The twenty-six French and two German graves it originally contained have been removed and it now contains sixty-four UK, twenty-seven of whom belong to the 20th, 21st and 24th Manchesters, whose memorial plaque is in Mametz. Look uphill past the top left-hand corner of the cemetery and that is the direction of Sassoon's raid towards Kiel Trench.

Return to the junction with the D938 and rejoin Itinerary Two.

Memorial to Manchester Regiment, Mametz

Approach to Devonshire Cemetery, with the memorial tablet on the left

Devonshire Cemetery 1 July 1916 Headstones: Poet W.N. Hodgson

Capt D.L. Martin with two other men of the Devonshires

Turn left on the D938 signed to Maricourt and Péronne. 300m later fork right up the track to the car park and walk up the remainder of the track to the cemetery.

• *Devonshire CWGC Cemetery, Mametz/20.0 miles/10 minutes/Map K45*

All the burials here, except three, are of Devons killed on 1 July, including the ill-fated **Captain Martin** (buried in a grave with two other Devon Privates). Another Devons' officer who had a premonition of death and who was proved right is also buried here. He is the poet **Lt William Noel Hodgson, MC** (won at Loos), Bombing (grenade) Officer of the 9th Battalion. In his last poem entitled *Before Action*, and published (not written as is commonly believed) two days before the attack, the final line of the final verse reads, 'Help me to die, O Lord.' Hodgson, son of the Bishop of St Edmunsbury, had been educated at Durham School and Christ College, Oxford. A brilliant scholar (with a First in Classical Moderation), he was also a fine athlete. This popular all-rounder (known as 'Smiler') had, as well as writing poetry, produced some accomplished prose, published under the pseudonym of Edward Melbourne. He, and as many of the 160 Devons that died that day as he could gather in, were buried by the Chaplain to the 8th and 9th Devons, the **Reverend Eric. C. Crosse**. 'Nearly all the casualties were just by the magpie's nest', Crosse wrote later to a fellow officer. 'I buried all I could collect in our front line trench.' Crosse survived to serve with the 7th Division on the Asiago Plateau from August to November 1918 and wrote an account of its actions there (*'The Defeat of Austria as seen by the 7th Division'*). He then went on to Marlborough College.

Today a **stone plaque** outside the cemetery entrance gate proclaims: 'The Devonshires held this trench, the Devonshires hold it still'. This is a modern version of the wooden sign, bearing the same legend, which stood on the same site for many years. The stone was unveiled on the seventieth anniversary of the battle on 1 July 1986 by the Duke of Kent, Col in Chief of the Devonshire and Dorset Regiment and President of the CWGC.

Return to the D938 and continue right towards Péronne. Stop at the small cemetery on the left.

• *Gordon CWGC Cemetery/20.3 miles/5 minutes/Map K47/OP*

This small cemetery contains six officers (2nd Lieutenants) and ninety-three men of 7th Division and 2nd Gordon Highlanders, all killed on 1 July and buried in their own support trench in a double semi-circle around the Cross of Sacrifice. There are also three artillerymen killed on 9 July buried in the cemetery. Stand in the gateway to the cemetery. To a first approximation a line over the left-hand back corner leads directly to Dantzig Alley Cemetery and a line over the right-hand back corner leads to Montauban. It was within this arc that the biggest advance along the whole front of 1 July 1916 was made. A night visit to this cemetery can be very atmospheric. The height of the hedge is such, that by standing close to it and looking over the top, one has the impression of standing in a trench.

Continue past a junction on the left with the D254 and at the next crossroads with the C3 turn left downhill and stop at the cemetery on the left.

• *Carnoy CWGC Military Cemetery/21.4 miles/10 minutes/Map N7*

The cemetery, which contains 837 burials, was begun on 15 August 1915 by 2nd KOSBs and 2nd KOYLIs. In it is buried **Capt W. P. Nevill** of the 8th East Surreys who, when on leave shortly before the Somme offensive, bought footballs for each of his four platoons. He offered a prize for the first football to be kicked into a German trench during his company's assault on Montauban on 1 July. One football was inscribed 'The Great European Cup. The Final, East Surreys v Bavarians. Kick off at Zero'. Nevill (an Old Boy of Dover College) kicked off, but did not survive to award his prize. Two of the footballs were retrieved and one is in the National Army Museum and the other in the Queen's Regimental Museum at Howe Barracks, Canterbury. Their Sergeants have a silver football in their mess. Near Nevill's grave are three unusual headstones. On the first are two 2nd Lieutenants, on the second are two Lieutenants and on the third two Captains. They are all East Surreys killed on 1 July 1916. Also buried here is a Chaplain, the **Rev Charles Plummer** attached to 61st Infantry Brigade, and one of the family of four Newfoundlanders called Ayre (qv) to be killed on 1 July. He is **Captain B. P. Ayre**, who was serving with the Norfolk Regiment. Also buried here is **Lt Colonel F.E.P. Curzon,** age 57, 9 September 1916, who commanded the 6th Battalion RIR.

Continue to the T junction in the village, turn right uphill and fork left after 200m signed to Montauban.

You are now travelling in the direction of the attack of 18th Division on 1 July. The British front line crossed this road some 1,200m after the Y junction, with 7th Buffs to your right and 8th Norfolks across the road and to your left. It was some 600m over to the right of this road that Capt Nevill's platoon kicked their footballs on 1 July. The attack was successful. The divisional boundary excluded Montauban up ahead, and the village was taken by 16th and 17th Manchesters of 30th Division, the extreme right hand British division and the only one to take and hold all its objectives by mid-day. However, after Montauban fell to the Germans in March 1918, it was 7th Buffs and 11th Royal Fusiliers of 18th Division that recaptured the village on 25 August.

After the 1916 battles it was discovered that the much-loved Madonna of Montauban-de-Picardie had disappeared from the ruined church. It was not until April 1986 that the Mayor of Montauban, M. Froment, received a letter from a Miss Valerie Ives from Netherby in Yorkshire which explained her disappearance. The Madonna – or rather the bust that was all that remained of her – had been taken to England by a British Officer who gave it to a friend. She kept it in her library, mounted on a plinth with the inscription, 'Montauban Madonna – Battle of the Somme' and on her death it was inherited by Miss Ives who decided it should be returned to its rightful home. She brought the bust back to Montauban in November 1986 when it was restored to its place in the rebuilt church.

Continue on to the junction with the D64 and keep right to Montauban, passing through the village with the church on your left, keeping the new Liverpool and Manchester Pals memorial (passed earlier in this itinerary) on the right and out beyond to the crossroads with the D197. Go straight over.

The first wood on the left is Bernafay Wood, which was taken on 4 July. Then, after a gap of some 600m, the next wood is Trones Wood (*Bois des Troncs*) and as the road bends left, there is a memorial on the left at the edge of the wood.

Stop. Be careful to park off the road.

• *18th Division Memorial/25 miles/5 minutes/Map K41*

The first British soldiers to gain a foothold in the wood (broadly attacking from across the open ground to the right of the road) were 30th Division on 8 July, but it was finally cleared by 6th Northants, 7th Royal West Kents and 12th Middlesex of 18th Division on 14 July on the first day of Part III of the Somme Battle. Col Francis Maxwell (who won his VC in South Africa, then commanded 12th Middlesex, went on to command 27th Brigade and was killed on 21 September 1917 in the Ypres Salient) wrote home two days later,

> "To talk of a 'wood' is to talk rot. It was the most dreadful tangle of dense trees and undergrowth imaginable, with deep yawning trenches criss-crossing about it; every tree broken off at top or bottom and branches cut away, so that the floor of the wood was almost an impenetrable tangle of timber, trenches, undergrowth, etc., blown to pieces by British and German heavy guns for a week. Never was anything so perfectly dreadful to look at … particularly with its gruesome addition of corpses and wounded men – many lying there for days and days. Our doctor found one today who had had no food or water for five days … but so dense is the tangle that even if you find a wounded man … then leave him, you have lost him, simply because you can't find your way back to him."

Recaptured by the Germans in March 1918, it was again taken by 18th Division on 27 August 1918. At one time a plain wooden cross commemorated the men of 8th Berks, 11th Essex and 7th Royal West Kents who fell in the 1918 fighting. Now only the stone obelisk Divisional Memorial remains, with the same simple words as at Thiépval, 'This is My Command, that ye love one another'. The memorial was erected before the shattered wood had regrown.

Continue along the D64 to the junction with the small Hardecourt au Bois road to the right.

18th Division Memorial, Trones Wood

Headstone of Capt W.P. Nevill, Carnoy Mil CWGC Cem

Extra Visit to Maltkorn Farm (Map K42) & Private Memorials to Boucher, Lapage and Capitaine Cochin (Map K48)
Round trip: 2.4 miles. Approximate time: 20 minutes/OP

Turn right in direction of Hardecourt and continue to a memorial cross on the left.

This calvary marks the site of **Maltkorn Duclercq Farm** (sometimes known as Maltz Horn Farm), destroyed in the battles which took place here between 1 July and 9 August 1916. The farm made a salient in the German lines and it actually fell to 89th and 90th Brigades of 30th Division on 30 July as they advanced towards Faffemont (or Falfemont) Farm (Map L6 area). Standing by this cross the sharp-eyed can see the top of Pozières

Maltkorn Farm Calvary, with Trones Wood behind

> ***Extra Visit continued***
> wireless mast to the left of Trones Wood on the skyline. To the left of Trones Wood is Bernafay Wood, at the left hand edge of which is Montauban Church. *Continue towards the next junction,* before which on the right, up a track, is a memorial stone to **Marcel Boucher *'et son camarade'* Roméo Lapage** of the 153rd Infantry Regiment who were killed here on 28 July 1916. At the junction is a Private Memorial to **Capitaine Augustin Cochin** of the 4th Battalion, Chasseurs who was killed here in a brave action on 8 July 1916. The decorative cross is made from shells, machine-gun belt chains and incorporates the image of a soldier being carried aloft by angels.
> *Return to the D64 and continue on the main itinerary*

Continue. To the right of the road is the area where an exceptional VC was won.

• *SOA Capt Noel Godfrey Chavasse VC & BAR, MC/Map K43*

On 9 August 1916, Capt Chavasse, the dedicated Medical Officer of the 1/10th King's Liverpool Regt:

> "... attended to the wounded all day under heavy fire, frequently in view of the enemy, and during the night he searched for wounded in front of the enemy's lines. Next day he took a stretcher-bearer and under heavy shell fire carried an urgent case 500 yards into safety, being wounded himself on the return journey. The same night, with 20 volunteers, he rescued three wounded men from a shell-hole 36 yards from the enemy's trenches, buried the bodies of two officers and collected many identity discs. Altogether he saved the lives of some 20 wounded men, besides the ordinary cases which passed through his hands."

Chavasse was to carry out a similar act of repeated heroism, which earned him a bar to his VC (he was the only double VC winner to gain both his awards in World War I), at Wieltje in the Ypres Salient, but finally died of wounds on 4 August 1917 and is buried in Brandhoek New Military Cemetery in Belgium. There is a memorial to him in the village.

Continue and stop at the next cemetery on the left.

• *Guillemont Road CWGC Cemetery/26.8 miles/20 minutes/Map K44/OP*

Although Trones Wood was taken on 14 July, continuous and furious fighting went on for the area of this road until September. Lost again in March 1918, it was retaken by 18th and 38th (Welsh) Divisions on 29 August.

The cemetery contains over 2,200 burials, including the grave of **Lt Raymond Asquith**, of the 3rd Grenadier Guards, elder son of the British Prime Minister Herbert Henry Asquith, who managed to see his son on a visit to the front line on 7 September 1916. Also present was Raymond's brother, Herbert, a Captain in the Royal Artillery. Raymond was shot in the chest on the 15th, in Part 4 of the Somme Battle, leading his company into the attack. He died soon after in a nearby dressing station. Raymond was said to be one of the most promising men of his generation. He was a barrister and had been President of the Union at Oxford, won the Craven, Derby and Ireland Scholarships, a First in Greats and a Fellowship at All Souls. A. A. Milne called him 'the most brilliant man I have ever met', Winston Churchill referred to him as 'my brilliant hero-friend', John Buchan said, 'he moved among us like a being of another world'. When he heard of his son's death, the Prime Minister wrote, 'Whatever pride I had in the past, and whatever hope I had for the future, by much the largest part of both was vested in him. Now all that is gone'.

Buried in the same row is **Lt the Hon Edward Tennant**, of the 4th Grenadiers. 'Bim' was a talented poet, author of poems such as *Worple Flit, Home Thoughts from Laventie,* and *The Mad Soldier*. This popular young officer (1 July 1916 was his 19th birthday and he was killed, by a sniper, on 22 September) would have admired Raymond Asquith, who, although considerably older (at 37) was part of the same social set. Their generation was known as 'The Coterie', and they were the children of the esoteric group of witty, privileged members of a few select families known as 'The Souls'. They were even related by the second marriage of Raymond's father to Margot Tennant, Bim's aunt. His mother, Pamela Glenconner, wrote *A Memoir* to her beloved son, which was published in 1919. In the row behind is the grave of **Lt Col John Collier Stormonth Darling** of the Cameronians, killed on 1 November 1916 while he was commanding the 9th HLI, age 38.

Walk to the seat in the back wall of the cemetery.

Some 300m straight ahead, away from the road is a shallow valley, once a major German trench line. The single track Albert to Péronne railway ran just behind that, from left to right, and the wood on the skyline is Delville Wood. At the left-hand end of Delville Wood it should be possible to spot Longueval church. Also in the valley is the Private Memorial to 2nd Lt Marsden-Smedley (Map K30). The wall that surrounds the memorial can be seen, provided the crops in the field are not too high, in the middle distance just to the right of a line to the water tower at the edge of Delville Wood.

Return to your car and continue towards the village of Guillemont to a grassy path to the left. This is the best access route to the Marsden-Smedley memorial.

Extra Visit to the Private Memorial of 2nd Lt George Futvoye Marsden-Smedley/Map K30 Round trip: 0.8 miles. Approximate time: 20 minutes

Turn left down the narrow track (which can be muddy when wet) and continue bearing to the left. Continue to the memorial on the left.

Entrance to Guillemont Road CWGC Cem

Extra Visit continued

George Marsden-Smedley was educated at Harrow where he became an outstanding athlete. Instead of taking up his place at Trinity College, Cambridge, George joined the Rifle Brigade on leaving school in 1915. During his short period at the front, George often wrote to his family. He described leaving Southampton for France on 16 July, arriving at his battalion (the 3rd) which was then in reserve (somewhere near Albert). He discussed the Eton-Harrow Cricket Match, demanded a supply of mouth organs for his men and chocolates from Fortnum & Mason for himself. He talked of getting 'The Boche fearfully alarmed', of the Hun being pounded by our bombardment and on the day before he was killed, knowing the big attack that was being planned would take place on the morrow, promised his mother 'a better letter... possibly

Private Memorial to 2nd Lt G.F. Marsden-Smedley, with Guillemont Road Cem behind

Extra Visit continued

in three days time'. On 18 August the 19-year-old Subaltern led his platoon on an attack on Guillemont Station. This is believed to have been about 100m from the memorial. He single-handedly charged a machine gun post which was holding up the company but after shooting one of the Germans was himself shot. He fell on the German parapet, which was on the site of the present memorial. His body was never found and he is commemorated on the Thiépval Memorial. The memorial was erected by his parents but fell into disrepair. When the family read our description of the memorial as being 'neglected' they decided to renovate the memorial, the surrounding brick wall and the wrought iron gate. This they did with the help of the WFA. The memorial bears the inscription 'Lovely and pleasant in life, in death serene and unafraid, most blessed in remembrance'. A small plaque to the left of the gate says that for further information contact John Smedley Ltd, Lee Mills, Matlock DEA 5AG the old family business. The memorial was re-dedicated on 19 July 1997 in a moving ceremony attended by some 30 family members, including the instigator, George's nephew Christopher Marsden-Smedley, who lost two cousins in the Second World War.

Return to the main road and pick up Itinerary Two

Continue into the village and stop at the church with a memorial in front of it.

• *16th Irish Division Memorial/27.5 miles/5 minutes/Map K32*

The struggle for the village was a long and bitter one. As early as 30 July, elements of the 2nd Royal Scots Fusiliers got into the area but were forced out. Another assault on 8 August had some success, but it was not until 3 September that the village was cleared by 20th Light Division,

Memorial to 20th (Light) Division, Guillemont

16th (Irish) Division Memorial, Guillemont

supported by a brigade of 16th Division.

The German author **Ernst Junger**, born at Heidelberg in 1895, ran away from home at the age of 17 to serve with the French Foreign Legion. When the war broke out he returned home and joined the German Army. His war memories were published under the title *Orages d'Acier* ('Steel Storms') and in them is an entire chapter on Guillemont. Junger always seemed to be in the thick of things, and was wounded fourteen times during the war. On 22 September 1918 he won Germany's highest award for gallantry, the *Pour le Mérite*. Only thirteen other Lieutenants won this coveted decoration during the entire war. On 23 August 1916, he wrote that, as his unit was being transported by lorry, 'Jokes flashed around, accompanied by general bursts of laughter from one vehicle to another'. But as they approached nearer the front a German intelligence officer told them of 'of a new and harder world ... of monotonous days spent huddling in the trenches to escape shellfire, uninterrupted attacks, fields covered with corpses ... expressionless faces ... a macabre impression.' The nervous laughter ceased.

Junger fought again in the Wehrmacht in WW2. He had an ambivalent attitude towards Nazism, sometimes seeming to embrace, sometimes to oppose, its ideology. He went on to win many awards for his literary and international personal achievements (such as the Peace Medal at Verdun in 1979). He died on 17 February 1998 at the age of 102 in Wiflingen, Germany, where he had been in retirement for the past 50 years.

Continue to the crossroads with the D20. Turn right onto the D20, signed to Combles. Continue through the village and stop at the memorial on the right.

• *French 265th Infantry Regiment Memorial/ 28 miles/5 minutes*

This obelisk memorial commemorates the action of **Capitaine Hippolyte Marie Joseph Fockedy** and soldiers of the 265th Infantry Regiment of XI Corps who fell on 28 August 1914. It was erected by Old comrades and *Souvenir Français*.

Continue to the crossroads with the D20E.

• *20th Light Division Memorial/28.1 miles/5 minutes/Map K33*

This memorial, unveiled on 25 April 1995, replaced the old, leaning and crumbling memorial that was identical to the Division's memorial in Langemarck in the Ypres Salient. The division took part in the capture of Guillemont.

Extra Visit to the 'Dickens Cross' Private Memorial Map L3. Round trip:1.7 miles. Approximate time: 15 minutes

Continue on the D20 to a cart track to the left signed to the Dickens Cross.

About 400m up the track is a wooden cross to Major Cedric Charles Dickens (grandson of Charles Dickens) of the 1/13th (Kensington) London

Extra Visit continued

Regt, killed near here on 9 September 1916 during the attack on Leuze Wood. The inscription reads, 'In loving memory of our darling Ceddy'. The cross originally stood in a small copse some distance up and to the left of the track. In it are the traces of trench lines. It was erected by his mother, Lady Dickens, and she planted the area with British flowering shrubs and small trees and, until the outbreak of World War II, made an annual pilgrimage to the cross. Attempts were made after the war to re-inter the body in a Commonwealth War Graves Commission Cemetery, but it could not be found. Dickens is therefore commemorated on the Thiépval Memorial. In September 1995 the cross was moved, with the family's consent, to its present location nearer to the road, in a complicated compensatory re-allocation of land after the building of the TGV railway line. The old wooden cross is now again surrounded by attractive shrubs and bushes. To the right of the D20 is Leuze Wood (known, of course, to Tommy as 'Lousy Wood'), the objective of the Kensington's attack.

Return to the junction with the D20E and rejoin the main itinerary.

Turn left on the D20E, in the direction of Ginchy. Continue into the village.
Following the general offensive in this area of 8 August 1916, 7th Division took the village of Ginchy on 3 September, only to lose it again the same day. It finally fell on 9 September to 49th Brigade of 16th Division.

Continue to the church, which is normally open. Stop and enter.

• *Private Memorials to Major Dickens & Lt Irwin, Ginchy Church 28.8 miles/10 minutes/Map K17/18*

To the right of the altar is a brass plaque with a French inscription which reads, 'To the glory of God and to the memory of Major Cedric Charles Dickens 1/13 Kensingtons the London Regt and of the million dead of the British Empire who fell in the Great War 1914-1918 and who, for the most part, rest in France. RIP.'

To the left of the altar is another brass plaque, with a Latin inscription which translates:

> Pray for the soul of Charles Patrick Michael Irwin, beloved son of Charles Trevor Irwin and Beatrix his wife and brother of Katharine Irwin of Oakley near Basingstoke of the 3rd Bn the RIF who was killed in the attack on Ginchy in France on 10 September 1916, in his 19th year, whose soul belongs to God. Amen.

Lt Irwin is buried in Delville Wood CWGC Cemetery.

Continue along the road to a memorial on the right, just before the power line.

The Dickens Cross and detail, Leuze Wood

Memorial to Lejoindre & Fister, Ginchy

Plaque to Maj Dickens, Ginchy Church

• *Private Memorial to Lejoindre & Pfister/29.2 miles/5 minutes/Map K16*

An avenue of flowering shrubs leads to this neglected and sad French memorial to *Médaille Militaire* and *Croix de Guerre* winners, Georges Lejoindre and Georges Pfister and their comrades of the 18th Régiment d'Infanterie fallen on the field of honour in the fighting for Flers and Ginchy on 26 September 1914.

Return to the village. Turn right at the crossroads signed to Longueval and then at the Y junction fork right to Longueval.

Straight ahead is the village of Longueval and Delville (Devil's) Wood with its prominent water tower. Across the field to the left is a small row of houses running down from the wood. Waterlot Farm stood at the left hand of that row. During the war it was a sugar refinery and a strongly defended German position. Once in British hands (it was finally taken on 17 July 1916) it was

Bas reliefs in the Delville Wood Museum, showing the bitter struggle for the wood in July 1916

Monument to the last original tree, Delville Wood

Memorial to Welsh VCs., Delville Wood

heavily bombarded by the Germans. Rebuilt after the war, it was demolished again in the early 1990s.

Continue to the South African Memorial area and park in the extensive car park by the Visitors' Centre.

• *Delville Wood: South African National Memorial, SOA Sgt Gill VC, Museum, Memorial to Welsh VCs Cpl Davies & Pte Hill, Original Hornbeam Memorial, Bookshop & Cemetery/32 miles/ 50 minutes/Map K 12/13/14/14a/14b/15/RWC*

In the car park is a **CGS/H Signboard** about the South African participation here.

In 1916 the wood, known as Bois d'Elville, was a major German defensive feature. On the left of the road is **Delville Wood Cemetery, Longueval,** which was made after the Armistice by concentrating ten or more cemeteries from the Somme battlefield. There are 5,493 burials and almost two-thirds, 3,590, are unknown. 151 graves are those of South Africans. One grave of note is that of **Sgt Albert Gill**, KRRC, who won a posthumous **VC** when rallying his platoon by standing up in full view of the enemy. Another is **Lt Charles Patrick Michael Irwin** of the 3rd Bn Royal Irish Fusiliers, attd 7th Bn, on Special Memorial A8, killed in action at Ginchy on 10 September age 19, who is commemorated on a plaque in Ginchy Church (qv). **Lt Niel Shaw Stewart** of D Coy, 3rd Bn the Rifle Bde, killed leading C Coy in the attack on Guillemont on 21 August 1916, age 22, and commemorated on a plaque in Rancourt *Souvenir Français* Chapel (qv), is also buried here. The British Parliament decreed that private memorials could not be erected. However, overseas, this could only apply on land ceded or granted to the Commission, i.e. cemeteries or memorial sites. Thus one way around the ruling for families wishing to erect a memorial to their lost one was to do so in a foreign church.

On the right of the road is Delville Wood itself, the South African National Memorial and the Museum built in 1985/86. The Visitors' Centre was extended in 1994 when the whole complex was still run by dedicated curators Tom and Janet Fairgrieve. The centre provides drinks and light snacks and has a picnic area, good toilets, an exceptional book stall and a stock of battlefield artefacts.

The museum is **open daily**, except Mondays, February-March and mid-October-end November 1000-1545 and 1 April to mid-October 1000-1745. Closed December, January, and French holidays. ☎ (03) 22 85 02 17.

The battle for the wood was a complex one and is well told in the museum and in booklets available there. The South African Brigade was attached to 9th Scottish Division and when the latter took Longueval village on 14 July in Part 3 of the Somme Battle, the Springboks were given the task of taking the wood. At dawn on 15 July the assault began with a fearsome artillery duel. By nightfall all four South African regiments were committed, the main direction of their attack being from the south-west – that is from the direction of the cemetery and Longueval village – and only the north-west corner of the wood remained in enemy hands. Waterlot Farm, however, was still held by the Germans. Five days of hand-to-hand fighting followed. It rained every other day and enemy artillery fire reached rates exceeding 400 shells a minute. The landscape was a tangled mess of broken tree stumps, knotted undergrowth, huge shell holes and mud and water all overlaid with bodies of soldiers of both sides (many of whom still lie in the wood). Though the South Africans were told, and tried, to take the wood 'at all costs', they did not quite manage to do so, and when they were relieved by 26th Brigade on 20 July, only 143 men of the original 3,150 came out of the trenches. It was not until 25 August 1916 that 14th (Light) Division finally overcame all enemy resistance in the wood.

Lord Moran, later to become Churchill's doctor, but then serving with the 1st Bn the Royal Fusiliers in the trenches immediately south of Delville Wood during the battle, describes in his book *The Anatomy of Courage*, how his men attempted to help some of their fellows buried by shell fire:

> "Shells were bursting all around and in the black smoke men were digging. Muffled appeals for help, very faint and distant, came out of the earth and maddened the men who dug harder than ever, and some throwing their spades away, burrowed feverishly with their hands like terriers. It was difficult to get the earth away from one place where they said someone was buried without piling it where others were digging also. We were getting in each other's way. We were afraid too of injuring those buried heads with the shovels and always through our minds went the thought that it might be too late. Then there was a terrific noise, everything vanished for a moment and when I could see, Dyson and the two men working beside him had disappeared. They were buried."

Following the Gulf War and Afghanistan there has been considerable debate about 'friendly fire'. The Royal Fusiliers had been under friendly fire during this incident.

In the 1918 battles the Germans over-ran the area on 24 March, and 38th (Welsh) Division retook the wood on 28 August.

The memorial (unveiled by the widow of General Louis Botha on 10 October 1926) is topped by a **sculpture of Castor and Pollux** holding hands. Designed by Alfred Turner, it symbolized the unity of the English and Afrikaans speaking peoples of South Africa. A replica overlooks Pretoria from in front of the Government Buildings, designed, as was the Delville Wood Memorial, by Sir Herbert Baker ARA. Behind the arched memorial is a Voortrekkers Cross, which replaces the traditional Cross of Sacrifice. The Stone of Remembrance in front of the memorial is to South Africa's dead of World War II. **The museum**, unveiled on 7 June 1984 by then Prime Minister P. Botha and built around the cross, is a replica of the Castle of Good Hope in Capetown. Its five bastions bear the names of other castles in Capetown. Just to the left inside is a magnificent coloured replica of the **P.L. Cart de la Fontaine (qv) CWGC plaque**, specially

Delville Wood, Castor & Pollux South African Memorial, with the museum beyond

made for this museum. The museum has delicately engraved glass windows round an inner courtyard and dramatic *bas reliefs* in bronze depicting the days of bitter fighting for the wood. Exhibits depict South Africa's World War I role in Delville Wood, the German South West and East African campaigns, her VCs, and the role of South Africa in other wars, notably World War II and Korea. The combined losses of these conflicts totals 25,000.

The rides in the wood have stone markers with the names of streets given during the war: Rotten Row, Bond Street, Regent Street, Princes Street, etc, and for Brigade HQ. One tree, a **hornbeam**, remains from the terrible days of 1916. It is to the left and rear of the museum and in front of it is a **memorial stone** unveiled by the South African Ambassador in 1988. To the left of it is a **small stone to the two Welsh VCs, Cpl Joseph Davies**, 10th (Service) Battalion and **Pte Albert Hill**, both of the RWF, whose acts of conspicuous gallantry took place here on 20 July 1916. Davies survived until 1976 and Hill died in the USA in 1971.Their plaque was unveiled by members of the Regiment in July 2001.

Continue into Longueval on the D20 and stop at the crossroads.

To the left is the village *Poilu* war memorial and on the opposite corner is

• *Pipers' Memorial/32.2 miles/10 minutes/Map K14c*

The memorial was proposed by members of the Somme Battlefield Pipe band, formed in 1989 under the Honorary Presidency of Ian C. Alexander of the War Research Society, to perpetuate the memory of the Pipers of various regiments who fought in WW1. Longueval was chosen for the site as it was captured by the 9th Scottish Division in July 1916 and through it many pipers marched. The project was supported by the Mayor, Jean Blondel. A world-wide fund was launched and Andy de Comyn, a Midlands-based sculptor, carved the 4-metre high white stone statue of a Piper, with black pipes, stepping over sandbags, on the base of a cairn. On the surrounding wall, constructed by a local builder, are the cap badges of each regiment who lost a Piper during the War, carved by the CWGC. Ian and his team worked indefatigably to raise the £35,000 needed to complete the project. The statue was unveiled on a sunny 20 July 2002 by Lt General Sir Peter Graham,

Blessing of the Pipers' Memorial, Longueval, 20 July 2002 with memorial instigator, Ian C, Alexander

KCB, CBE, late Colonel of the Gordon Highlanders, and Maj General Corran Purdon, CBE, MC, CPM, President of the RUR and London Irish Rifles Associations, at an impressive ceremony during which the pipe tune by George Stoddart, called Longueval, was played and the moving poem *The Piper* by Ron Venus was said.

THE PIPER

'Take my pipes', the Piper said
'And lay me down to sleep.
The sights I've seen have broke my heart
And caused my soul to weep'.

'Take my pipes', the Piper said
'And wrap me in my plaid.
The sights I've seen have made me cold
And all I feel is sad'.

'Take my pipes', the piper said
'And my heavy tartan kilt.
My friends have gone and left my side
Dragged down by mud and silt'.

'Take my pipes', the piper said
'And play them far away.
Their sound's too sweet to carry far
Upon this dreadful day'.

'But stay ...! Don't take my treasured pipes
I'll need them by my side
When I take up my Scottish lads
To the land on the other side.'

Pipe and drum bands had gathered from around the world - the Huntley & District from Aberdeen, the London Scottish and the London Irish, representatives from the Black Watch (with their Drum Major), the Highlanders and the Royal Scots, the Royal Corps of Signals, the Somme Battlefield, the President of the American Pipe Band Association, bands from Belgium, Germany and from Holland - to attend this special event. The colourful column, of 105 Pipers and over 75 Drummers, formed up at Delville Wood and marched along the road you have just driven to the rousing sound of the pipes and drums to the village. After the ceremony the massed bands played a poignant selection of tunes to the well over 1,000-strong enthralled audience in the tiny village square.

Turn right onto the D197 signed to Flers and the New Zealand Forces Memorial.

At the Y junction 250m later fork left signed to the memorial and continue right.

Off the road to the right, near a calvary, is the area where 'Billy' Congreve VC was mortally wounded.

• *SOA/Wounding of Billy Congreve VC/Map K11*

It was in this area that a most unusual VC was won by the son of a VC winner. William La Touche Congreve was born on 22 March 1891, the eldest son of Lt General Sir Walter Norris Congreve who won the VC during the Boer War battle of Colenso. Coincidentally, Lt the Hon Frederick Hugh Sherston Roberts also won the VC in the same action and he, too, was the VC son of a VC father – Earl Roberts. At the time of Billy's action his father was in command of XIII Corps on the Somme.

Billy Congreve, a popular and energetic Brigade-Major in the Rifle Brigade, had once before been recommended for the Victoria Cross for gallant action in the Battle for St Eloi in April 1916 and had been awarded the Distinguished Service Order. He already had the Military Cross for gallantry at Hooge in 1915. On 1 June 1916, Billy married Pamela Maude, daughter of the actor Cyril Maude and a great friend of Gilbert Talbot (after whom Talbot House in Poperinghe was named). After a brief honeymoon, Congreve returned to his regiment in time for the 1 July Somme Battle. On 20 July he was hit by a sniper on the outskirts of Longueval and was taken to Corbie for burial (visited on Itinerary Three). His citation quoted 'Acts of Bravery: 6-20 July' during which 'by his personal example he inspired all those around him with confidence at critical periods of the operations'. On 1 November the young widow, who was pregnant with Billy's child, received on her husband's behalf, the VC, the DSO and the MC from King George V, the first officer to have won these three awards for gallantry. He was also awarded the *Légion d'Honneur.*

Continue past the calvary to the memorial and stop.

• *New Zealand Memorial/32.6 miles/5 minutes/Map H26*

There is a **CGS/H Signboard** by the column. It marks the area from which the Division set out on the historic battle of Flers-Courcelette on 15 September 1916, Part 4 of the Somme Battle, when tanks were used for the first time, and together with the 14th and 41st Divisions entered Flers (2,400m away to the right at right-angles to your line of approach) behind 'a solitary tank'. The track behind the memorial leads away to the right and into Flers and can be walked, following approximately the same route as the tanks did on 15 September 1916. The wood immediately behind you is Delville Wood. The New Zealand Memorial to the Missing on the Somme is in Caterpillar Valley Cemetery. The Division fought for twenty-three consecutive days on the Somme, advanced over 2 miles, captured 5 miles of the enemy front line and had 7,000 casualties. This memorial was unveiled in October 1922 by Sir Francis Bell, the Leader of the Legislative Council in New Zealand.

Return to the Calvary. Turn right at the calvary junction and continue down the track to the D107 road.

Across the road, slightly left 650m away, is Caterpillar Valley Cemetery.

Turn right and continue to the beginning of High Wood, known locally as Bois

New Zealand Memorial, Longueval

High Wood: Memorial to 47th (London) Division

Glasgow Highlanders Cairn

Cameron Highlanders and Black Watch Memorial

Memorial tree to Public Schools Bn, 20th Royal Fusiliers

des Fourcaux. Park. There is a (probably muddy) track to the right along the side of the wood. Drive up it for 400m. There is a memorial on the left.

• *Cameron Highlanders & Black Watch Memorial/33.9 miles/10 minutes/Map H25*

Following the failure of the cavalry at High Wood and subsequent ineffective attempts to nibble away the German strongholds such as High Wood, it was decided to try mining. 178th Tunnelling company placed 3,000lb of ammonal 25ft below and about 50ft behind the German front line and on 3 September 1916, 30 seconds after the mine was blown, the Black Watch charged and occupied the crater. They were driven out by German counter-attacks. Another charge of 3,000lb was placed close by the old crater and fired on 9 September. It blew into the first crater and both were occupied and held by the 1st Northants. When you face the memorial, the craters, filled with water, are just behind it and to the right. The memorial commemorates not only the Cameron Highlanders who fell here in September 1916, but all who fell throughout the war. The Black Watch inscription is on the back of the memorial.

Return to the main road, turn right and drive 100m. Stop at the memorial on the right.

• *47th (London) Division Memorial/34 miles/5 minutes/Map H24*

The original wooden memorial here was unveiled on 13 September 1923 by Lt General Sir George Gorringe and Maj General Sir William Thwaites commemorating the action of the Division on 15 September 1916. Its replacement stone 'porch' memorial was renovated in the 1980s from money raised by the Divisional Association, but in the mid 90s it was in such poor condition that it, too, was replaced by the current cross. It was the 47th Division that finally took High Wood and one of the assault formations was the 1st Battalion, Prince of Wales's Own Civil Service Rifles. They were told that they were to attack at 0550 hours on 15 September and that they would be supported by two tanks instead of having an artillery barrage. At zero hour the

Entrance loggia, London CWGC Cem, High Wood

tanks had not arrived and the attack went in without them – and without artillery support – resulting in many casualties. The unit history records:

> "Meanwhile the tanks had not shown up – though one of them later on, after nearly smashing up Battalion Headquarters, got stuck in a communication trench and materially interfered with the removal of the wounded. Its pilot got out and going into Battalion Headquarters asked the Commanding Officer where High Wood was. The CO's reply is not recorded. The other tank eventually got into action somewhere in front of D Company's objective and then caught fire."

Although High Wood was won by mid-day, only 150 men of the Battalion reached their objective.

Continue a further eighteen paces and stop on the right.

• 20th Battalion Royal Fusiliers Tree/34 miles/5 minutes/Map H23

The oak tree at the edge of the wood was planted in memory of the battalion ('The Public Schools Battalion') who were killed here on 20 July 1916.

Continue a further 100m and stop on the right.

• Glasgow Highlanders' Cairn/34.1 miles/5 minutes/Map H22

The cairn commemorates the unsuccessful attack of 9th (Glasgow Highlanders) Battalion, Highland Light Infantry of 15 July 1916. Privately erected by Alex Aiken, (he brought much of the material out in the boot of his car) whose book *Courage Past* deals with the attack, it was inaugurated in November 1972. One hundred and ninety two stones from near Culloden individually commemorate each man killed and form a cairn of 5ft 7in tall, the minimum recruiting height for the battalion. The square stone on top was a Glasgow paving stone. The Gaelic inscription reads, 'Just here, Children of the Gael went down shoulder to shoulder on 15 July 1916.'

Continue to the cemetery on the left and park.

• London Cemetery & Extension/34.2 miles/15 minutes/Map H21 OP

The original cemetery was begun in September 1916 by the burial of forty-seven men 'in a large shell hole' by 47th Division, and was later enlarged by the addition of other graves to make a total of 101. That area is immediately to the left of the main entrance, where there is also a memorial to seventy-eight NCOs and men, the locations of whose graves are not known. The cemetery was further extended after the Armistice and is the third largest on the Somme, containing over 3,330 graves of which more than 3,100 are unknown. There is also a World War II plot in the cemetery.

Death makes no political distinction, and just as Herbert Asquith, Liberal MP and Prime Minister, lost a son on the Somme (qv), so did Arthur Henderson, leader of the Labour Party at the time (and who was to win the Nobel Peace Prize in 1934). **Captain David Henderson** of the Middlesex

Regiment, attached to 19th London Battalion, was killed in High Wood on 15 September 1916, aged 27 and is buried here.

Go to the far end of the cemetery behind the main hedge and stand in the left-hand corner facing forward.

The key to the German positions on the British right flank was the high ground here of the Longueval-Bazentin-Pozières Ridge on which the woods and villages had been fortified. You are now standing in a German goal, with your goal posts the woods of Bazentin and Delville. Just beyond the left-hand edge of Bazentin-le-Grand Wood is the northern end of Caterpillar Valley and it was from there that the cavalry came forward in the attack of 14 July, heading for the goalkeeper. Very few made it to the net. To the extreme left and slightly behind you is Delville Wood. Now looking clockwise you can see: Longueval Church spire at the edge of Delville Wood; Caterpillar Valley Cemetery on the ridge; the unusual bulk of Montauban Church on the skyline; Bazentin-le-Grand Wood slightly right of straight ahead and to the right the wireless mast at Pozières Windmill. Looking straight ahead between the woods there is a valley some 300m away and it was there that the Cameron Highlanders formed up for the September attack on High Wood. To the left another, shallower, valley runs between you and Delville Wood towards High Wood and it was up that valley that the Deccan Horse charged in July.

Continue on the D6 to Martinpuich.

Just before the village **Martinpuich CWGC Cemetery** is signed to the left and in the local cemetery on the corner are five beautifully tended CWGC graves, one group of three (including **Able Seaman J. Wilkinson**, Drake Battalion, RND, age 21, 25 March 1918 'who was buried by the enemy in Martinpuich German Cemetery No 1 but whose grave is now lost') and two single graves.

Continue to the crossroads and turn right onto the D6E signed to le Sars. Stop at the gateway beyond the church in front of the Mairie/school.

• *47th Division/German Memorials/35.7 miles/5 minutes/Map H20/19*

The village was taken by the 15th (Scottish) Division on the afternoon of 15 September 1916. The 47th Division Memorial (with battle honours inside the arch) also comprises the covered loggia behind it and to the left. The school playground was presented to the village by Lt Gen Sir George Gorringe on Sunday 13 September 1925 when the 47th Div memorial gateway was unveiled. On the local memorial behind the gateway is a **German Memorial Plaque to the 109th RIR.**

Return to the crossroads and go straight over. At the fish pond turn left signed to Bazentin. Stop just before the next fork to the right.

• *Martinpuich Bunker/36.7 miles/5 minutes/Map H17*

The large, well-preserved bunker is in the field to the right.

Turn round and return to the crossroads. Turn left on the D6 signed to

Martinpuich bunker

Canadian Memorial, Courcelette

Courcelette. Note the World War I pickets holding up the wire fences in this area. *At the crossroads with the D929 go straight over on the D107 to a small turning to the right at the local cemetery.*

• *German Headstone/38 miles/5 minutes*

To the left of the entrance gate along the grass bank is a grey German headstone which has been pushed down the bank. Its inscription is very worn, but the words '**Lt Hermann Mayer Kol** Fuehrer Lieben bruder der 5 Dez 1914 bei Thiépval' can be made out. It is remarkable how quickly permanent memorials and headstones were erected by regiments in the early days of the war. The Germans began the cemetery at St Symphorien near Mons immediately after the battle. This headstone is probably the sole survivor of a number of markers and may not originally have been at this site at all. It might have been at Thiépval.

Continue along the D107 to the cemetery on the right.

• *Adanac Military CWGC Cemetery & Maple Leaf Gate/39.1 miles/10 minutes/Map H3*

The gate to this cemetery contains the Maple Leaf emblem, indicating that it is first and foremost a Canadian cemetery (its name is Canada backwards!) and indeed it contains 1,071 Canadian burials in its 3,172 graves (1,712 of which are unidentified). **Two Victoria Cross winners** lie here. One is **Piper James Cleland Richardson** of the 16th Bn, Manitoba Regiment, the Canadian Scottish (Richardson was born in Scotland). On 8 October 1916 Richardson's company

Heavy tank Mk IV

Gun-carrier tank Mk I

Medium A Whippet

Heavy tank Mk V

Tank Memorial, Pozières. To the left the WWI tanks at each corner. The wireless mast to the right is a useful landmark

Australian Memorial at the site of the Windmill, Pozières

was held up by very strong wire at Regina Trench and came under intense fire. Piper Richardson, who obtained permission to play the company 'over the top' strode up and down outside the wire playing his pipes, which so inspired the company that the wire was rushed and the position captured. Later the piper was detailed to take back a wounded comrade and some prisoners, but after proceeding some distance he insisted on turning back to recover his pipes which he had left behind. He was never seen again. Richardson's inspiring playing recalls other pipers who performed similar morale-raising acts: Piper Laidlaw at Loos (who also won the VC); and Lord Lovat's Piper, Bill Millin, who piped the Commandos onto the shores of Normandy at SWORD Beach on 6 June 1944. The other **VC is Sgt Samuel Forsyth** of the New Zealand Engineers, att, 2nd Bn, Auckland Regt who, on 24 August 1918, led attacks on three machine-gun positions in Loupart Wood and took the crews prisoner. He was later wounded attempting to get support from a tank that was then put out of action, so he led the tank crew and some of his own men in an attack which caused the enemy machine gun to retire and enabled the advance to continue. At this moment Forsyth was killed by a sniper.

Turn round, return to the crossroads, turn right onto the D929 and stop 100m later at the memorial on the right.

• Canadian Memorial, Courcelette/40.7 miles/5 minutes/Map H10

The village of Courcelette is some 1,000m north west of this memorial which commemorates the actions of the Canadian Corps from September to November 1916. It was the 2nd (Canadian) Division, formed in England in April 1915, that drove the Germans from this area on 15 September, aided by a tank called "Crème de Menthe" that evicted the enemy from a sugar factory nearby. This simple octagonal block of Canadian granite is the standard memorial erected on all sites where the Canadians performed with exceptional valour on the Western Front, after it was deemed that the winning design in a competition for a Canadian Memorial – the Vimy Ridge pylons – and the runner up – the Brooding Soldier at Vancouver Corner – were too expensive to duplicate. The area around the memorial was re-landscaped in 1985-6 following a severe winter in 1984 which damaged trees and shrubs. The Canadian assault was, broadly, towards you along the line of the road. The Thiépval Memorial and the Pozières wireless mast can be seen from here.

Return to your car and continue to the Pozières wireless mast and park.

There are two memorials here. The Tank Corps one is on the left of the road, the Australian one to the right of the road.

• Tank Corps Memorial/41.6 miles/5 minutes/Map H16

There is a **CGS/H Signboard** about tanks here. It was at the battle of Flers-Courcelette, Part 4 of the Somme offensive, that tanks went into action for the first time. This obelisk, with its four superb miniature tanks, is a memorial to the fallen of the Corps, and its fence is constructed from tank 6-pounder gun barrels and early driving chains. This point was one of several where the tanks mustered ready for the attack after assembling behind Trones Wood on the night of 14 September.

Walk (carefully!) across the road.

• *Australian Memorial, Pozières Windmill/RB/41.6 miles/5 minutes/Map H15*

The ruins of the old windmill can still be seen sticking out of the mound of earth. This was the high point of the Pozières Ridge, so bitterly and bloodily fought for by the Australians. Over the month of August when Haig, pushed by Joffre, was indulging in piecemeal attacks, it was the 1st, 2nd and 4th Australian divisions that hammered towards the high ground of the ridge along the Albert-Bapaume road (the one you are driving along). In forty-five days the Australians launched nineteen attacks and lost 23,000 officers and men.

Australia had immediately supported Britian when the war broke out and recruiting started on 10 August 1914. Forces were raised locally through the State Military HQ and, thus, the Australian Imperial Forces (AIF) consisted almost entirely of Pals Battalions – albeit the geographical areas were much larger than in Britain. This local recruiting was followed after the war by local settling. The Australian Government had a number of programmes to help returned soldiers, including offering specially selected land areas to those prepared to settle them. These were administered by State Governments, supported by a Federal Grant of £625 per settler. One such soldier settlement area was around Stanthorpe, 104 miles south-west of Brisbane in south-east Queensland, and the intensity of their battle experience is reflected in the names of the new settlements that the Australian Pals founded – Pozières, Amiens, Bapaume ... all joined by a railway line that had been opened in 1920 by the Prince of Wales. It had been a gruelling tour for the Prince, lasting 210 days, visiting over 200 towns and places and travelling 46,000 miles. One of his main aims was to 'mingle with war veterans.' Their boisterous obsession with touching the future Edward VIII left him 'black and blue'.

The site was bought by the Australian War Memorial Board and the inscription reads:

> "The ruin of Pozières windmill which lies here was the centre of the struggle in this part of the Somme Battlefields in July and August 1916. It was captured on 4 August by the Australian troops who fell more thickly on this ridge than on any other battlefield of the war."

In fact, Australian casualties over the whole war were 215,000, which as a percentage of troops in the field, was the highest of any Allied force. Ten days after the Aussies left the Somme the tank made its debut. The memorial was re-landscaped by the CWGC in 1986 and in 1993 a **Ross Bastiaan bronze**

plaque, sponsored by the Returned Services League, was unveiled by Lt Gen J. C. Grey, Chief of the General Staff.

It was here that Australia's first VC winner of WW1 (gained at Courtney's Post in Gallipoli on 20 May 1915 as a Corporal) won the MC on 6 August 1916. He was perhaps Australia's most famous and best-loved soldier, **Albert Jacka** (qv) – obstreporous, outspoken to his superiors, non-conformist, popular and always ready to settle a dispute with his fists. Now promoted to Lieutenant (he would never rise higher than Captain) Jacka led a platoon (known as 'Jacka's Mob') which was reduced by a fierce German attack to a mere seven men. These he launched at the 60 or so Germans opposing them and although two of the Australians were soon killed and every other man wounded (Jacka himself was hit seven times) he continued brandishing his revolver and personally killed at least twelve of the enemy. This brave action inspired his fellows, many in the process of being taken prisoner, to counter attack. Many believe that Jacka's action was worthy of a bar to his VC. C.E.W. Bean described it as 'the most dramatic and effective act of individual audacity in the history of the AIF.' Fearfully wounded and disfigured, Jacka was sent to the UK to convalesce but returned to his battalion in December, in time to take part in the Bullecourt action the following May (qv).

It was also the scene of an incident on 5 August 1916 during which **Captain Percy Herbert Cherry** of the 26th AIF fired at a German officer who replied with a simultaneous shot. Cherry's helmet deflected the shot but he mortally wounded the German, who asked him to post the letters in his pocket. This he agreed to do. There is now a project by a group of local enthusiasts known as Le Digger-Cote to immortalise the scene in a sculpture as a memorial to all the heroic Australian actions that took place here, and funds are being raised. Cherry vies with Jacka for awards. He had the MC and was awarded the VC

Stanthorpe Railway Line, Queensland. The names of the stops are from World War I battlefields

posthumously for his actions at Lagnicourt on 26 March 1917. He was killed by a shell the following day.

Continue downhill into Pozières. At the crossroads with the D147 turn left and park by the track leading to the left, signed to Sunken Road and 2nd Canadian Cemetery. Walk (or drive if it is very dry) up the track.

• *Butterworth Trench (Map K1), Sunken Road (Map K2) & 2nd Canadian (Map K4) CWGC Cemeteries/42.9 miles/20 minutes*

This track forms the approximate line of a trench that was named after a talented composer, **George Butterworth**. Son of Sir Alexander Butterworth, he studied at Eton and Trinity College before attending the Royal College of

Recreated dugout, Tommy Café

Music and worked with Cecil Sharp and Vaughan Williams, both of whom influenced him strongly. He was an active member of the English Dance and Folk Music Society. His best known works are his song cycle *The Shropshire Lad*, from A. E. Housman's poems, and the lyrical *Banks of Green Willow,* which both show his love of simple folk melodies and his sensitive scorings for strings. At the outbreak of War, Butterworth enlisted in the ranks of the Duke of Cornwall's Light Infantry and in November was posted to the 13th Battalion, the Durham Light Infantry as a 2nd Lieutenant. He served in the Armentières sector in early 1915 and was soon promoted to Lt. In July 1916 he was recommended (for the second time) for the MC and later for a third time on the night of his death. On 1 August the Brigade went up to the line for the fourth time in a month and it was at this stage that the trench that was officially named for him was dug between the British and German line. The Brigade made two attacks on 4 August, one a failure, the other successful. The second, led by Butterworth from the trench that bears his name, was a 'bombing' attack and 100yd was gained. During the attack Butterworth, 'a brilliant musician in times of war and an equally brilliant soldier in times of stress', according to his Brigadier, Page-Croft, was shot dead by a bullet through the head, a month after his 31st birthday. His hastily buried body was subsequently lost, and Butterworth is commemorated on the Thiépval Memorial (qv). It is a hauntingly beautiful experience to take a small tape recorder with a cassette of one of Butterworth's works, find his name on the memorial, and quietly listen to the music under the awe-inspiring arches of Lutyen's massive creation.

Continue along the track to the cemetery on the right.

Sunken Road CWGC Cemetery was one of the last cemeteries to be finished, it contains 214 burials, 148 of them Canadians, 61 Australians and 5 UK.

Walk across the track.

2nd Canadian CWGC Cemetery was also one of the last cemeteries to be completed. It has a bronze Maple Leaf Canadian insignia on the entry gate and the 2nd (Eastern Ontario) Battalion used it from the beginning of September 1916 to mid-October.

Return to the main D929 road and turn left. Immediately on the left is a café.

• *Tommy Café/Dugouts/43.7 miles/Map H14/RWC*

This used to be the Burma Star Staging Post Café run for many years by the redoubtable Madame Brihier. It is now run by Dominique and Melanie Zanardi and offers snacks and light meals throughout the day (coaches must book in advance) ☎ (03) 22 74 82 84. The café walls are covered in wartime photographs, posters etc and in the garden is a recreated trench/dugout system, complete with uniformed models, many weapons and artefacts and sound effects (admission free).

• *End of Itinerary Two*

ITINERARY THREE

• **Itinerary Three** starts at Amiens Cathedral and heads east across the battlefields of 1918, via the Australian National Memorial at Villers Bretonneux. It continues east into the French sector of the 1916 fighting and then north behind the German second line to the Butte de Warlencourt and ends in Bapaume.
• **The Route: Amiens** – cathedral, station area, French National Cemetery, St Acheul; Longueau railway; Longueau British CWGC Cemetery; Glisy Airport; the 'Nearest Point to Amiens'; first Tank Versus Tank Battle; Adelaide CWGC Cemetery; Villers Bretonneux – château, school, *Mairie*, marker stone, Australian National Memorial; Corbie – church, Communal Cemetery & Extension, Colette Statue; Von Richthofen Crash Site; Australian 3rd Div Memorial; Beacon CWGC Cemetery; 58th (London) Div Memorial; Chipilly CWGC Cemetery; Bray – Côte 80 French National Cemetery, German Cemetery; P'tit Train Terminus, Froissy; Proyart – miniature Arc de Triomphe, German Cemetery; Col Rabier Private Memorial; Foucaucourt Local Cem; Lt Col Daly, 6th AIF Memorial; Estrées Memorial; Assevillers New CWGC Cemetery; Hem Farm CWGC Cemetery; 'HR' Private Memorial; Maurepas 1st RI Memorial; V. Hallard Private Memorial; Charles Dansette Private Memorial; Maurepas – French National Cemetery, Memorial; Combles – Communal Cemetery Extension, Guards Cemetery; Guards Memorial, Lesboeufs; Capt Meakin Private Memorial; Gueudecourt Newfoundland Memorial; AIF Grass Lane CWGC Cemetery; SOA Lt Col R. B. Bradford VC; German Memorial, Le Sars; Butte de Warlencourt; Warlencourt CWGC Cemetery; Bapaume.
• **Extra Visits** are suggested to: Marcelcave French National Cemetery; Capt Mond/Lt Martyn Private Memorial, Le Hamel Australian Memorial/RB; Heilly Station CWGC Cemetery and Private Memorial to L Cpl O'Neill; French National Cemetery, Bray; Bray Military CWGC Cemetery; Bray Vale CWGC Cemetery; Bray Hill CWGC Cemetery; Carey's Force Action; Ruined Village of Fay; German Cemetery, RB/Lt McCarthy VC, Capt Delcroix, Bourget & 158th RI, 1st Chass à Pied; Vermandovillers; German Trenches; French National Cemetery, Lihons; Murat Monument; Chaulnes - US & French Nurses, Ger 16th Bav Memorial; Fay - Ruined Village, Memorials to Capt Fontan, Abbé Champin & 41st RI 1940; French National Cemetery, Dompierre; French National Cemetery/383rd RI Memorial, Cléry; Gaston Chomet Private Memorial; Heumann/Mills/Torrance Private Memorial; 41st Div Memorial; Bull's Road CWGC Cemetery; French 17th/18th RIT Memorial.

• **Planned duration**, without stops for refreshment or extra visits: **8 hours 10 minutes.**
• **Total distance: 75.4 miles.**

• *Amiens Cathedral/0 miles/15 minutes/RWC/Map 1/6*

Follow signs to Cathedral Parking (well-placed throughout the City) and park.

On 28 August the Germans took Péronne and the citizens of Amiens trembled as the enemy fought their way towards the city, then occupied by Moroccan troops who were sent to take up defensive positions at Villers Bretonneux. A fierce fight was put up at Proyart, but the Germans counter-attacked and swept their way into Amiens on 31 August 1914, and, as recorded in a notice posted by the Mayor, M. Fiquet, seized twelve hostages from the town council, who, unlike German hostages taken in other towns, such as Senlis, were unharmed. They requisitioned half a million francs worth of supplies to sustain them on their drive towards Paris. Most of the force, after pulling down the French *tricolore* and hoisting the German flag on the town hall and raiding the safes in the savings bank, proceeded on their way *'nach Paris'*, but a garrison was installed with a town major on 9 September. A curfew was imposed, motor cars were requisitioned and 1,000 young men were sent into captivity. Following their defeat on the Marne, the Germans withdrew, and on 12 September the French Army, under General Amade, returned.

Although damaged by air attacks during the next 3½ years, it was not until the German offensive of 1918 that the city again came under a major attack. From April to June it endured an almost continuous artillery bombardment, most citizens were evacuated and the Pope was asked by the Bishop to intercede with Kaiser Wilhelm to save the cathedral from the shelling. The Germans did not reach Amiens. They were stopped at Villers Bretonneux (see

Amiens Cathedral plaques: CWGC (left), US 6th Engineers, Carey's Force (right)

below). On 17 November 1918 a Mass of Thanksgiving was held here to celebrate the end of the war. **Open daily**. There is an entrance fee for guided visits. ☎ (03) 22 71 60 50.

Designed by Robert de Luzarches, the Cathédrale de Notre Dame was begun in 1220 as a suitable resting place for the relic brought back from the Fourth Crusade by Walon of Sarton – the forehead and upper jaw of John the Baptist. It also houses relics of Saint Firmin, the first Bishop of Amiens. The cathedral is regarded as one of the finest and most harmonious examples of Gothic architecture and, at 142m long and 42m high, has the greatest volume. Ruskin called it 'the Bible of Amiens' as its stone façade and wooden choir stall contain so many carved pictures of Bible stories. Edward III attended mass in the cathedral on his way to the Battle of Crécy and Pte Frank Richards DCM, MM of the 2nd Bn, RWF, author of *Old Soldiers Never Die,* visited it in August 1914. Richards was 'very much taken up with the beautiful oil paintings and other objects of art inside. One old soldier who paid it a visit', he reported, however, 'said it would be a fine place to loot'. A huge restoration and cleaning project was started in 1994.

During World War I elaborate precautions were taken to protect the

Carlton-Belfort Hotel, Amiens

cathedral and its priceless art treasures – all portable items (including the stained glass, which was taken by firemen from Paris) being removed for safekeeping. The choir stalls were enclosed with reinforced concrete and sandbags (a precaution that was to be repeated in World War II), as was the principal façade. Although it received nine direct hits by bombs and some shells, none caused serious damage. During the Spring 1918 offensive, when the Germans reached Villers-Bretonneux and Amiens came under such fearsome bombardment that over 2,000 houses were hit and all the inhabitants fled, the British war correspondent Philip Gibbs described it under the moonlight, '… every pinnacle and bit of tracery shining like quicksilver, with magical beauty'. It contains the standard CWGC memorial plaque, twenty-eight of which were designed for erection in cathedrals and important churches in Belgium and France by **Lt Col M. P. L. Cart de Lafontaine, FRIBA** and made by Hallward. The Amiens plaque was the first to be unveiled (by the Prince of Wales, then President of the CWGC) in July 1923. It is slightly different from the others, as it bears the Royal Coat of Arms alone and commemorates the war dead of Great Britain and Ireland who were killed in the diocese. The plaques in other churches also bear the coats of arms of the Dominions. In Amiens there are separate plaques for Australia, Canada, Newfoundland, New Zealand, South Africa and the USA. A replica of the Amiens plaque is in the reception area of the CWGC headquarters in Maidenhead, and a similar plaque is in Westminter Abbey. There is a private memorial to Lt Raymond Asquith (see Itinerary Two).

Return to your car, turn left out of the car park and then right, direction St Leu and right again at the traffic lights following Gare SCNF signs. Keep in the left hand lane.

• *Amiens Station/Carlton-Belfort Hotel/0.5 miles*

The square in front of the station is the Place Alphonse Fiquet (named after the Mayor of Amiens in August 1914). The station and the 104m, twenty-six-floor-high tower opposite were both designed by August Perret. He gave his name to the tower, which was once the tallest office building in the western hemisphere. It is an excellent landmark. The station restaurant was once renowned for its gourmet cuisine and the Prince of Wales lunched there after inaugurating the Thiépval Memorial on 31 July 1923. No stranger to Amiens, the young Grenadier Guards Officer had frequently dined in Amiens' popular restaurants when he had been in the Somme area during 1916. When the Prince himself could not get away, Raymond Asquith borrowed … "Wales' excellent Daimler" and whipped off to Amiens where he "ate and drank a great deal of the best, slept in downy beds, bathed in hot perfumed water, and had a certain amount of restrained fun with the very much once-occupied ladies of the town."

Stand with your back to the station. The hotel on the opposite left corner was the famous Carlton-Belfort Hotel, whose façade had altered little since

1918 until a change of ownership and a facelift in the late 1980s. Up to then a wartime sign, 'No Lorries Through Town' could still be discerned on the wall to the right of the main entrance on rue de Noyon. Apart from the wartime industrial activity which thrived in the city, its function as staff HQ's and its many temporary hospitals, Amiens was known chiefly as a place of relaxation for the Allied soldiers. Among **notables** who visited (and wrote about) the Carlton-Belfort were Siegfried Sassoon, Edwin Campion Vaughan, Robert Graves, Cecil Lewis, and Mick Mannock. Many famous war correspondents and artists were based at or visited Amiens, and other popular haunts were the Hôtel du Rhin (*continue down the rue de Noyon and turn left* when you reach the Place René Goblet, with its World War II memorials to the Martyrs of Picardy and to General Leclerc). A regular patron of the Hôtel du Rhin in the days leading up to 'The Big Push' in 1916 was the cartoonist Bruce Bairnsfather, who was based at the administrative HQ at Montrelet as a lowly Staff Officer. The very name, he wrote, 'at once conveys visions to [one's] feverish mind of the gladdest nights that were then permissible'. John Masefield, commuting between Amiens and Albert while researching for his book on the Somme, 'dined on duck at the Rhin' at a dinner given by Nevill Lytton for the US Ambassador, Gen Bliss the US CGS and Calvin Coolidge, the future President.

Bruce Bairnsfather cartoon. 'A Hopeless Dawn. Just back off leave. Amiens is only 34 hours more in the train now. You know that because you can see the cathedral quite clearly.'

Sir William Orpen, KBE, RA, describes, in his book *An Onlooker in France* 1917-19, how he dined at the Rhin with the Canadian General Seely and Prince Antoine de Bourbon, Seely's ADC. Orpen did a portrait of Seely while his friend, Alfred Munnings, who was official artist to the Canadian Cavalry Brigade, was painting an equestrian portrait of the prince. Philip Gibbs and other foreign correspondents found refuge there on the night when Amiens was under its greatest threat in April 1918. Bombs crashed around the hotel and the guests, who had voted whether to 'Stay or Go', stayed, but spent the night 'in the good cellars below the Hôtel du Rhin, full of wine casks and crates'. Outside raged 'a roaring furnace'. The Restaurant Godbert (62 Rue des Jacobins, but no longer a restaurant) was a favoured restaurant – 'The food was excellent and we all had money to burn', wrote Dennis Wheatley. But when he visited it on 1 April he found it rather like the *Marie Celeste*. It had closed suddenly when Amiens was being threatened and the Provost Marshal rounded up officers in all the main restaurants and ordered them back to their units at once. 'Every table in the big restaurant had been occupied and on all of them were plates with half-eaten courses. On some there were only hors d'oeuvres, on others pieces of omelette, fish, game, savouries and ice-cream that had melted. Beside the plates stood glasses mostly full or half-full of red or white wine.' Perhaps the Godbert's popularity had something to do with 'little Marguerite, [who] made eyes at all the pretty boys who craved for a kiss after the lousy trenches'. The poet, **Capt T. P. Cameron Wilson** of the Sherwood Foresters (commemorated on the Arras Memorial, qv), recalls the therapeutic effect of other waitresses with affection, including 'Yvonne, bringing sticky buns', in his delightful *Song of Amiens*:

Lord! How we laughed in Amiens!
For there were useless things to buy ...
And still we laughed in Amiens,
As dead men laughed a week ago.
What cared we if in Delville Wood
The splintered trees saw hell below?
We cared ... We cared ... But laughter runs
The cleanest stream a man may know
To rinse him from the taint of guns'.

Some encounters with the female population of Amiens were not so innocent. When most civilians evacuated in March 1918, a few enterprising girls remained. Wheatley found one such after his disappointment at the Godbert who had remained on duty 'Because I makes much money now there are few girls here'. It was not his first encounter with the oldest profession and he thoroughly recommended the dignified Madame Prudhomme's brothel. Such delights had been available in Amiens from the outbreak of war. **Private Frank Richards** had passed through the city on 13 August 1914 on his way to Mons. At that time General French was staying at the Hôtel Moderne (of which no trace remains) and Richards was billeted in a school, outside which was a fifty-deep queue of young ladies waiting to entertain the soldiers. Richards was 'sorry to leave' on 22 August. 'About the 16th August', he reports, he had 'attended a funeral of two of our airmen who had crashed; all the notabilities of the town were present.' This was the funeral of Lt Perry and AM Parfitt, who are buried in St Acheul Cemetery (see below). He also describes the bringing of

> Gen Grierson's body from the railway station to the town hall. He was Chief-of-Staff to General French. All sorts of stories were going around regarding his death. One was that he had been poisoned when eating his lunch on the train, but I believe now it was just heart failure from the strain and excitement. We took his body back to the railway station where a detachment of Cameron Highlanders took it down-country.

Lt-General Sir James Grierson, who was actually commander of II Corps, was buried in his home town of Glasgow.

The 64-year-old French Academician and novelist, Pierre Loti (the *nom de plume* of Louis Marie Julien Viaud), who had served with the French navy and

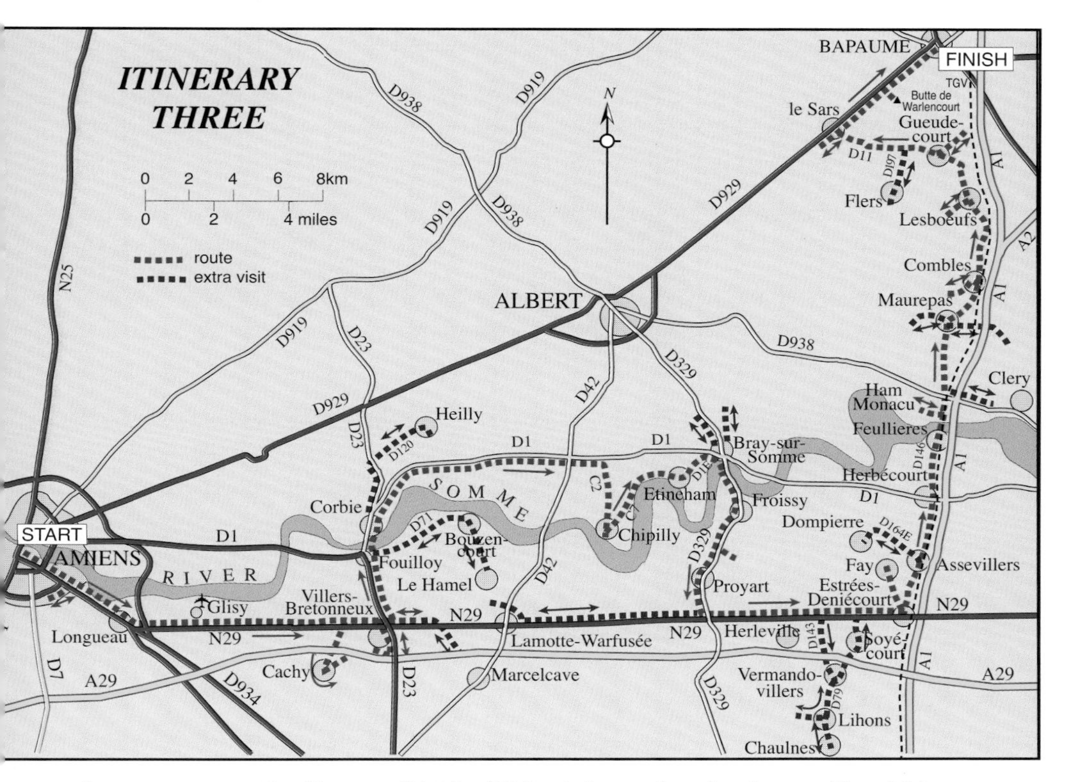

who was put on the Reserve List in 1910, at the outbreak of war offered his services to General Galliéni as a liaison officer. On 2 October he recorded his 'first day of service as a liaison officer' in his diary and travelled through the early battlefields left by the Germans' rush for Paris. He lunched in Amiens before visiting GHQ at Doullens and returned there that night. He found the town criss-crossed with parades of soldiers, singing, holding flowers that the young girls had given them. He did not return to the area until 1917 (when he again visited Amiens) – after tireless negotiations with the Turks, the Belgians, in Alsace, in Salonika and many parts of the French line, during which work he kept up a prodigious writing output. This indefatigable patriot was eventually forced to retire, exhausted, at the age of 68 on 1 June 1918. Another famous French writer, Jean Cocteau, stayed at the Hôtel du Commerce (32 rue des Jacobins) while waiting to be posted to his hospital near Villers Bretonneux in June 1916 (qv). On the 25th of that month, the Fourth Army Commander took time off from his planning of the Big Push to attend the 167-strong annual Old Etonian Dinner in Amiens.

For today's visitor to the city – and Amiens makes an ideal base for touring the battlefield if you follow Approach Two – there are a variety of restaurants and hotels, such as (with restaurant) *** Interhotel Carlton ☎ (03) 22 97 72 22; ** Express by Holiday Inn ☎ (03) 22 22 38 50; ** Hotel-restaurant Le Prieuré

☎ (03) 22 71 16 71; Ibis Centre ☎ (03) 22 92 57 33; * Hotel-restaurant Balladins ☎ (03) 22 53 90 70 and (without restaurant) *** Relais Mercure Cathédrale ☎ (03) 22 00 20. More detailed lists of hotels and restaurants are available from the Metropolitan Tourist Office, 6 bis rue Duseval. ☎ (03) 22 71 60 51.

Turn left at the traffic lights, past the station, on the N29 direction Longueau. Continue to the large school, Lycée Robert de Luzarches on the left and immediately turn right on the Boulevard de Pont Noyelles, which becomes Boulevard de Bapaume. Ignore the first sign to the left to the Cimetières de St Acheul and take the second left on Rue de Cottency. Continue to the cemetery and stop at the entrance on the left.

• *French National Cemetery, St Acheul, Graves of Perry & Parfitt/ 1.7 miles/10 minutes/Map 1/7*

There is a **descriptive board** (in French) just inside the entrance. In this French cemetery, with its impressive memorial incorporating a sensitive sculpture of a mourning female figure, there are 2,739 French, 12 British, 10 Belgian and I Russian soldiers of World War I. The British plot, just inside the entrance and to the left, includes the graves of the first airmen to be killed on French soil – on 16 August 1914. They are **2nd Lt Evelyn W. Copland Perry**, RFC, age 23, the personal message on whose headstone reads, 'First on the roll of honour. All Glory to his name' and **Air Mechanic H. E. Parfitt**, age 21, the crew of a Royal Aircraft Factory BE8. Perry was the last of his Squadron (3 Sqn) to take off from Amiens airport at Glisy en route for Mons, when his machine stalled, plummeted to earth and burst into flames. Other contenders for 'first casualties' were **Lt C. G. G. Bayly** and **2nd Lt V. Waterfall** of 5 Squadron RFC. They were killed on 22 August, six days later than Perry and Parfitt, but they were actually killed as a result of enemy action on a reconnaissance flight over Mons. They are buried in Tournai Communal Cemetery.

Return to the N29 and turn right signed Longueau. Pass under a railway bridge, over a waterway which marks the junction of the Rivers Avre, Noye and Somme and then across a bridge over a large railway complex.

• *Longueau/4 miles*

This area became a major administrative centre, supplying the Somme battlefront and it was from it that railway engineers worked eastwards to repair the railways destroyed during the 1914 German advance and subsequent shelling.

Continue uphill on the N29, passing the Hôtel de Ville of Longeau on the right, to a cemetery by traffic lights on the right at the junction of Rue des Alliés.

• *Longueau British CWGC Cemetery/4.5 miles/5 minutes/Map 1/8a*

Unusually, the register box is incorporated at the bottom of the Cross of Sacrifice in this small cemetery. It was begun in April 1918 when the British line was re-established before Amiens and used by fighting units and field ambulances until the following August. Plot IV was made after the Armistice by concentrating thirty-six graves from other cemeteries and the surrounding battlefield. Three US, one French and thirty-nine German graves have been removed. Now there are 68 soldiers, and airmen from the UK, 66 from Canada, 65 from Australia, 3 from the West Indies including 1 unidentified, and 14 unknown. Two graves were moved here as late as 1934.

Continue to a series of roundabouts and follow Cambrai motorway signs, green CWGC signs to Villers Bretonneux Aust Memorial and then St Quentin/Abbeville motorway signs.

You will pass near the convenient and comfortable *** Novotel, with outdoor pool and pleasant terrace and garden (☎ (03) 22 46 22 220), and nearby **Campanile (with excellent value buffet style meals, ☎ (03) 22 53 89 89) and *'Formula 1' (☎ (03) 22 47 03 04) and Hotel Première Classe (☎ (03) 22 46 12 12).

Continue on the N29 to the airfield on the left.

• *Glisy Airport/5.6 miles/Map 1/8*

The area was used by the RFC/RAF as an airfield from the first days of the war and is currently both a commercial and club field. In the early 1980s a new bar complex was built and a **memorial to the Red Baron** (originally destined to be erected at his crash site (qv) but rejected by local authorities) which used to stand in the old bar, went missing and is now thought to be in the hands of an Amiens collector. During the fighting of March 1918, General Sir John Monash, who commanded the Australian 3rd Division that played such a large part in the fighting up ahead at Villers Bretonneux, had his HQ in this vicinity. Maurice Baring, in Flying Corps HQ, 1914-1918, describes arriving at Amiens by train on 12 August where he was greeted with the scornful statement, *'Ah! les aviateurs, ils n'ont pas besoin d'aller à la guerre pour se faire casser la gueule ceux-là.'* ('Oh! airmen – that lot don't need to go to war to break their necks.'). 'After lunch' he went to the 'Aerodrome' and arranged supplies of 'water carts, ... pegs for the aeroplanes, ... a certain consignment of B.B. Oil', and then 'slept on our valises on the grass on the Aerodrome.' On the morning of the 13th, the first three squadrons of the RFC's total complement of four squadrons arrived, Harvey-Kelly (see also Vert Galand in Approach Two) being the first to land in his BE2A. They had taken off from a field above the White Cliffs of Dover, on the road to St Margaret's Bay. Today a memorial stands at the entrance to that field, with the inscription, 'The Royal Flying Corps contingent of the 1914 British Expeditionary Force, consisting of Nos 2, 3, 4 and 5 Squadrons flew from this field to Amiens between 13 and 15 August 1914.' In the afternoon Prince Murat (qv) reported as their Liaison Officer and on 14 August Sir John French arrived to look at the squadrons. The airfield was also used during World War II.

Continue (noting that the road runs due east), crossing the railway twice in the next 5 miles.

Note the tall column of the Australian Memorial which becomes more and more clearly visible to the left along this road.

Continue downhill past a wood on the right to a small crossroads with the D153. Turn right and stop as near to the crossing as practical.

• *The Nearest Point to Amiens/10.5 miles/5 minutes/OP*

The German attack on 21 March 1918 forced the British and French armies into a hurried retreat, troops pouring towards you on their way back to Amiens. Up ahead of you on the crest is the village of Villers Bretonneux and it was not until 28 March that the German advance (which had begun some 50km away at St Quentin) was stopped 3km east of the village – i.e. the other side to where you are now – mainly due to the efforts of the 1st Cavalry Division. Short of troops, and with Amiens in great danger, Haig looked 100km north to Flanders and ordered down the Australians. Thirty-six hours after the German onslaught began again at dawn on 4 April it seemed as if Villers Bretonneux would be taken, but Lt Col H. Goddard commanding the 9th (Australian) Brigade, newly based in the town, ordered the 36th Battalion forward in a bayonet charge. The advancing Germans broke and withdrew and, before they could attack again, one of their aerial heroes, the 'Red Baron' (qv) was killed.

By 10 April, Haig knew the situation was critical and he begged Foch to take over some portion – any portion – of the front held by British and Commonwealth forces, stretched to the point of exhaustion. Foch agreed to move up a large French force towards Amiens. The next day (12 April), still waiting for them to arrive, a worried Haig issued his famous 'Order of the Day':

> "To all Ranks of the British Forces in France. Three weeks ago today the Enemy began his terrific attacks against us on a 50 mile front .... Many amongst us are tired .... There is no other course open to us but to fight it out! Every position must be held to the last man: there must be no retirement. With our backs to the wall, and believing in the justice of our cause, each one of us must fight to the end...."

In the dawn mist of 24 April the German 4th (Guards) Division and the 228th Division, supported by thirteen tanks, tried again. It was to be one of the first actions in which the Germans had used tanks and the first action in which tank fought tank.

This time the enemy got into and through the village, despite the determined resistance by 2nd West Yorkshire Regiment at the railway station, so that by 2000 hours that evening the front line ran at right angles to the N29 along the D523 (where you now are) across your front to your left and right. It was the nearest point to Amiens that the Germans reached. That evening at 2200 hours the Australian 13th Brigade counter-attacked in the area on the right but were caught in fierce fire by German machine guns of 4th (Guards) Division set up in the wood to your right – Abbey Wood.

In a remarkable action which won him the **VC, Lt C. W. K. Sadlier** led a small party into the wood and destroyed six machine-gun positions, thus allowing the attack to continue. An hour later the Australian 15th Brigade, in the light of flames from the burning château in the village, attacked in a pincer movement through the area beyond the railway line to your left.

Turn right on the D523 towards Cachy and immediately before the motorway bridge turn sharp left towards Villers Bretonneux. Continue and pull in and stop just before the 70 sign on the right with Villers Bretonneux church on the skyline ahead.

• *First Tank versus Tank Battle Monument, Cachy/12.1 miles/10 minutes/Map 1/14*

The historic tank versus tank action took place in the fields to your left and to your right on the slope up towards Villers Bretonneux on the morning of 24 April 1918. At 0345 hours German artillery began an HE and gas shell barrage on British positions in the town and on the feature on which the Australian National Memorial now sits. The attack began at 0600 hours and, led by thirteen A7V tanks, the Germans inflicted heavy casualties on the East Lancashires of 8th Division in the area around the railway station. By 0930 four A7Vs were making their way across the fields towards where you now are. Earlier that morning three British

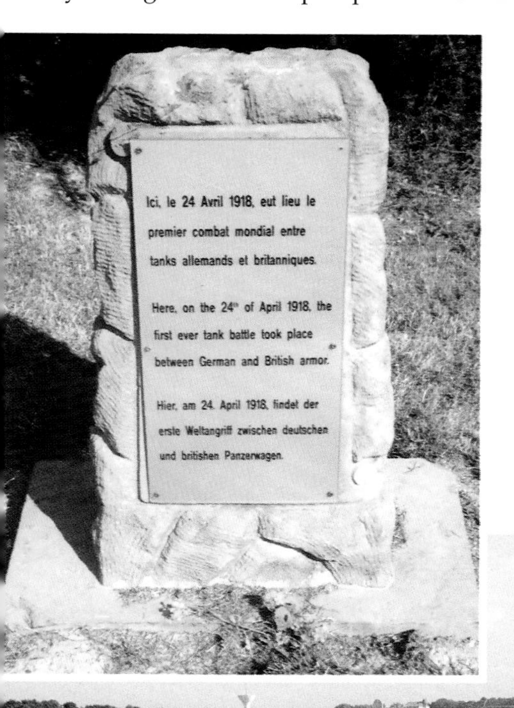

Memorial on the site of the first tank versus tank battle, Cachy. Villers Bretonneux is on the crest

Mark IV tanks, lagered in the wood through which you drove from the N29, were ordered to move to this area forward of Cachy. They too were moving this way at about 0930. Commanding one of the British tanks was **Lt Frank Mitchell** and in his book, *Tank Warfare*, he told what happened:

> "Opening a loophole I looked out. There, some three hundred yards away, a round squat-looking monster was advancing, behind it came waves of infantry, and farther away to the left and right crawled two more of these armed tortoises .... So we had met our rivals at last. Suddenly a hurricane of hail pattered against our steel wall, filling the interior with myriads of sparks and flying splinters ... the Jerry tank had treated us to a broadside of armour-piercing bullets ... then came our first casualty ... the rear Lewis gunner was wounded in both legs by an armour-piercing bullet which tore through our steel plate ... the roar of our engine, the nerve-wracking rat-tat-tat of our machine guns blazing at the Bosche infantry and the thunderous boom of the 6 pounders all bottled up in that narrow space filled our ears with tumult while the fumes of petrol and cordite half stifled us."

Mitchell's tank attempted two shots at one of the A7Vs. Both hit but seemed ineffective, then the gunner tried again 'with great deliberation and hit for the third time. Through a loophole I saw the tank heel over to one side then a door opened and out ran the crew. We had knocked the monster out.'

When the war was over, Mitchell, tongue in cheek, recalling that the tanks were called 'landships', and that naval crews are entitled to prize money for sinking enemy ships, applied for prize money for himself and his crew for having knocked out an enemy 'landship'. The War Office descended into a puzzled silence and then turned the application down.

Before the day was over seven of the new British Whippet tanks charged into the German infantry and the advance stopped. The Germans, however, were now poised on the high ground. If Amiens were to be saved they had to be moved.

Just after dawn on 25 April the two attacking Australian brigades met on the other side of the town, taking almost 1,000 prisoners. It was ANZAC Day and Amiens was safe. After the action the Australians recovered one of two German tanks that had broken down and shipped it to Brisbane as a souvenir. The village was almost obliterated by the fighting and so great was the destruction that a sign was put up in the ruins proclaiming, 'This was Villers-Bretonneux'.

Walk to the bottom of the hill.

On the left is the small **Memorial to the Tank Action** with a caption in three languages, English, French and German, stating that 'Here on 24 April 1918 the first ever tank battle took place between German and British armour.'

Return to your car, turn round, return to the N29, turn right and continue to the CWGC Cemetery on the left.

• *Adelaide Cemetery/14 miles/10 minutes/Map 1/13a/ABT3*

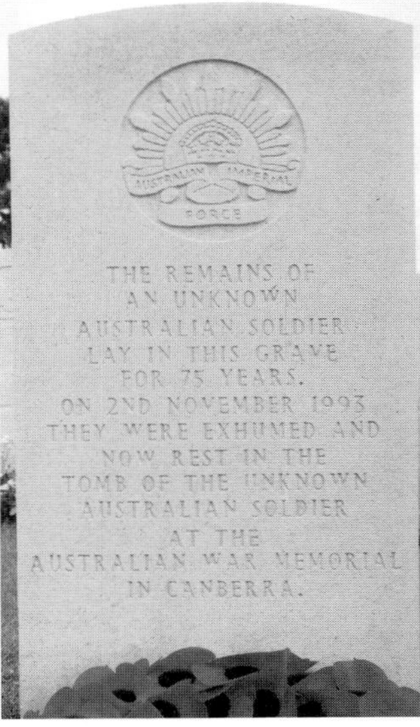

Original grave of the Australian Unknown Soldier, Adelaide CWGC Cem

The cemetery, which has the most delightful and varied array of plants, was started in early June 1918 and used by 2nd and 3rd Australian Divisions. By the Armistice it contained ninety graves and then 864 other graves were concentrated here. There are now over 500 Australians, 365 soldiers and airmen from the UK, including **Lt Col S. G. Latham, DSO, MC and Bar,** age 46, killed on 24 April while commanding the 2nd Battalion the Northampton Regiment, and 22 Canadians. The 113th Australian Infantry Brigade, the 49th, 50th, 51st and 52nd Australian Infantry Battalions and the 22nd DLI all at one time erected wooden crosses here to commemorate their dead in the actions of Villers Bretonneux. In Plot III, Row M, Grave 13 is a most unusual headstone. It records the fact that 'The remains of an Unknown Soldier lay in this grave for 75 years. On 2 November 1993 they were exhumed and now rest in the Tomb of the **Unknown Australian Soldier** at the Australian War Memorial in Canberra.'

Continue, again crossing the railway, and 800m later there is a ruined château on the left.

Just before it is a **Memorial to the Villers Bretonneux Déportés of WW2.**

• *Villers Bretonneaux Château/14.7 miles/Map 1/13/ABT2*

This is the château whose flames lit up the attack of the Australian 15th Brigade on the night of 24 April. After the War it was used as the HQ of the Australian Graves Registration Unit. Local opinion has it that after the war the owner of the château collected a considerable sum of money in reparations and decided to spend it elsewhere. When Henry Williamson returned to the Somme in 1929, he met in an estaminet in Albert the 'son of a millionaire, who had made his "pile" since the war by buying for "cash down" the sites of shattered buildings, and rebuilding with the generous reparation grants later on'. The speculator himself then owned over fifty houses, shops, and three motor cars.

Continue some 300m to the crossroads with the D23 signed left to the Australian Villers Bretonneux memorial. Turn right along the rue Maurice Seigneurgens. Turn right at the first crossroads along rue Driot to the next crossroads. Go straight over. The road is now called rue Victoria. Stop at the school on the left.

• *Villers Bretonneux School & Franco-Australian Museum/15.4 miles/20 minutes/WC/Map 1/15/16/ABT1*

A plaque on the school wall records that the building was 'the gift of the children of Victoria, Australia, to the children of Villers Bretonneux as a proof

Iris Empress of India

Iris Pink Horizon

Blue Iris

Iris Flamenco

Yellow Rose

Paeony Karl Rosenfield

Oriental Poppy

Cerianthus Sub

Campanula Telham Beauty

Campanula Persicifolia

Delphinium Black Knight

Delphinium Sumn Skies

Dianthus

Polygonum Bi Sorta

London Pride

Osteospinum

The ruins of Villers Bretonneux Château

Villers Bretonneux School and pupils, with a detail of the memorial plaque on the school wall

To the left – Adelaide Cemetery, 21 May: A selection of the flowers on one day out of 365 in one of 140 CWGC cemeteries on the Somme

Interior of the Franco-Australian Museum, Villers Bretonneux

Bronze model of the original Australian 2nd Division Memorial at Mont St Quentin

of their love and good will towards France.' 1,200 of their fathers, uncles and brothers gave their lives in the recapture of the village on 24 April 1918. Inside the school is a permanent exhibition of photographs of Australia. The memorial obelisk in front of the school records the story of the school building project, from the visit by the President of the Australian Council on 25 April 1921, to its inauguration on 25 May 1927. The left wing of the school is marked 'Salle Victoria'. This hall is panelled in wood, surmounted by carvings by an Australian artist of Australian fauna, recently individually illuminated. A plaque by the entrance records the dedication of the museum – which is on the top floor – and which was founded by Marcel Pillon in 1975. It has since been taken over by the council and completely refurbished. It is run by M Jean-Pierre Thierry, for many years the Research Officer at the *Historial* and has a centre of documentation, with an audio-visual presentation and a small book stall. The collection now includes some superb photographs, personal items, ephemera, artefacts, a bronze of the original 2nd Division memorial at Mont St Quentin which was destroyed by the Germans and the flag used to drape the coffin of the Australian Unknown Soldier during rehearsals for the ceremony of removing it to Australia. The family of kangaroos once housed in the Town Hall have taken up residence at the entrance here. **Open:** Wed-Sat 1000-1200 and 1400-1800. Tues 1400-1800. Closed on public holiday (except 11 November). ☎ (03) 22 96 80 79. Entrance fee payable. Well worth a visit.

Return to the crossroads and turn left on rue de Melbourne. Stop at the large town hall on the right in Place Charles de Gaulle.

• *Villers Bretonneux Town Hall/RB/15.7 miles/5 minutes*

The main château in the centre of the town was also destroyed and it has been replaced by the Town Hall and memorial garden on the right. In front of it is a **Ross Bastiaan bronze tablet** unveiled on 30 August 1993 by the Governor General of Australia, the Hon Bill Hayden. Inside the Town Hall is a room devoted to the various connections between the village and Australia – Villers Bretonneux is twinned with Robinvale in Australia and there are still many joint activities.

Robinvale was named after **Lt Robin Cuttle** from Ultima, Victoria, Australia. In 1914 Robin volunteered but was inexplicably rejected. Not to be deterred he went to England and applied to join the RFC. Again he was rejected - because of his size: he was 6ft 8ins tall. So he joined the RFA in July 1916 and served as a Lieutenant throughout the Somme battles. Whilst attached to the 9th Scots Guards at the Butte de Warlencourt in November 1916 he was awarded the MC when he assisted in capturing many German guns. In 1917 he reapplied to join the RFC and by early 1918 was flying over France with C flight of 49th Squadron as an observer. Whilst returning from a reconnaissance and bombing mission on 9 May 1918 his plane was shot down. His body was never found and in 1923 members of his family came to France to try and find where he was buried. With the help of members of his squadron and local people they found bomb pieces similar to those carried by Robin's plane and aircraft wreckage by a crater at Caix near Villers Bretonneux. Back in Australia in October 1924 the expanding railway reached Ultima and a name was needed for the new station. Robin's mother, Margaret, hung a sign over the station which said 'Robin Vale' ('farewell Robin' in Latin). The mother's tribute to her dead son was eventually accepted as the name for the new township which, after initial hardships, prospered. In 1977 Alan Wood the local MP visited Villers Bretonneux and the links between the two townships were formed.

Cuttle is commemorated on the Arras Flying Services Memorial (qv).

To the left of the car park is the beautifully maintained local war memorial with a stone memorial to the Australians in front and a sunburst gate.

Return to the crossroads with the N29 and turn right.

N.B. At this stage the American, Canadian and French actions of 1918 may be followed by turning right on the D23. See '1918 Itinerary' for further instructions.

Drive to the parking area by the local cemetery on the right and pull in as near as possible to the small entrance at the far end.

• *Villers Bretonneux Local Cemetery Allied Graves, Demarcation Stone 16.1 miles/10 minutes/Map 1/18*

Just inside the wall is a CWGC plot containing 6 graves from 1918, 4 of them Australian.

Walk to the marker some 300m along the road.

After the war the Touring Clubs of France and Belgium erected 240 demarcation stones along a line agreed by Maréchal Pétain's General Staff to be the limit of the German advance along the Western Front. 'Here the Invader was brought to a standstill 1918', is the inscription. Four still remain in the Somme area. The authors, knowing that the Germans had actually penetrated as far as 'OP1' on the far side of the village, asked the local *Souvenir Français* organisation why the stone had not been placed there. 'They were there for less than 24 hours', was the reply. Local historians now wish to move the stone to what they consider to be the correct site.

Extra Visit to the French National Cemetery at Marcelcave (Map 1/19) Round trip: 3.8 miles. Approximate time: 20 minutes

Continue on the N29 to a right turn, signed to Cimetière Nationale de Marcelcave. Turn right and stop at the cemetery on the left.

Marcelcave, 'Les Buttes', Cemetery, in the area where **Jean Cocteau** served, was created in 1916 after the 1 July Somme Battles. It contains 1,610 burials, many concentrated from other smaller cemeteries in 1922 and 1936.

Extra Visit continued

It was completely re-landscaped in 1980. Like John Masefield, Jean Cocteau, who had been exempted from military service in 1910 because of his poor health, volunteered for the Red Cross in 1914. Like Masefield, Cocteau continued his writing and other artistic activities during the war, notably writing *Thomas l'Imposteur* about the French Marines, from his experiences at Nieuport and Coxyde in Flanders. He moved to the Somme in June 1916 and joined Evacuation Hospital No 13 at Marcelcave on 28 June in time for the 1 July Offensive. It was one of the most important French hospitals on the front and a great rail connection. From 28 June to 11 September 27,211 wounded passed through it, of which 4,170 were retained for further treatment, 829 of whom died – hence the formation of the cemetery. During his stay at the hospital, Cocteau wrote regularly to his mother, describing the hospital as *'le district des plaintes'*. He comments on the number of aeroplanes (*'Brouillard épais tissé par mille avions'* – thick fog, interlaced with 1,000 aeroplanes) and takes many photographs on Kodak film. On 16 July he is distressed by the death of Josselin de Rohan, *'mort tout près de nous'* (killed very close to us) on 14 July. Rohan was the son of the Dowager Duchess of Rohan and brother of Marie Murat. On 27 July Cocteau left the Somme to travel to Italy and to continue work on such diverse projects as the ballet *Parade* and the revue *Le Mot*. At Christmas time that year he recalled the horrors he had seen and described, in his poem *No l 1916*, a 'war crèche' where the baby Jesus is all alone because the Three Kings were fighting, Mary was working at a hospital, Joseph guarded a road, the ox had been eaten, the donkey carried a machine gun, the Star was a signal and all the shepherds were dead and buried.

Return to the marker stone and pick up the main itinerary.

Return to the crossroads and turn right on the D23 signed to the Australian Memorial. Stop by the memorial.

• *Australian National Memorial & CWGC Military Cemetery Villers Bretonneux/RB/17.7 miles/35 minutes/Map 1/11/12/OP/ABT4*

Outside the cemetery is a CGS/H Signboard with the reproduction of a photo from the Museum of an archetypal 'Digger'.

It was an extraordinary coincidence that the two Australian brigades which encircled Villers Bretonneux should meet in the early hours of 25 April 1918 because three years earlier on that morning, then a Sunday, the Australian Imperial Forces had landed at Gallipoli. What happened on that terrible day lives on in the nation's memory, and every year young Australians make their

Australian National Memorial and CWGC Cemetery, Villers Bretonneux, with headstone of Jean Brillant, VC

way down to the Gallipoli Peninsula to commemorate what came to be known as ANZAC Day (see *Major and Mrs Holts Battlefield Guide to Gallipoli*). It is remembered at Villers Bretonneux too, for here is the Australian National Memorial which commemorates 10,797 Australians who gave their lives on the Somme and other sectors of the Western Front and have no known grave. Until the end of the 1980s Australian veterans regularly visited the village at this time. In the cemetery, known as Fouilloy Cemetery, lie 1,085 UK, 770 Australian, 263 Canadian, 4 South Africans and 2 New Zealand burials. There are some memorable private inscriptions on the Australian graves, which merit careful reading, e.g. **Pte C.J. Bruton**, 34th AIF, age 22, 31 March 1918 [II.C.5/7], 'He died an Australian hero, the greatest death of all'; **Pte A.L. Flower**, 5th AIF, 29 July 1918 [III.B.6.], 'Also Trooper J.H. Flower, wounded at Gallipoli, buried at sea 05.5.1915'. In VI.AB.20 lies **Jean Brillant, VC, MC**, 22nd Bn French-Canadian, age 22, 10 August 1918. His headstone, engraved in French, records that he volunteered in Quebec and 'Fell gloriously on the soil of his ancestors. Good blood never lies.' His wonderful citation is in the Cemetery Report. There is a hospital named after Brillant in Quebec.

Within the left-hand hedge at the edge of the lawn before the main memorial, there is a **Ross Bastiaan bronze plaque**, unveiled on 30 August 1993 by the Governor General of Australia. From this point the heights on the left can be seen, with the tall chimney of the Colette brickworks near which the Red Baron was shot down.

Unveiled by King George VI on 22 July 1938, the impressive main **Memorial** consists of a wall carrying the names of the missing and a 100ft-high central tower which can be climbed with due caution. If the gate to the tower is locked the key maybe obtained from the *Gendarmerie* on the N29 at Villers Bretonneux. If you intend to go up, allow an extra 20 minutes. The memorial was designed by Sir Edwin Lutyens and, due to delays occasioned by lack of funds, it was the last of the Dominion memorials to be inaugurated. The original plan for the memorial had included a 90ft-high archway, but this was omitted, presumably for financial reasons. It bears the scars of World War II bullets (deliberately retained as an historical reminder) and the top of the tower was struck by lightning on 2 June 1978 and extensively renovated. By facing directly away from the memorial, the cathedral and the Perret Tower in Amiens can be seen on a clear day. How near the Germans came!

The war correspondent **Philip Gibbs** described how,

> "The Germans came as near to Amiens as Villers-Bretonneux on the low hills outside. Their guns had smashed the railway station of Longueau, which to Amiens is like Clapham Junction to Waterloo. Across the road was a tangle of telephone wires, shot down from their posts. For one night nothing – or next to nothing – barred the way, and Amiens could have been entered by a few armoured cars. Only small groups of tired men, the remnants of strong battalions, were able to stand on their feet, and hardly that."

Later he reported:

> "Foch said 'I guarantee Amiens'. French cavalry, hard pressed, had come up the northern part of our line. I saw them riding by, squadron after squadron, their horses wet with sweat. To some I shouted out *'Vivent les Poilus'* emotionally, but they turned and gave me ugly looks. They were cursing the English, I was told afterwards, for the German break-through. *'Ces sacrés Anglais!'* Why couldn't they hold their lines?"

Gibbs acknowledges that:

> "Amiens was saved by the counterattacks of the Australians, and especially by the brilliant surprise attack at night on Villers-Bretonneux under the generalship of Monash."

In one of the strange coincidences of war, Gibbs was relieved to bump, quite accidentally, into his 'kid' brother Arthur who had become lost from his unit and was bringing up his field guns towards Amiens. 'I had never expected to see him alive again, but there he was looking as fresh as if he had just had a holiday in Brighton.'

Continue on the D23 to Fouilloy. Turn right at the T junction with the church onto the D1 and follow signs to Péronne and 'Toutes Directions' towards Corbie. After some 200m there is a sign to the D71 to the right.

Extra Visit to the Private Memorial to Capt Mond & Lt Martyn (Map Side 1/20a), Australian Memorials at Le Hamel/RB (Map 1/24a,b). Round trip: 10.5 miles. Approximate time: I hour

Turn right, signed Hamelet on the D71 and continue to the centre of the village.

This is **ABT5** (Australian Battlefield Tour point 5 – from Villers Bretonneux an 'Australian' tour may be followed using a route described in a commemorative pack issued by the Office of Australian War Graves and available at Villers Bretonneux). Some 60 new British Mark V tanks and 4 resupply tanks of the 5th Tank Brigade assembled here on 3 July 1918 and at 1030 moved south-east to their start points for the battle of le Hamel due to begin at 0310 the following morning, the attack to a first approximation being in your direction of travel. As an entirely Australian idea proposed by Monash, and executed solely under Australian auspices, the success of the operation was a major boost to Australian self-belief. Having trained the infantry and tanks together and making maximum use of artillery and aircraft, the Australians saw Monash's plan as a blueprint for all future allied success. The action was over in under 100 minutes. Hamel was taken and 2,000 Germans were killed or captured while Australian casualties were some 1,400.

Continue towards Vaire.

In **Vaire Communal Cemetery** are four Australian soldiers of 8 August 1918 buried together.

Continue to Vaire and turn right towards le Hamel.

It was to the right of this road that **Private Harry Dalziel**, a Lewis Gunner of the 15th AIF, won the **VC**, capturing a German machine gun and killing two. He was twice wounded in the action but survived until 1965.

Continue through le Hamel to the T junction by the local War Memorial and turn left. Follow the road to the left signed to Bouzencourt on the C7. Continue to the memorial on the left.

The memorial is just before the village and surrounded by a small, well-tended garden. The French inscription translates, "To the memory of **Capt Francis Mond, RFA and RAF and Lt Edgar Martyn RAF** of 57th Squadron who fell gloriously in this area battling against three German aeroplanes on 15 May 1918. Per ardua ad astra." They were flying in a DH4 and are buried in Doullens Communal Cemetery Extension No. 2 (qv). On the

Memorial to Capt Mond & Lt Martyn, RAF, Bouzencourt

Extra Visit continued

heights beyond the memorial can be seen the tall brickworks in the area where the **Baron von Richthofen** came down.

Continue to the bottom of the road to turn and return to le Hamel. On entering the village turn left uphill following the sign to Monument Australien, and left again. Continue to the large parking area on the right.

The Australian Corps Memorial Park, ABT16/OP. Stand with the sign 'Bus car parking' to your right and look over the Valley of the Somme. At 12 o'clock on the skyline is the Australian 3rd Division Memorial, at 11 o' clock is the chimney of the Richthofen crash site brickworks, at 10 o' clock are the twin towers of Corbie church, from which direction the attack came.

On 4 July 1918 this was a German position known as the Wolfsberg and was on the final objective line for the assault. Apart from being a great success, a novel aspect of the attack was that the Australians were resupplied by parachute. The choice of 4 July for the attack had been influenced by the hoped for participation of the recently arrived American 131st and 132nd Regiments, but Pershing ruled this out, though four companies did take part incurring 100 casualties. It was from these positions that the Australians set out on 8 August in the Allied offensive that marked the beginning of the end for the Kaiser, a day that Ludendorff called *Der Schwarze Tag* (The Black Day).

The land for this memorial was donated to the Australians on the 80th anniversary of the Battle of le Hamel. The park contains picnic,

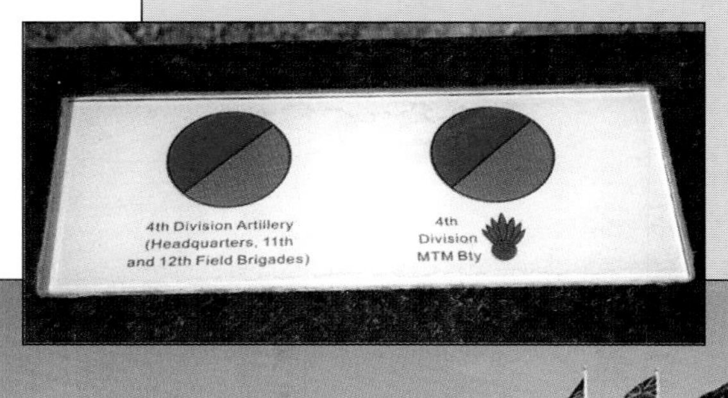

Australian Memorial, le Hamel, with divisional insignia

Extra Visit continued

toilet and drinking facilities in the edifice in the car park that (regrettably) can be seen for miles around, and there are informative speaking panels (unfortunately minus their buttons in 2002) which give a very positive Australian view of the Somme battles.

A path then leads towards the main memorial, telescope, orientation tables and more informative panels (e.g. re the **VCs of Harry Dalziel** (qv) and **Tom Axford**, the knighting of General Monash in the field). There is a recreated trench system and, in front of the main memorial walls surmounted by the divisional and unit badges of the AIF. On the black marble memorial which stands out boldly from the surrounding gentle countryside, is a huge engraved sunburst, a quotation from C.E.W. Bean and a portrait of Lieutenant-General Sir John Monash on the reverse.

Return towards le Hamel.

On descending towards the village the top of the Australian National Memorial at Villers Bretonneux may be seen straight ahead.

Turn left and then right and stop by the church on the left.

In front of the church is a fine **Ross Bastiaan commemorative bronze plaque** about the Battle of le Hamel, sponsored by Hugh and Marcus Bastiaan, John and Hazelle Laffin and Carbone-Lorraine Aust. On a wall to the right of the Church is a **May/June 1945 plaque with an anchor to the Senegalese** who had a medical facility nearby. This is rue du General Monash.

Return to the D23, turn right and rejoin Itinerary Three.

Continue into Corbie, crossing the River Somme en route and follow signs to Centre Ville passing the picturesque, fairy castle-like Hôtel de Ville and war memorial on the left.

The château was built in 1863 and bought by the town in 1923.

After 100m park in the Place de la République.

N.B. On Saturday there is a market in the square so it will not be possible to park here. The key to the church is held in the Tourist Office on the corner. Its opening hours vary according to the season, but it is usually closed on Sundays - other than in July and August - and often on Monday mornings. It shuts for lunch from 1200-1430. Over the road is the excellent restaurant La Table d'Agathe with superb regional dishes. Closed Sunday night and Monday and the first two weeks in July. ☎ (03) 22 96 96 27.

Walk along rue Charles de Gaulle to the church.

• *Congreve Plaque, Corbie Church/19.7 miles/5 minutes/Map 1/10*

Corbie has a fascinating history. It was attacked by the Normans in 896AD, in 1415 Henry V, desperately seeking a Somme crossing, was attacked here by a small force of French Knights, in 1475 the town was taken and burnt by Louis

X1, in 1636 it was taken by the Spanish who were chased out by Louis XIII and Richelieu, and it was badly damaged in the French Revolution.

In the distinctive twelfth-century church of Saint-Etiennes, whose architecture shows the transition between Roman and Gothic styles, is a plaque, designed by Sir Edwin Lutyens, to 'Billy' Congreve VC (qv).

Return to the Place de la République, turn left past the splendid 'Porte d'Honneur' to the Abbey, following the D1 signed to Péronne, to the Hospice de Corbie on the left. Turn right following the green CWGC sign. Park at the cemetery.

• *Corbie Communal Cemetery & Extension/20.4 miles/10 minutes/ Map 1/20*

Just at the top of the steps leading to the cemetery, a headstone is inscribed, **'Major W. La Touche Congreve, VC, DSO, MC,** Rifle Brigade. 20 July 1916. *Légion d'Honneur.* In remembance of my beloved husband and in glorious expectation.'

Congreve, affectionately known as 'Billy', was the VC winner son of a VC winner father, Lt Gen Sir Walter Congreve VC, CB, MVO (who was commanding XIII Corps on the Somme at the time of his son's death). A conspicuously brave, and immensely popular officer, Billy Congreve kept a forthright diary until 17 January 1916, (which has been edited by Terry Norman as *Armageddon Road*), when Congreve was killed at Longueval by a sniper (qv). He had been married on 1 June 1916 to Pamela Maude. Her poignant message on her husband's headstone refers to the fact that she was pregnant. She christened their daughter Gloria. A fellow officer described Billy as 'absolutely glorious'.

Return to the Hospice junction, turn right and continue to the female statue at the Y junction.

• *Colette Statue/20. 8 miles*

The statue, known as 'Colette' (after the young citizen of Corbie who founded the Clarisse Religious Order), was unveiled in the presence of the Bishop of Amiens and the Curé of Corbie to commemorate citizens of the town who were killed in World War I. Colette managed to found seventeen monasteries in her life-time, during the difficult times of the Hundred Years' War.

Extra Visit to Heilly Station CWGC Cemetery & Private Memorial to L Cpl O'Neill/Map 1/22/23

Round trip: 4.8 miles. Approximate time: 25 minutes

Take the left fork on the D23 and after approximately 0.8 miles, fork right on the D120 signed Méricourt l'Abbé. After 1.5 miles turn right following

Extra Visit continued

green CWGC signs at a crossroads where Heilly is signed to the left.

The railway ran through here from Amiens to the front and Heilly was the site of one of the Casualty Clearing Stations to which ambulance trains were due to run after the battle of 1 July 1916. As you turn right, the station house can be seen on the C11 to the left. This is a particularly lovely cemetery – in a quiet, rural setting, with beautiful flowers and shrubs – and unusual, partly due to the vastly greater number of casualties that arrived at the CCS than were anticipated. Men had to be buried two or three to a grave – a rare occurence in a British cemetery. There was not, therefore, room to engrave the men's regimental badges, and so many of them are incorporated into the colonnaded brick wall on the right as you enter. There is also a private memorial erected by his comrades to **L Cpl J. P. O'Neill** of 13th NSW battalion, AIF, who was killed on 6 January 1917 when a grenade accidentally exploded.

It was to this CCS that Henry Williamson's fictional hero Phillip Maddison was brought and there is a totally realistic description of Maddison's wounding after going over the top at Ovillers, his crawling painfully back to find basic treatment at the First Aid Post, then being wheeled on a stretcher to the Advanced Dressing Station at Albert, being encouraged by an RC padre, given an injection and then lifted into a Ford ambulance and driven to Heilly. There he 'was carried into a hut for officers', laid on a rubber sheet and covered with a blanket, fed tea, bread and butter and jam and given 'the latest number of the Bystander'. This was the magazine which carried the popular cartoons of Bruce Bairnsfather, known as *Fragments from France* and which featured 'Old Bill' (see page 91).

Return to the Colette statue and continue with the main itinerary.

Keep to the right on the D1 signed to Péronne and Bray, passing on the right a picnic site (Pointe de Vue de Sainte Colette) with tables and benches and a superb view over the River Somme. Continue towards a brickworks on the left with a tall chimney.

• *Von Richthofen Crash Site, Vaux-sur-Somme/22.5 miles/5 minutes/Map 1/21*

Some 200m before the chimney is a **CGS/H Signboard** on the right summarising the last flight of Manfred von Richthofen and believed to be on the site of his crash. Another CSG/H Signboard is on the site of his airfield at Cappy. The precise location of the Baron's crash is still open to some debate, but many qualified experts place it in the vicinity of the brickworks.

Corbie Comm Cem with headstone of 'Billy' Congreve, VC, DSO, MC

Continue to the brickworks.

The chimney is visible for miles around and makes a good reference point.

The 'Red Baron', Baron Manfred von Richthofen, was credited with eighty kills. His squadron, Jasta II, was known as the 'flying circus' because of the bright colours of their planes. Richthofen's own Fokker triplane DR-1 425/17 was vermilion. They were based at Cappy, just south of the River Somme and south east of Bray. On Sunday 21 April 1918 the squadron went up at mid-morning, after Richthofen had posed for a photograph for a mechanic, despite the superstition held by many pilots that being photographed just before a mission meant that one would not return. The Baron did

Private Memorial to L/Cpl O'Neill in Heilly Station CWGC Cemetery and headstones with double burials

Australian 3rd Division Memorial

not. After an active dog fight with British RE 8s and Camels led by Capt A. Roy Brown, a Canadian with eleven kills, von Richthofen crashed near this spot, coming down from your right. Brown claimed the victory. So did Australian Lewis gunners of 14th Artillery Brigade near Vaux. Subsequent research gives credence to the Australian claim. Even the angle at which the fatal bullet

The brickworks near where Manfred von Richthofen (the 'Red Baron') was shot down

entered the Baron's chest – from below, not above (as Brown was flying) – points to a hit from the ground. What is indisputable is that Richthofen's apparel and possessions and his red tri-plane were soon stripped, as by a plague of locusts by souvenir hunters. Many items found their way to Australia and several have since been donated to the Australian Imperial War Museum. Von Richthofen was buried in Bertangles (Map 1/5, Approach Two) on 22 April, with ceremony, by the Australians. In 1925 his remains were re-interred in Fricourt German Cemetery (Map J34) and from there were transferred to his family home in Schweidnitz, in eastern Germany. Contemporary accounts claim that only the skull had been removed and P. J. Carisella, American author of a book on the Baron's death, states that he unearthed the rest of the skeleton in Bertangles in 1969 and that he presented it to the German Military Air Attaché in Paris.

Continue. Park on left by memorial.

• *Australian 3rd Division Memorial/24.3 miles/5 minutes/Map 1/23a*

The obelisk is similar to the 1st Division Memorial at Pozières (Itinerary One). It lists the battle honours of the Division, including The Windmill (Pozières), Bray and Proyart (both the latter are seen on this Itinerary). The Division, raised in Australia, was formed on Salisbury Plain in July 1916 and reached Flanders under General Monash in December that year and the Somme in March 1918. The memorial overlooks the ground across the other side of the Somme where four Australian Divisions (2, 3, 4 and 5) attacked roughly parallel to your direction of travel in the early morning fog of 8 August 1918. This side of the Somme were the British 18th and 58th Divisions. It was a remarkable assault, with fine co-operation between infantry, cavalry, tanks and aircraft. Determined efforts had been made to keep preparations for the attack secret and it was launched without a preliminary bombardment.

The British front (the Fourth Army – III Corps under Butler where you are now, to the south, the Australian Corps under Monash and then the Canadian Corps under Currie) stretched about 23km south from around Albert which is over to your left. The unsuspecting German Second Army of six weak divisions, without a single tank, were suddenly confronted by 360 heavy tanks, 96 Whippet light tanks, 1,900 aeroplanes (against 365) and accompanying bombardment from 2,650 guns and a total force of 16 divisions. In his book, *Wings of War,* **Rudolf Stark**, serving with *Jagdstaffel 35*, tells how he flew over the front of 8 August, and how the sky was full of aircraft:

> "There are fights in the upper air. There are fights in the lower air. The numerical superiority of the enemy gives him the advantage, so it does not matter where we fight .... But the ground swarms with men in brown. They crouch in every shell hole and run forward along every hollow. Grey squat things roll through their midst – tanks. Here, there, everywhere."

Except at the extremities, an advance of more than 8km was achieved everywhere. Although the Germans recovered quickly, and the attack lost its momentum after the first day, for Ludendorff, the German Commander, it was the final straw that broke the back of his determinaton to win.

In Germany more than 1½ million workers were on strike, the spreading influenza epidemic was weakening his armies, the civilian population was starving and Ludendorff was suffering from nervous exhaustion. Although the gains by the Allies on 8 August did not compare to the territorial conquests of the Germans in their March Offensive, the *'Kaiserschlacht'*, the shock of 8 August loosened the Germans' grasp upon the initiative and it passed to Foch.

By looking across the Somme River towards the high ground the facilities building at le Hamel can be seen.

Continue on the D1, passing on the right a sign to CWGC **Dive Copse Cemetery** (Map 1/23b). This was begun during the 1916 battles.

Continue to the next cemetery on the right.

• *Beacon CWGC Cemetery/26.0 miles/5 minutes/Map 1/23c*

The cemetery report here records that the

> "... first fighting in this part of the Somme took place on 26/27 March 1918 when the Third Army withdrew to a line between Albert and Sailly-le-Sec. This line was held until 4 August when it was advanced nearly to Sailly-Laurette and on 8 August, the first day of 'The Battle of Amiens', Sailly-Laurette and the road to Morlancourt were disengaged."

Burials began here as the Third Army withdrew before the German onslaught of March 1918. Others were made by the 18th Div Burial Officer on 15 August. The cemetery was then greatly increased after the Armistice by the concentration of 600 graves from the battlefields and small cemeteries around. There are some 570 UK burials and 190 Australian.

Continue over the crossroads with the D42 and turn right at the next crossroads onto the C2, signed to Chipilly.

This road runs down towards the Somme at Chipilly where a spur (roughly a direct extension of this road) juts south into a bend of the river. On 8 August 1918 the Allied assault south of the Somme made advances of 8km or more in the day, but at Chipilly village and on the spur the Germans made a stand. 58th (London) Division supported by 131st Infantry Regiment of the 33rd (American) Division made a joint assault here at 1730 hours on 9 August. The Americans lined up parallel to, and 50m to the right of, this road, having had to march in double-time for 7km to reach the start-line. In the following action, supported by the 4th (Australian) Division attacking the village from south of the river, both Chipilly and the spur were captured – the latter, it is said, by a six-man Australian patrol. **Corporal Jake Allex** of 33rd Division won the

Congressional Medal of Honour for single-handedly destroying a German machine-gun post, killing five of the enemy and taking fifteen prisoners.

Continue downhill on the C306 to the church road junction in Chipilly.

• 58th (London) Division Memorial/29.2 miles/5 minutes/Map 1/26

There is a **CRP Signboard** beside the memorial. This striking memorial, sculpted by Henri-Désiré Gauque, 1858-1927, a well-known French sculptor who excelled at animal figures, is of a soldier saying goodbye to his dying horse and is reminiscent of the famous Mantania painting *Farewell Old Man*. Unusually it commemorates not only 58th Division, but also the French, Canadian and Australian action of 8 August. The Americans were not mentioned, presumably because on 8 August they were in reserve. When the Australians came to enter the village from the south they found that the Germans had blown both bridges across the river. With typical Aussie ingenuity they took the girders from the longer bridge and balanced them on the piers of the shorter to restore the crossing.

Turn left past the church and continue uphill on the C7, signed to Etinehem and almost immediately there is the local cemetery on the right.

• Chipilly Communal Cemetery & Extension/29.4 miles/5 minutes/Map 1/28a

In the cemetery are a number of British and French military graves from July 1916. The plot was started in August 1915 and used until March 1916. It contains fifty-five UK burials (including a Rifleman who was drowned whilst swimming in the Somme) and four French. The extension was used between March 1916 and February 1917. The cemetery has extensive views over the Somme Valley from the back wall.

58th London Division Memorial, Chipilly

Continue. The route that you are following is that fought along by the American 131st Infantry from 9 to 19 August 1918. Keep to the left of the river and drive to Etinehem village. This was taken by the Americans and Australians on 13 August.

At the junction with the V2 take the C2 signed to Albert along Rue du Moulin. Turn right following signs to the French National Cemetery.

• *French National Cemetery, 'La Côte 80' (Hill 80)/32.3 miles/10 minutes/Map M6*

As has happened with most of the French cemeteries on the Somme, this is now landscaped *'à l'Anglaise'*, with flower beds in front of the rows of graves. This is a concentration cemetery, which contains 955 French burials and 49 British, as well as the tomb of **Abbé Thibaut**, Chaplain to the 1st Infantry Regiment. He was a *Chevalier de la Légion d'Honneur,* and was mortally wounded in the assault on Frégicourt on 26 September 1916. He died at Maricourt the following day. The monument, erected by the officers, NCOs and men of the Régiment de Cambrai, bears a plaque with the Abbé's portrait. To the right and left of it are two rows of Australians from August 1918. The other CWGC graves, of mixed nationality and units, are near the flagpole in the centre and are from 1916. Like many French cemeteries, Hill 80 was the site of a military hospital. Serving there in 1916 was the French humanist writer, man of letters and other arts, and Member of the *Académie Française,* **Georges Duhamel**. Duhamel, born in Paris in 1884, studied medicine before being drawn into a literary and artistic life. However, when war broke out, he joined the 110th Regiment of Line as a medic. His experiences are described in *Vie des Martyrs* and *Civilisation*. In the latter he describes the area around Hill 80: the churned up mud made by 2,200 horses being taken daily to drink from the Somme, the tented city marked by vivid red crosses, the circle formed by 30 balloons, the continual puffs of smoke from lines of artillery fire. His adjutant warns him,

> "You will see passing here more wounded than you have hairs on your head, and more blood flowing than there is water in the canal. All those who fall between Combles and Bouchavesnes are sent here."

Continue to the D1 crossroads and turn right towards Bray. On entering the town go downhill to the German Cemetery (Cimetière Militaire Allemand/Deutscher Soldatenfriedhof) on the left and park near the boules pitch. Climb the steps to the cemetery.

• *Bray German Cemetery/33.6 miles/10 minutes/Map M7*

Enclosed by a hedge are the 1,079 graves and 43 bodies in a mass grave. A new stone monument surmounted by a black cross bears the names of the missing. There are no flowers in this stark, sad cemetery, with its black crosses which bear four names. There are only three German cemeteries in the triangle formed by the N29 Amiens-Albert-Bapaume road, the N336 Amiens-Villers Bretonneux-Assevillers road and the A1 Bapaume-Assevillers motorway. In the same triangle there are some eighty British CWGC Cemeteries.

Continue to the church in the town.

• *Bray/33.8 miles/RWC*

Bray was the 1916 junction of Rawlinson's Fourth Army to the north (the side of the river you are now on) and Fayolle's Sixth Army to the south. An important administrative centre and railhead, it suffered badly from the attentions of German aeroplanes. In the March 1918 assault it was easily taken by the Germans on 26 March, due to a mix-up in Fifth Army orders. On the night of 23 August, 40th Battalion of 3rd (Australian) Division attacked along the river and recaptured it. Among the units simultaneouly attacking along the road from Etinehem was the 15th (London) Regiment, otherwise known as the 1st Civil Service Rifles. It was commanded by **Lt Col Rowland Feilding, DSO**, whose book *War Letters to A Wife*, published in 1929, is one of the most telling personal accounts of the war. Bray was adopted by the town of Eastbourne after the war.

There are **commemorative plaques** in the nave of the church.

Extra Visit to the Bray group of cemeteries/Map M8, 9, 10, 11
Round trip: 4.9 miles. Approximate time: 25 minutes

Turn left at the church and continue to the cemetery on the left.

This is the **French National Cemetery of Bray-Sur-Somme**, completely renovated in 1990. It contains 1,044 French soldiers, of which 102 are in a mass grave, and one British soldier. Before it, on a well kept garden and lawn, is a fine *Poilu* memorial.

Continue, and take the second road to the right, following the green CWGC sign. Continue to the cemetery, signed to the left.

This is **Bray Military Cemetery**, begun in April 1916 by fighting units and Field Ambulances. In September 1916, the front line having been pushed further east, it was used by XIV Corps main Dressing Station and in 1917, 5th, 38th and 48th CCS came forward and used it. In May 1918 the village and cemetery fell into enemy hands but were retaken by 40th Australian Bn on 24 August and used again. After the Armistice there were more concentrations and it now contains 739 UK burials, including **Sgt M. Healy, DCM, MM and Bar and (the extremely rare) Albert Medal**, of the 2nd Royal Munster Rifles, 31 Australians, 13 Indians, 3 Canadians, 2 South Africans, 79 unknown and, unusually, 8 Egyptian labourers. On 1 March 1917 Sgt Healy,

> "... with a total disregard for his own personal safety and solely prompted by the desire to save his comrades, rushed to pick up a live bomb which had been thrown by a Private and which struck the parapet and rolled back into the trench near Lt Roe and the Private. Sgt Healy, fearing the party could not escape in time, made a most gallant effort to seize and hurl the bomb from the trench. It exploded, however, and mortally wounded him. This was the last of Sgt Healy's many acts of gallantry and devotion to duty."

Healy died the following day of his wounds, age 25.

Turn round and return to the junction and turn right on the D329. Continue to the cemetery on the right.

Extra Visit continued

This is **Bray Vale British Cemetery**, attractively landscaped on two levels. It was begun in August 1918 and enlarged after the Armistice by the concentration of isolated graves. It contains 256 UK, 17 Australian, 3 Newfoundland, 1 Canadian and two unknown burials. On the lower level there are many burials unknown by name, but identified by Regiment, from 1 July to October 1916, including two which read, '**A Drummer of the Great War**. South Lancashire Regt.' **Maj G. A. Gaffikin**, RIR, killed on 1 July 1916, age 30 has a quotation from Leigh Hunt's Abou Ben Adhem on his headstone, 'Write me as one that love[d] his fellow men'.

Turn round and return to the junction with the D147. Turn left and continue to the cemetery on the left.

This is **Bray Hill British Cemetery**. This tiny cemetery was made by 58th (London) Division on 31 August 1918 as they advanced from Corbie. It originally contained forty-one graves and after the Armistice sixty-three graves were concentrated here. The two German graves were later removed. It now has 102 UK (65 of the London Regt) and 2 Australian burials.

Return to the crossroads in Bray and rejoin Itinerary Three.

Turn right onto the D329 direction Montdidier and Proyart. Some 300m later cross the River Somme. Continue through Froissy and turn left into the car park at the large sign to the P'tit Train Museum.

• *P'tit Train/Railway Museum, Froissy-Dompierre/35.1 miles/5 minutes/Map 1/34*

The Picardy Association for the Upkeep of Old Vehicles has lovingly restored 7km of this 1914-18 narrow gauge (60cm) 'portable' Decauville track. The system was invented around 1880 by the industrialist Paul Decauville and adopted in 1888 by the French artillery to move guns and ammunition. Verdun, Toul, Epinal and Belfort all had a network connecting their forts to the main Citadel. The Froissy-Cappy line, of which this was a part, was capable of moving 1,500 tons of ammunition per day. Dompierre, at the other end of this stretch of the line, was captured by French Colonial troops on 1 July 1916. The present route was laid down for use by local industry and the tunnel constructed after the war. Rides can be taken on genuine World War I rolling stock (made for eight horses or forty men) pulled either by a World War I steam locomotive or a Maginot line diesel engine. The zig-zag climb up a steep incline, the haul up the 3km-long ramp, the journey through the 300m-long tunnel – all add to the excitement.

The museum has been extended and sophisticated and the entrance to the station is through it. Opening hours vary through the season but basically it is

World War I steam locomotive on the Froissy-Dompierre railway

closed (other than for reserved groups from April to October) from end September to end May and on Mondays throughout the year. Then it is open on Sundays in May, June and September and for the rest of the week in July and August. The fare includes entrance to the Railway Museum, which has the most comprehensive collection of 60cm railway material. ☎ (03) 22 44 55 40 for details of special steam days.

Continue on the D329 signed to Proyart.

The road from here to its junction beyond Proyart with the N29 Amiens-Assevillers road, some 5km ahead, runs across the front of the Australian Division's attack (from your right) of early August 1918. Following the dramatic success of the first day's advance of some 10km on 8 August from the start line some 12km to your right, the next 2km – to where you now are – took almost two weeks. On 23 August the 1st (Australian) Division under General Glasgow attacked right to left across this road and in what is known as the Battle of Proyart, the Aussies captured the village of Chuignes (some 2.5km to your left east), a 14in German naval gun and 2,000 prisoners.

Continue to the junction and turn left following signs to the German Cemetery.

• German Cemetery, Proyart/36 miles/5 minutes/Map 1/28

This is the third of the cemeteries in the Amiens-Bapaume-Assevillers triangle (the others being Bray and Fricourt) and contains 4,643 burials. Stark black crosses, mostly with four names, bear the name, rank and date of death when known. They are interspersed with Jewish headstones. Most of the burials are from 1918. Unusually there does not appear to be a mass grave.

Return to the D329, continue and stop at the magnificent memorial on the right.

• Proyart Miniature Arc de Triomphe Memorial/36.7 miles/10 minutes/Map 1/27

This memorial, almost incongruously impressive for such a small, rural village, is a replica of the Arc de Triomphe in Paris. Under the arch stands a *Poilu*, with the triumphant cry, *'On les a'* inscribed at his feet. The great French rallying cry at Verdun was *'On les aura'* (we'll get 'em'). Proyart's Poilu says, 'We've got 'em!'

'Arc de Triomphe' Memorial, Proyart

Beautifully executed bas relief sculptures flank each side of the arch, a miniature cannon stands on the lawn in front of it and the gateposts are surmounted by bronze *Poilus'* helmets and carry the sign of the *Légion d'Honneur*. Altogether it is one of the most photogenic memorials on the Somme.

Continue on the D329 to the crossroads with the N29.

Extra Visit to Site of Carey's Force Action (Map 1/25) & Heath CWGC Cemetery (Map 1/25a). Round trip: 12.6 miles. Approximate time: 30 minutes

Turn right at the crossroads and enter the village of Lamotte Warfusée.
It has the most splendid fretwork-effect Art Deco church spire. The church was designed by prize-winning Paris architect Godefroy Tessière with stained glass windows by Jacques Gruber. It was consecrated on 12 July 1931. Many devastated Somme villages were aided after the war by towns and villages in Normandy whose regiments had fought in the area – e.g. the 329th that liberated Lamotte came from le Havre, which paid for books for the new library in the village in 1919. Among their fund-raising efforts was a concert by 'The Band of HM Royal Garnisson [sic] Artillery'.

At the traffic lights by the small church on the right, turn right on the D42 and after 100m turn left on the D122 signed to Corbie. Drive 500m to the first Z bend and stop.

Extra Visit continued

In March 1918 the German advance towards Amiens was so rapid that, fearful for the safety of the city, General Gough decided to occupy an old French defensive position, 'The Amiens Defence Line', which had been constructed in 1915. It was 8 miles long and ran across the St Quentin-Amiens road immediately west of this village. On the night of 25/26 March an ad hoc force about 3,000 strong was gathered to occupy the position under the command of Major General C. G. S. Carey and it became known as **'Carey's Force'**. Among the patchwork of small units involved were two companies of American 6th Regiment Engineers from the US 3rd Division, totalling some 500 men who had been building bridges at Péronne. They were the first American soldiers to fight in a full-scale battle since their own Civil War in the 1860s, and they have a memorial plaque in Amiens Cathedral (qv). The Americans occupied the line from the road to the wood about 1 mile to your right (north) and came into action on the night of 27 March against German patrols in the town. You are standing on their front line positions. They resisted German attacks on 29 and 30 March and stayed in the line until relieved on 3 April. The Prime Minister, Lloyd George, referred disparagingly to the rapid withdrawal of Gough's 5th Army and gave undue importance to the action of Carey's Force by saying that 'it closed the gap to Amiens for about 6 days' and that it had been formed on the initiative of General Carey. In fact it, and other similar forces, had been formed by the much-maligned Gough – Carey's Force had been created while Carey himself was on leave in England.

Turn round and return to the N29. Turn left and continue to the CWGC Cemetery on the right.

This is **Heath CWGC Cemetery**, so named from the wide expanse of country on which it stands. It has an attractive, somewhat pagoda-shaped shelter with a dramatic line of pollarded trees behind it. Not made until after the Armistice, this British and Commonwealth cemetery stands on the site of a French military cemetery, started in August 1914, that contained 431 French and 1,063 German graves which were all removed. After the war, 1,813 bodies were buried here from the Bray-Harbonnières battlefields and it now contains 958 Australian soldiers and airmen, 839 UK, 9 Canadian, 6 New Zealand, 2 South African, 369 unknown and 24 Australian and 19 UK Special Memorials. Among the large Australian contingent, lie **Pte Robert Matthew Beatham, VC** of 8th Bn Aust Inf, killed 11 August 1918, age 24 and **Lt Alfred Edward Gaby, VC** of 28th Bn Aust Inf, killed the same day, age 26. Beatham attacked four German machine guns, killing ten and capturing ten men and was killed while bombing a further machine gun. Gaby captured four machine guns and fifty prisoners at Villers Bretonneux on 8 August.

Continue to the crossroads with the D329 and rejoin Itinerary Three.

Turn left onto the N29, direction Péronne, and continue downhill on the N29 to a bend in the road at the bottom. Stop at the memorial on the left.

• *Colonel Rabier Private Memorial/Foucaucourt Local Cem/39.0 miles/5 minutes/Map 1/28b*

This monument is to Col Rabier, Commandant of the 55th Infantry Brigade. According to the inscription, which is a message from General Castelnau of the Second Army, the Colonel led, with the greatest energy, the 24 September 1914 attack on Foucaucourt-Herleville. He died gloriously at the head of his brigade.

Continue to the local cemetery further on to the right.

In it is a CWGC Plot (Map 1/28a) of eight graves, all of 1918, at the rear including that of **2nd Lieutenant Attwater MGC**, 22 March 1918, age 29, with the personal message 'Until we meet. Your little son Mervyn'. French military graves include **Gustave Lemoine** who was killed in Paris in the Garde Mobile in 1871 *'Triste destin de la Guerre'* (Sad fate of war), **Daniel Delavenne**, 8 August 1916 and **Noel Viguane Garin**, killed in Indo-China in 1945.

Continue to the turning to the right on the D143e.

This leads to Herleville, where there is a **bronze plaque** below the local war memorial outside the church, (Map 1/49), to **'Lieutenant-Colonel C.W.D. Daly, DSO** and 413 officers and men of the 6th AIF' killed in France 1916-1918. It was funded and presented by a former member of the 6th Battalion, The Royal Melbourne Regiment, Ron Austin in 1992, and is the highlight of his annual pilgrimage. Ron publishes military books through his company Slouch Hat Publications. The village and the woods to the north were captured after very heavy fighting on 23 August 1918 and in the woods **Lieutenant W.D. Joynt** of 8th AIF won the **VC** and **Lieutenant Norm Tutt** was awarded a bar to his MC, won at Gallipoli as a CSM. The 6th Battalion had fought through Gallipoli, the Somme in 1916, Flanders in 1917 and back again to the Somme in 1918. Few original members survived.

Continue to the crossroads with the D143.

Extra Visit to the German Cemetery (Map 1/30), Memorials to Capt Delcroix & 1st Chasseurs à Pied, to P.V. Bourget & 158th RI, RB to McCarthy VC (Map 1/48)at Vermandovillers, Murat Monument & French Cemetery at Lihons (Map 1/29), French & US Nurses, German Memorial, Chaulnes (Map 1/46/47) & German trenches at Soyécourt (Map 1/31). Round trip: 10.6 miles. Approximate time: 60 minutes.

Note that the proposed new third airport to serve Paris (believed by some to be the EC's idea of a third London airport)would affect much of the area

Plaque to Lt Col C.W.D. Daly, DSO, and 6th Bn AIF, Herleville

Colonel Rabier Private Memorial, Foucaucourt

Non-standard Ross Bastiaan Plaque to Lt L. McCarthy, VC, Vermandovillers

Memorial to Prince Murat, Lihons

Extra Visit continued

covered by this Extra Visit, **including several war cemeteries**. As a protest, in 2002, villages which would be threatened by the huge development blanked out their names on local signposts - a telling visual reminder of what would be lost.

Turn right on the D 143, direction Soyécourt. Stop at the cemetery on the left.

This vast **German cemetery** at **Vermandovillers** is the largest of any nationality on the Somme with 9,400 graves and 13,200 buried in fourteen mass graves. In one of the latter is buried the German expressionist, poet and short-story writer, **Alfred Lichtenstein**. A Prussian Jew, son of a factory owner, he satirised the life of the bourgeoisie in Berlin. After obtaining a law degree, Lichtenstein entered his year's obligatory military service in October 1913 and was caught up in the Great War at its outbreak. Serving with the 2nd Bavarian Infantry Regt, which was immediately called to the front, Lichtenstein died of wounds at Vermandovillers on 24 September 1914, after being hit by a sniper. He was 25 years old. Despite his early death, Lichtenstein wrote several powerful war poems, the most enduring being *Die Schlacht bei Saarburg* ('The Battle of Saarburg') written only days before his death. It describes in vivid detail the horrors of being under machine-gun and artillery fire and in it he, like Alan Seeger and many other war poets, anticipated his own death:

I brace myself in the greyness
And face death.

Also buried in Vermandovillers is **Reinhard Johannes Sorge,** the young, brilliant German Expressionist playwright. Sorge, whose works all contained a strong religious theme, was born in 1892, and by 1914 had decided to become a priest. But in October 1915 he had been called up into the 56th Infantry Regt and was serving in Belgium. On 20 July 1916 he was mortally wounded by a grenade at Ablaincourt. His innovative and influential play, *Der Bettler* ('The Beggar') was produced to enormous acclaim by the famous producer Max Reinhardt on 22 December 1917.

Among the black crosses, with white, almost fluorescent names, are some magnificent willow trees.

Continue into the village of Vermandovillers and at the crossroads turn left towards the church.

This is *Place du Souvenir*. Beside the Place sign is a brass plaque on a stand to **Pierre Victoire Bourguet** (erected by his sons on 6 September 2000) and to the 158th RI with a sketch map showing the site of their action at Boyau du Duc on 6 September 1916. To the right of the church is a large cross with a calvary. The inscription translates, 'In this place **Capt Jean Delcroix**, Commander of the 14th Coy of the 327th RI, *Chevalier de la Légion d'Honneur,*

Extra Visit continued

fell gloriously for France on 6 September 1916 at the head of the brave soldiers that he commanded.' This memorial was recently moved here from a field outside the village.

Beside it is a small stone monument in memory of 11 officers, 24 NCOs and 133 corporals and chasseurs of the **1st Bn, Chasseurs à Pied** who fell from 17 August to 23 December 1916 in the battles of Soyécourt, Vermandovillers, Deniécourt and Ablaincourt.. The memorial goes on to describe how on 6 Sept 1916 the 1st Bn of Chasseurs, after a rapid advance of 1,500m, fought a hard battle at Vermandovillers which cost them 8 officers, 10 NCOs and 58 chasseurs killed. They took 200 prisoners, six 240 mm guns and in the face of violent counter-attacks held this ground in front of the cemetery until relieved on 11 September 1916. On the side of the monument is a plaque with a photo to **Chasseur François Lamy,** 6 September 1916.

On the wall of the *Mairie* of Vermandovillers (just round the corner from the church) is a non-standard **Ross Bastiaan bronze commemorative plaque** at the top of which is the emblem of the Victoria Cross. It is in tribute to **Lieutenant Lawrence McCarthy, VC**, whose only child, Lawrence, was engaged to Ross Bastiaan's mother before he was killed on Bouganville in 1944. She later married and when Ross was born the Australian veteran VC treated him like a grandson, filling his young mind with stories of the Great War and of Australian achievement in it. He was undoubtedly the inspiration for the wonderful series of commemorative plaques that Ross has raised wherever Australians served with distinction in two World Wars. This one was raised at Ross's sole expense. The plaque describes how on 23 August 1918 McCarthy showed singular bravery and initiative in single-handedly capturing 460m of German trenches, 5 machine guns and over 50 prisoners at the nearby Bois à Fame.

Turn round and turn left at the crossroads. At the next junction, turn right onto the D79, signed Rosières and Lihons.

The French Front Line of 1 July ran between Vermandovillers and Lihons, at the southern extremity of the line. Continue to the local cemetery on the left on the outskirts of Lihons.

Turn left immediately past the cemetery up a small but well-surfaced road and follow it round as it bends to the left. Stop at the brown metal gates in a laurel hedge on the right, just before the road ends.

Here is the **Private Memorial and grave of Maréchal de Logis Prince Louis Murat**. According to the inscription, he was Louis Marie-Michel Joachim Napoléon, born at Rocquencourt on 8 September 1896, volunteer, Maréchal de Logis (this equates, perhaps, to a British quartermaster, a non-commissioned rank, whose functions were to find billets) of the 5th Regt of Cuirassiers à Pied, son of Prince Murat of Pontecorvo, grandson of Joachim

Extra Visit continued

Murat (Napoléon's brother-in-law), grand-nephew of Napoléon 1, died for France on 21 August 1916. 'Like them, he served his fatherland'. Further inscriptions record how his father, Napoléon, Prince of Pontecorvo, and his mother, Marie Cécile Ney, erected this memorial to their son, 'because of his faith and his gentleness God chose him for a sacrifice and clothed him with His glory. Although he was the youngest of all, his youth was nowhere apparent in his actions', and how Princes Charles and Paul Murat, in memory of their brother Prince Louis, restored the monument in 1961 and gave the site to the commune of Lihons. The local council accepted the responsibility of maintaining the tomb and the surrounding grove – hence the tarmacadam road and the immaculate garden surrounding the monument. Below the magnificent monument, surmounted by an exuberant Imperial eagle, is Murat's tomb. Extensive researches in France, the UK, the USA and Canada with the Murat family and the International Napoleonic Society have not established the relationship between Prince Louis and the 'Prince Murat' and his cousin mentioned by Maurice Baring at Glisy Airport. Unfortunately Baring gives no christian names, so the complicated Murat family tree by Prince Lucien, which shows no fewer than nine contemporary Prince Murats, does not help!

Return to the main road and turn left following signs to the French National Cemetery.

The Lihons French National Cemetery, which was started in 1915 and completely renovated in 1988, contains 6,581 French and six British graves. There are 1,638 bodies in the four mass graves, in No 1 of which is thought to be the American poet, **Alan Seeger** (see Itinerary Four).

Follow signs to Chaulnes on the D337.

Chaulnes was a heavily-fortified German defensive position, held by them despite many courageous French attempts to retake it, from 29 September 1914 onwards.

Here one of the most innovative German poets of the Great War, **August Stramm**, fought in January 1915 as Commander of 9th Coy, 3rd Battalion of Reserve infantry Regiment 272. He was killed on the Russian front later in the year.

On entering the town continue down to the crossroads and stop on the left hand corner of rue Ernest Boitel.

On the wall is an exuberantly painted *bas relief* figure of a nurse with a sick child round a drinking fountain. It is in memory of the collaboration of the **American Red Cross and the *Union des Femmes de France* and *Croix Rouge Francaise*** working in Chaulnes, 1917-1919.

Turn round and drive back up to the road to the right, turning into a large open square and green. Drive past the church on the right.

Drinking fountain Memorial to American and French Nurses, Chaulnes

Extra Visit continued

Opposite is a dramatic and brightly painted reclining *Poilu* below a female figure (see page 266).

Turn right along rue de la Sablonnière and follow the road right round to the outskirts of the village to a large white stone on the left.

This is a rare **German memorial to the 16th Bavarian Infantry Regiment**, moved here from a German cemetery (and indeed originally there were important memorials in most German cemeteries) by young German volunteers in 1992. In it was found a bottle containing a list of German soldiers (now in the *Historial*).

Return to Lihons and continue on the D79 through Vermandovillers to Soyécourt. In the centre of the village turn left to the church.

On the local war memorial before the church is **a plaque which commemorates Jersey's help** in the village's post-war rebuilding.

Drive north downhill past the church on rue de Wallieux. At the bottom of the hill turn up the track to the left, just before house No 5 on the right.

In the tip of the copse to the right are well-preserved German trenches. These trenches at the **Bois de Wallieux** have been acquired by the CGS/H and have been sympathetically preserved. At the entrance is a **CGS/H Signboard** and a fenced-off trail leads through the tranquil and evocative wooded area. Wooden bridges pass over the trenchlines and craters to preserve them from erosion by too many feet passing through them. Sadly the aesthetically-pleasing green chicken wire fence is not strong enough to be vandal-proof and several of the contemporary photographs have been stolen from their stands. The path leads to a crater in which there appear to be some fractured tree stumps. This is the metal sculpture by Ernest Pignon-Ernest commissioned by the State (with the support of the CGS) to mark the 80th Anniversary of the Armistice of 11 November 1918.

Continue to the N29, turn right and rejoin the main itinerary.

Memorial to 16th Bavarian Inf Regt, Chaulnes

Continue towards Estrées Deniécourt.

There are brown informative lozenge-shaped signs pointing to the left to Fay on the D164 and then to the right to Bois de Waillieux (Soyécourt).

Extra Visit to Fay (Map 1/27a,27b) Round trip: 2 miles. Approximate time: 20 minutes.

Turn left following the brown sign with a red poppy to the church in Place du Souvenir Francais. Stop

To the right of the door is a **plaque to Officiers of the Gendarmerie and Capitaine Fontan**, Fay 18 December 1914 and to the left to **Abbé Ernest Champin, Sous-Lieutenant of the 329th**, Fay 4 July 1916 and above a small plaque to the **41st RI** who had a bitter engagement against the enemy here on 7 June 1940.

Continue following the poppy sign to the enclosed site on the left.

This is the original site of Fay, the only destroyed French WW1 village not to have been rebuilt on its original site. Around the landscaped site are **CGS/H Signboards** showing pictures of the village left in its ruined state and rebuilt where you now see the houses and church.

Return to the crossroads with the N29 and rejoin Itinerary Three.

Continue on the N29 into Estrées Deniécourt. Stop at the Mairie on the right and walk across the road to the memorial on the corner to the left.

• *Lt Col Puntous Memorial, Estrées/43 miles/5 minutes/Map 1/32*

The front line of 1 July was some 2km to your rear (towards Amiens). One of the factors contributing to French success in the Somme offensive was their use of small units in independent actions, moving according to circumstance and terrain rather than in line with a pre-ordained pattern. The action here was typical. The French 329th Infantry Regiment advanced up the road as you have done, led by their commanding officer, Lt Col Puntous, who was killed, together with a number of his officers, NCOs and soldiers, on 4 July 1916. The inscription describes the *'Chevalier sans peur et sans reproche'* (a phrase originally used to describe Pierre de Terrail, Seigneur de Bayard, an illustrious French officer of the fifteenth/sixteenth centuries) who took Estrées with an irresistible élan.

The village was heavily defended by the enemy who counter-attacked with violence. The brave Colonel resisted all these assaults except that from

Memorial to Lt Col Puntous, C 329th IR, Estrées

the left and the Regiment was overcome. The next day it regrouped under Lt Col Albert who, in a memorable bayonet charge, ejected the enemy from the village. The Michelin Guide reports that:

> "The village had to be captured house by house. On the evening of July 4, after three days of fighting, the Germans held only the eastern part of the village. For the next twenty days about 200 of them hung on desperately to it, holding back the assailants with machine-guns posted in the cellars, which fired through the narrow vent-holes. To overcome this resistance, which prevented all advance north or south, it was necessary to sacrifice these houses, and for six consecutive hours 9-in, 11-in, and 15-in shells pounded this small area. Only fifteen survivors were found in the ruined foundations; the rest of the German garrisons had been wiped out. This terrible struggle utterly destroyed the village."

The memorial was erected by the *Anciens Combattants* of the 329th RI of Le Havre on 5 June 1933. Today it is beautifully maintained by *Souvenir Français.*

Continue to the roundabout. Turn left signed to Assevillers and continue on the D146 to the crossroads in the village. Follow the green CWGC sign to the right on the D146E signed to Péronne. Stop at the cemetery on the left just short of the TGV railway line.

High Speed Train passing Assevillers

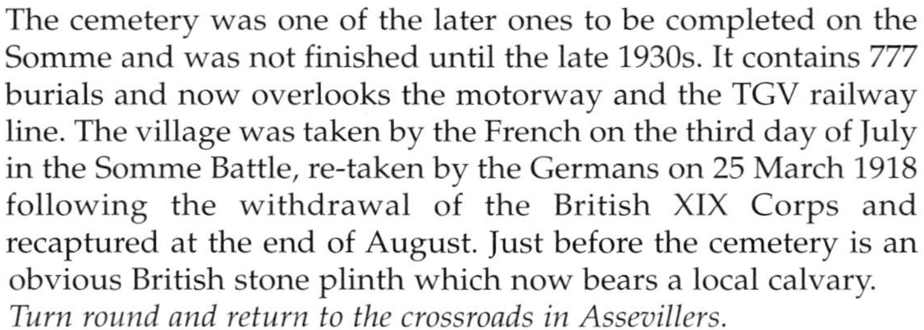

• *Assevillers New British Cemetery/45.2 miles/5 minutes/Map 1/33a*

The cemetery was one of the later ones to be completed on the Somme and was not finished until the late 1930s. It contains 777 burials and now overlooks the motorway and the TGV railway line. The village was taken by the French on the third day of July in the Somme Battle, re-taken by the Germans on 25 March 1918 following the withdrawal of the British XIX Corps and recaptured at the end of August. Just before the cemetery is an obvious British stone plinth which now bears a local calvary.

Turn round and return to the crossroads in Assevillers.

Extra Visit to the French National Cemetery at Dompierre-Becquincourt/Map 1/33. Round trip: 4.4 miles. Approximate time: 15 minutes

Go straight over and then take the D164E left to Fay/Cappy and fork right at the T junction signed to Becquincourt and immediately left. Follow signs to Dompierre-Becquincourt. Turn left past the small chapel and pharmacie and left on rue de Péronne. Continue through the village to the Poilu memorial. Turn right on the D71 signed to Chuignes. The cemetery is on the left.

The cemetery was built in 1920 for the casualties from the Somme Battles

Extra Visit continued

of 1914-18, concentrating burials from local civilian cemeteries in the region and later exhumations from the battlefield. It contains 7,032 World War I burials, of which 1,671 are in four mass graves.

To the right of the entrance past the usual information board, is an unusual and elaborate **memorial from the Italian residents of Dompierre** (stone masons who came to help with the reconstruction) to their French comrades who died for the Fatherland. To the left of the entrance are some beautiful, cone, or shell-shaped fir trees. Also in Dompierre is the terminus (which does not have a station building like Froissy) of the Froissy-Dompierre Decauville railway (see above). The Swiss writer **Blaise Cendrars**, born in 1887, was a francophile who, after travelling in Russia and the USA, took part in the literary life of Paris and wrote some highly influential avant-garde poems. When the war broke out he joined the French Foreign Legion and fought in Champagne and on the Somme. On 26 September 1915, he lost an arm, but his wartime memories were not published until 1946, as *'la main coupée'*. The book describes his 1915 experiences in the Dompierre-Frise-Feuillières-Curlu area. He describes a night patrol to Curlu to make contact with the next Regiment in the line. It was not until after the war that he realized, to his chagrin, that among its officers was the 'genial master of Cubism, Georges Braque', a friend whose hand he would 'dearly have liked to have shaken'.

Return to the D146 and rejoin Itinerary Three.

Turn right and continue on the D146 through Herbécourt.

This village, in the German second line, had been taken the day before Assevillers in July 1916 and its history in 1918 was a similar story.

Continue on the D146 signed to Feuillières going downhill into the Valley of the Somme, crossing the river and its fragmented pools and eel farms in the picturesque village of Feuillières.

The village is a paradise for fishermen getting away from it all in their weekend cabins and has an immaculate local WW1 memorial.

Cross the lock on the Somme Canal, over the Somme bridge and after some 400m turn left on the D146E following CWGC signs to Hem-Monacu. Continue through the village to the cemetery.

• *Hem Farm Military Cemetery/ 50.5 miles/10 minutes/Map N6*

The 5th (Australian) Division crossed the Somme here by hastily constructed bridges during their advance on Péronne of 30 August 1918. The cemetery contains 138 of their dead, 88 South Africans, 4 Canadians and 1,563 British. There are two **VC holders** buried here. **2nd Lt George Edward Cates** of the 2nd Rifle Brigade, was killed on 9 March 1917 while deepening a captured

German trench, when his spade struck a grenade. When it started to burn he put his foot on it and it immediately exploded. By sacrificing his own life he saved those of his companions in the trench. Cates is also commemorated on the Rifle Brigade Memorial in Winchester Cathedral. On 1 September 1918, during the attack on Mont St Quentin, **Pte Robert Mactier** of the 23rd (Victoria) AIF:

> "... rushed out of [his] trench, closed with and killed the machine-gun crew of eight men and threw the gun over the parapet. He then moved to another strong-point and captured six men. He disposed of a third machine-gun, but in tackling a fourth was killed. This action enabled the battalion to capture Mont St Quentin a few hours later."

Return to the D146. Turn left and continue to the crossroads with the D938.

Extra Visit to the French National Cemetery (Map O2) & 363rd Infantry Regiment Memorial (Map O3), Cléry
Round trip : 1.4 miles. Approximate time: 15 minutes

Turn right onto the D938 and go under the motorway. Turn left to the cemetery and stop at the memorial at the entrance.

This commemorates the feats of the Regiment between 7 August and 2 September 1916. The cemetery contains 2,332 burials, of which 1,129 are in two mass graves and is a concentration of graves from the old front line in this area. Inside the cemetery are large boards showing maps of all the French cemeteries in the area and of the Somme Battlefield, with photographs.

Return to the crossroads and rejoin the main itinerary.

On the high ground to the right over the motorway is the French National Cemetery at Cléry.

Continue over the crossroads for 100m.

• 'HR' Memorial/52.1 miles/5 minutes/Map 01

On the left-hand bank of a small road junction is a small memorial, with the inscription 'HR, 12 August 1916'. It bears a *Souvenir Français* roundel, but all information about the subject has been lost.

Continue on the D146 to Maurepas. Stop at the cemetery at the fork on the outskirts of the village.

• French National Cemetery, Maurepas/53.7 miles/5 minutes/Map L8

This cemetery was formed in 1921 from two temporary cemeteries at Maurepas and at Suzanne, about 12km away. Besides two mass graves which contain 1,588 bodies, there are another 2,070 French, 19 Russian and a Rumanian burial. The first cross seen on entering the cemetery is that of Sgt Leclerc. It was his namesake General who liberated Amiens in 1944.

Memorial to French 1st Inf Regt, Maurepas

Private Memorial to Charles Dansette, Combles

Private Memorial to Victor Hallard, Maurepas

Entrance to Combles Comm Cem

Extra Visit to the Edouard Naudier Private Memorial (Map O4). Round trip: 3.4 miles. Approximate time: 10 minutes.

Turn right onto the road past the cemetery to Leforest on the C5. Continue through Le forest on the D146E, under the TGV line and the motorway, turn sharp right and continue on a narrowing road for half a mile to the monument on the left, opposite a junction to the right.

The inscription on the broken column monument reads, 'Our beloved son, **Edouard Naudier**, tax collector, died for France at Hospital Farm. 1890-1916. Eternal regrets of all the family'. The Ferme de l'Hôpital is the farm on the rise to the left of the monument.

Return to the French Cemetery and rejoin Itinerary Three.

Continue to the T junction at the square in Maurepas.

Extra Visit to the Gaston Chomet Private Memorial (Map K49). Round trip: 1.4 miles. Approximate time: 5 minutes

Turn left on the D146B on Rue Général Frère. Keep to the right of the church and follow signs to Hardecourt au Bois on the D146E. As the road begins to rise, the memorial is on the top of a bank to the left and is often very overgrown.

The stone monument is to French soldier Gaston Chomet of the 160th RI, killed at Maurepas on 30 July 1916. The memorial has been restored by the Albert branch of the *Souvenir Français* but already has a chipped corner on the inscription panel.

Return to the square in Maurepas and rejoin the main itinerary.

Turn right and immediately left.

There is a **CGS/H Signboard** here which describes how the reconstruction of the village, completely destroyed during the battle, was funded by the Pouret family whose son was killed in action here on 30 July 1916.

Continue to the small memorial to the left in the square.

• *1st RI Memorial, Maurepas/54.1 miles/5 minutes/Map L7*

This commemorates the fallen of the 1st (Cambrai) Infantry Regiment who, together with the Zouaves, entered Maurepas on 12 August 1916, taking the areas around the church and cemetery. The village had been strongly fortified by the Germans and it was not until 24 August that, with British help, it was wholly cleared, by which time it was totally destroyed. The inscription reads, 'To our comrades of the 1st RI who fell in 1916 for the deliverance of Maurepas'.

Continue round the square, past the Poilu memorial on the left and turn left again on the D146 direction Combles. Continue some 1½ miles to a junction to the right with the D146A. Stop by the memorial on the bank.

• *V. Hallard Private Memorial/55.5 miles/5 minutes/Map 4b*

The inscription translates, 'Here lies our beloved son Victor Hallard, known as Tredez, 110th Régt de Tirailleurs who died gloriously 12 September 1916 at the age of 28 years'. It has been renovated by *Souvenir Français.*

Continue into Combles on the D146 to the crossroads with the D20. Turn right signed to Rancourt and stop at the large memorial on the right just before the High Speed Train line.

• *Charles Dansette Private Memorial/56.4 miles/10 minutes/Map L4a*

The inscription on this important-looking memorial reads:

"Beneath this cross, erected to his memory, lies 2nd Lt Charles Dansette, born at Armentières and who fell gloriously for his country on 25 September 1916 at the age of 22 years. This élite officer who had always distinguished himself since the beginning of the campaign by his energy and his indomitable courage fell gloriously on 25 September 1916 leading his assault section against a German trench, which was brilliantly taken. "

There is also a quotation from Victor Hugo, 'Those who piously die for their fatherland have the right that the crowd should come to their tomb and pray.' On another side is a citation dated 18 April 1915, 'On 5 April 1915 during the attack on German trenches in the Pareid Wood proof was shown of an ardour and an enthusiasm which was a fine example for his men'.

Return to the crossroads. Turn right following the CWGC signs and stop at the cemetery on the left.

• *Combles Communal Cemetery Extension/56.9 miles/5 minutes/ Map L4*

This cemetery was begun by the French in October 1916, the first British burials being in December 1916 and enlarged after the Armistice. It contains 1,041 UK, 5 Canadian, 1 South African and 13 special memorials.

Turn round, return to the junction, turn right and follow the road down and round into the village to the imposing Hôtel de Ville with its splendid memorial and the CWGC sign pointing left to the Guards Cemetery.

• *Combles/57.4 miles/RWC*

During their two and a half years of occupation, the Germans had turned Combles into a formidable redoubt in their third line of defence. Much of the strength of the position was due to the extensive catacombs and tunnels beneath the church and under Lamotte Château which stood opposite. (For many years there was talk of opening up these works to the public, but as yet nothing has transpired.) The German writer, **Ernst Junger**, remembers

Combles with dread. He described the daily hour-long bombardment between 0900 and 1000 of a 'demented violence', when 'the ground shook and the sky seemed a giant's boiling cauldron'. Worst of all, however, was the stench:

> "There floated above the ruins ... a thick odour of corpses, for the shelling was so violent that nobody could look after the dead. One literally had death in one's nostrils ... this heavy, sickly smoke wasn't only nauseating, mixed with the acrid vapour of explosives it inspired an almost visionary exaltation, which only the close presence of death could produce."

The town held out as the Allied assaults of September 1916 inched their way past on either side. In a set piece attack on 25 September by the British in the north and the French in the south, the 56th (London) Division and the French 73rd and 110th Infantry Regiments cleared the town by the following morning, taking 1,200 prisoners. During 1917 when the British took over the front line down to the Somme, Combles became an important military railway centre and, to conceal the movement of men and material, long lines of high canvas screens were erected alongside the roads leading to the town. **Sir William Orpen RA**, who was sent to France in April 1917 as an official war artist, drew the screens in a picture called *The Great Camouflage, Combles*, now in the Imperial War Museum, London.

In the German advance of 1918 Combles fell on 24 March, despite stubborn resistance by the South African Brigade and then, when the tide again turned, it was retaken by 18th Division on 29 August.

The town was adopted by Portsmouth. Good basic food can be had in the Café Chez Joelle, 3 rue de la Montagne, ☎ (03) 22 85 07 51.

Turn left and keep to the left of the church. Continue to the cemetery on the right.

• *Guards Cemetery, Combles/57.8 miles/10 minutes/Map L5*

The cemetery was begun by the Guards Division in September 1916 and at the Armistice contained a hundred graves, nineteen of which were Foot Guards. There are now 150 burials, including **Gunner Squire Lawrence Taylor**, RHA, service number 111111, killed on 28 February 1917, aged 25. Taylor was with the famous 'L' Battery, which at Néry during the retreat from Mons in 1914 won three VCs. Also

Entrance and path to the Guards Cemetery, Combles

of 'L' battery, but after Mons, is **Major Guy Horsman, MC**, age 25, 28 February 1917, who served throughout the Gallipoli campaign. **Second Lieutenant L.L. Paterson** of the Post Office Rifles, age 24, 1 September 1918, has the inscription, 'His men wrote a rough cross "In memory of a very brave British officer"'. Seven Coldstream Guardsmen lie in a row, all killed on 11 December 1916.

Extra Visit to Private Memorial/Graves to Heumann, Mills & Torrance (Map L6). Round trip: .8 mile. Approximate time: 10 minutes

Continue to a farm on the right, where the metalled road peters out.

This is Faffemont (sometimes seen as Falfemont) Farm, although the original farm building was on the site of what is now a copse beyond and on a rise to the right of the present building.

Continue left on a track past the farm to the first pylon on the left. Stop.

The flat stone memorial is on private land and it is courteous to ask the farmer (who calls the pylon 'la Tour Eiffel') for permission to visit it. Be careful as you approach it not to damage any crops. The memorial is some 450m up the slope to the right, on a line between the pylon and the small copse and is completely invisible when there are tall crops. It is maintained by the Commonwealth War Graves Commission and is the grave of Capt R. Heumann, Sgt Major B. Mills and Sgt A. W. Torrance of the 1/2nd Londons, killed here on 10 September 1916 during their battalion's attack. Their burials are listed under CWGC Rancourt. After the war, Capt Dick Heumann's family bought the land and the families of all three men erected the flat headstone.

Turn round and rejoin itinerary three.

Return to Combles town hall. Turn left, continue 100m and turn right onto the D74, signed to Morval, then keep left on Rue de Morval and continue to Morval.

It was the capture of this village and Lesboeufs 2km ahead, both on high ground north of Combles, on 25 September 1918 that ensured the success of the assault on the Combles German redoubt on the same day. The road you are on runs directly across the front of the attacking Fourth Army (they came from your left) among whose troops were Guards, New Zealanders and Birmingham Pals (15th and 16th Battalion, the Royal Warwickshire Regiment). One of the Pals afterwards recalled the euphoria of victory on the morning of 26 September –

> "One of our fellows passed by, wounded and drunk. He had been having a rummage round a dugout. Said he had found bottles of beer and by his description, enough to keep the Army going. When he said he had had the lot before coming back we understood. He sold me a trench dagger and a pair of excellent field glasses for 11 Francs. He seemed very satisfied and so was I."

To the left is **Morval British CWGC Cemetery**, (Map L2) designed by Sir Reginald Blomfield, which contains burials from 26 August-6 September 1918. It was originated in September by V Corps.

Continue through Morval to the T junction in Lesboeufs signed left on the C5 to Ginchy and the Guards Cemetery. Follow the signs and stop at the cemetery on the right.

• *Guards Cemetery, Lesboeufs/62.7 miles/5 minutes/Map I4*

This large cemetery contains 2,827 UK burials, including 2nd Grenadiers from the 25 September attack, 202 Australian, 11 New Zealand, 4 Newfoundland, 1 Canadian and 88 special memorials. At the Armistice, there were forty graves and most of the burials are concentrations from the surrounding battlefield, made after the war.

Continue to the obelisk on the right.

• *Captain Meakin Private Memorial/62.9 miles/5 minutes/Map L1*

This sadly neglected tall column is to Capt Herbert Percy Meakin of the 3rd Coldstream Guards, attached to the Guards Trench Mortar Battery, killed near this spot on 25 September 1916. It is not a grave, and Capt Meakin is commemorated on the Thiépval Memorial.

Continue to the memorial cross on the right.

• *Guards Memorial, Lesboeufs/63.3 miles/5 minutes/Map K19*

The memorial stands immediately to the south of the German 1916 third line. The Guards Division was formed in September 1915 and was made up from four Grenadier battalions, three Coldstream, two Irish, two Scots and one Welsh. The memorial commemorates the action of 25 September 1916 when the division, in concert with 6th Division, captured Lesboeufs. During their three weeks holding the sector they sustained over 7,000 casualties. Ginchy Church can be seen straight ahead.

Return to the village.

The village of Lesboeufs was the scene of a remarkable stand by twelve machine guns of 63rd Machine Gun Battalion during the German 1918 Offensive, but it fell on 24 March. It was recaptured by 10th South Wales Borderers on 29 August.

Turn left past the church and fork left on the D74 signed to Gueudecourt.

The next 7km of this road, up to where it meets the Albert-Bapaume D929 at le Sars, runs effectively 1,000m to the left of and parallel to the 1916 final line reached by the British. The 1916 Somme offensive, coming from your left, finished in November.

Enter Gueudecourt and in the centre of the village turn right on the D574 Rue du Caribou signed to Beaulencourt. Continue to the Caribou memorial on the right.

• *Newfoundland Memorial, Gueudecourt/66.6 miles/10 minutes/ Map I2 OP*

Five Caribou memorials were erected by Newfoundland after the war and they became the responsibility of the Canadian Government when Newfoundland joined Canada in 1949. This memorial stands on the British line of 17 November 1916 (and there are some preserved trench lines within the memorial confines) therefore it is probably the nearest point to Bapaume reached throughout the entire 1916 offensive. Although the village from which you have come was taken on 26 September, this area was not secured until 12 October – by the Newfoundlanders. The advance stopped here and British and German forces (the latter straight ahead of you) faced each other until February 1917 when the Germans withdrew to the Hindenburg line.

By using the Holts' Battle Map and binoculars you can orientate, from the road outside the Caribou by looking up the road to Gueudecourt church which is at 12 o'clock. To the left on the horizon at 11 o'clock is Delville Wood, at just past 12 o'clock is High Wood, and at 1 o'clock is the wireless mast at Pozières. At 1.30 is the Thiépval Memorial and at 2 o'clock is the Butte de Warlencourt.

Turn round and return to Gueudecourt crossroads, then turn right on the D74, signed to le Sars. After some 700m follow a CWGC sign to the left. Park and walk up the track to the cemetery.

• *AIF (Australian Imperial Forces) Grass Lane Cemetery, Flers/ 67.7 miles/15 minutes/Map H11*

Australian medical units that had established themselves in nearby caves began the cemetery in November 1916 alongside a track known as Grass Lane. After the Armistice it was enlarged and now contains the graves of some 2,800 British soldiers, sailors and marines and approximately 400 Australians, 80 New Zealanders, 70 Canadians, 25 South Africans, 160 French and 3 German prisoners. A measure of the dreadful intensity of the fighting in the area is that two-thirds of the British burials are unknown. One that is known is that of **Sergeant Harold Jackson** of the East Yorkshires, who won the **VC** for individual actions in May 1918, four months before he was killed.

Return to the D74, turn left and continue to the crossroads with the D197.

Extra Visit to the 41st Division Memorial (Map H12), Bull's Road CWGC Cemetery (Map H13) & French 17th/18th RIT Memorial (Map H27) Round trip: 8.2 miles. Approximate time: 20 minutes

Turn left onto the D197 and drive into Flers. Stop at the memorial on the left.

This is the **41st Div Memorial**, an evocative bronze figure of a fully equipped Tommy which was immortalized by being the illustration on the cover of Rose Coombs' pioneering work *Before Endeavours Fade*. (The

Guards Memorial, Lesboeufs

Sadly neglected obelisk to Capt Meakin, 3rd Coldstream Guards, Lesboeufs

Newfoundland Caribou Memorial, Gueudecourt

41st Div Memorial, Flers

French Poilu Memorial, Flers

Extra Visit continued

village *Poilu* memorial nearby makes an interesting contrast in styles.) He is facing the direction in which his Division attacked on 15 September 1916 in Part 4 of the Somme Offensive.

It employed a new secret weapon – the tank. The Official History described how a tank helped to liberate Flers – 'firing as it went, the tank lurched up the main street followed by parties of cheering infantry'. It was commanded by **Lt Arnold** who won the MC and his **Gunner, Glaister** received the MM. The war correspondent **Philip Gibbs** described the action:

> "On that morning of September 15th, 1916, the front-line troops got out of their trenches laughing and cheering, and shouting again because the tanks had gone ahead, and were scaring the Germans dreadfully while they moved over the enemy's trenches and poured

Extra Visit continued

out fire on every side. One of them called 'Crème de Menthe' had great adventures that day, capturing hundreds of prisoners, and treading down machine-gun posts, and striking terror into the enemy. A message came back: 'Crème de Menthe is walking down the High Street of Flers with the British army cheering behind.'"

Sadly, the shock effect of the tanks did not last long.

"There were too few of them,' Gibbs maintained, 'and the secret was let out before they were produced in large numbers."

Turn left following the CWGC sign up the small road to the cemetery.

Bull's Road Cemetery contains 485 UK, 148 Australian, 120 New Zealand, 2 unknown and 15 special memorials.

Return to the D197. Turn left, continue through the village to the junction with the C5 to the left and stop at the memorial on the bank to the left.

This **memorial to the French 17th and 18th Infantry Regiments** of 82nd Territorial Division commemorates the Battle of Flers, Ginchy and Lesboeufs of 26 September 1914 and has a red, white and blue *Souvenir Français plaque.*

Return to the D197/D74 junction at Gueudecourt to rejoin the main itinerary.

Continue over the crossroads towards le Sars. As the road bends right and then left in l'Abbaye d'Eaucourt just before the D929 in this area is the site of a Victoria Cross action.

• *Site of Action of Lt Col R. Boys Bradford VC/ Map H6*

On 1 October 1916, here at l'Abbaye d'Eaucourt, **Lt Col (later Brig Gen) Roland Boys Bradford** of the 9th Bn, the Durham Light Infantry, when a battalion suffered very severe casualties and lost its commander, took command of it in addition to his own. By his fearless energy under fire of all descriptions and skilful leadership of both battalions, he succeeded in rallying the attack and capturing and defending the objective, an action which won him the Victoria Cross. Brig Gen Bradford was killed on 30 November 1917 at Cambrai and is buried at Hermies British CWGC Cemetery. His brother, **Lt Commander George Nicholson Bradford** RN, also won the Victoria Cross in April 1918, but was killed in the action which won him the award.

Continue to the crossroads with the D929 at le Sars. Turn left. Continue to the last building in the village on the left and turn up a small track to the left by a Calvary. Walk about 80m to the overgrown memorial behind the farm buildings to the left.

• *German 111th RIR Memorial, Le Sars/70.3 miles/10 minutes/Map H5*

This little visited memorial is one of the most important German monuments still remaining on the Somme battlefield. It is in the form of a large, sadly crumbling, stone, with fading inscription. A Teutonic cross can still be discerned on it and the words, 'RIR 111. *Einen Toten* [our dead]' and on the other side the battle honours of Fricourt, Mametz, Montauban and la Boisselle. The memorial is illustrated in the original Michelin Guide to the Somme which describes it as standing in a ruined German cemetery.

Turn round and continue along the D929, direction Bapaume.

Le Sars, which was completely devastated during the war, formed part of the German third line in 1916 and was not taken until 7 October when 23rd Division captured it attacking from your left. They attempted to continue right towards Bapaume but 1km further on were stopped by a formidable line of German defences on the Warlencourt Ridge, the last height before the town. Its central position was a solitary 50ft-high mound of chalk, said to be an ancient burial ground, known as the Butte, on Hill 122, which equated to the British as Mort Homme in the Verdun sector did to the French.

Continue through the village, past the local cemetery on the right.

It bears a CWGC *Tombes de Guerre* sign and in it lies **Sgt R. Hinds**, 1 September 1944.

As the road goes downhill out of the village, turn right onto the narrow road that leads to the Butte, which is signed. Keep to the left and park at the foot of the mound.

• *Butte de Warlencourt/71.5 miles/15 minutes/Map H7*

At the foot of the mound, which is fenced about, is a bronze sign whose French inscription reads, 'This site is sacred, respect it. Passers by you are entering this site at your own responsibility. British soldiers fell in 1916 in the Battle of the Somme and still lie here'. The danger warning is repeated in English and says that the Butte is the property of the WFA. There are steps up to the summit and metal railings. It can be very slippery.

This position was the very tip of the British advance in 1916. The attack that began just 10.5km back down the road at Tara-Usna on 1 July had gained an average of 77 metres a day to settle here on 17 November. The daily casualty rate averaged over 3,000. That is forty men for every metre of the advance – one man for every inch. Some of the fiercest fighting took place on and around the Butte. Riddled with tunnels, bristling with mortars and machine guns and guarded by waves of barbed wire, it stood firmly in command of the road to Bapaume. It was never taken and held by the British in 1916. Some reports say that it changed hands seventeen times, but it was not until 25 February 1917 during the German withdrawal that it was finally taken by the 151st Brigade.

In April that year the 6th and 8th Durhams placed individual battalion crosses on top of the hill to commemorate an action there on 5 November 1916 and after a protest by the brigade Commander, who said that it had been a

WFA plaque on the crest of Butte de Warlencourt

German 111th RIR Memorial, le Sars

brigade action, they were quickly joined by a large cross for 151st Brigade. Not to be outdone, the 9th Durhams added their own battalion cross. All four crosses were brought back to England after the war, the Brigade cross to Durham cathedral, where it rests today in the DLI Chapel in the south transept. A wooden cross was also placed on top of the Butte to commemorate the German defenders and two further crosses were erected at the base of the mound in memory of the South African 3rd and 6th Battalions. Later, in July 1917, King George V and General Byng visited the Butte. For many years after the war an ornate *Souvenir Français* cross, like the hilt of a sword, and a wooden cross to commemorate the German actions in the area, sat on the mound. Today they have been replaced by an important WFA bronze plaque which was inaugurated on 30 June 1990, when much of the dense vegetation was removed to return the Butte nearer to its 1914-18 appearance. Ten years later it had all grown up again. It carries a summary of the actions described above. A planned orientation table was not erected for security reasons.

Continue on the D929, past a sign that marks the front Line of 20 November 1916 to the cemetery on the right.

• *Warlencourt CWGC Cemetery/72 miles/5 minutes/Map H8*

This cemetery was not established until the end of 1919 when it was made by concentrating burials from the le Sars-Warlencourt battlefield. An idea of how many small burial plots there were may be gained from the fact that the largest single number of graves moved from one plot was seventeen, and there are over 3,000 burials in the cemetery.

Continue to Bapaume.

• *Bapaume/75.4 miles/RWC*

The town was occupied by the Germans as they pushed westwards in 1914 and held by them until 17 March 1917 when they retreated to the Hindenburg Line. It was then occupied by the Australian 2nd Division who found the German fires still burning. According to the Michelin Guide:

> "As they left they destroyed trenches, devastated the entire district, set death traps everywhere, stretched chains connected with mines across the roads and paths and set fire to shelters .... Not a house was spared."

A delayed-action bomb even exploded on 25 March, killing two members of the French Parliament. This systematic destruction, followed by further devastation in 1918, left the town totally destroyed. The Germans returned during the March Offensive of 1918 until ejected by the New Zealand Division, together with Welsh troops, on 29 August. Bapaume was 'adopted' by Sheffield after the war.

The unconventional war poet, **Arthur Graeme West**, despite defective eyesight, joined the 16th Public Schools Battalion of the Middlesex Regiment as a private in February 1915. He was killed by a sniper on 3 April 1917 in his trench near Barastre, to the east of Bapaume. In August 1916 he had been commissioned in the 6th Bn, the Oxs and Bucks. Educated at Blundells School and Balliol College, Oxford, he was an admirer of Bertrand Russell and veered towards atheism. His poems reflect his non-comformity to the usual patriotic and resigned public school attitude. 'God! How I Hate You, You Young Cheerful Men!', he wrote in early 1916. West is buried in Ecoust-St-Mein HAC Cemetery, 5 miles north of Bapaume.

Bapaume now boasts a completely modernized hotel, with gourmet restaurant – La Paix, 11 Avénue Abel Guidet, ☎ (03) 21 07 11 03. It belongs to the same group as the Royal Picardie in Albert and Le Prieuré in Rancourt. There are also several smaller restaurants which are handy for lunch breaks – but do not leave it much after 1300 hours or you might find that the chef has gone home (presumably for lunch!).

• *End of Itinerary Three*

ITINERARY FOUR

• **Itinerary Four** starts at Exit 13 from the E15/A1 Motorway, direction Péronne, at Assevillers and heads east to Péronne, over the Canal du Nord, through Rancourt to Bapaume.
• **The Route:** Assevillers; Belloy and the Alan Seeger Memorials; the French National Cemetery, Villers Carbonnel; the British and Indian CWGC Cemetery, La Chapelette; Péronne – the *Historial*, the town hall; Mont St Quentin, 2nd Australian Div Memorial; Bouchavesnes-Bergen – Private Memorials to French soldier Fuméry and French Aspirant Calle and the 106th Infantry Regiment Memorial, Marshal Foch Statue; Rancourt – German Cemetery, CWGC Military Cemetery, the French National Cemetery, the *Souvenir Français* Chapel; Sailly-Saillisel British CWGC Cemetery; the French Memorials, le Transloy; the German Cemetery and memorial, Villers au Flos; Bapaume.
• **Extra Visits** are suggested to: Biaches – Memorials in Biaches local cemetery, French Colonial Memorial/ 2nd Lt Brocheriou; Remains of German Cemetery, Flaucourt; French National Cemetery; Bullecourt – Museum, Slouch Hat Memorial, Digger's Park Memorial, Memorial to Missing.
• **Planned duration**, without stops for refreshment or extra visits: 3 hours.
• **Total distance: 28.3 miles.**

• *Péronne-Assevillers Motorway Exit 13/0 miles/RWC*

There is a motorway complex nearby with petrol station, shop, tourist information, cafeteria and fast food outlets. The *** Péronne-Assevillers Mercure Hotel, ☎ (03) 22 84 12 76 makes an ideal and comfortable starting base for touring the battlefield if using Approach One.

From the motorway exit, immediately turn left from the N29 towards Belloy-en-Santerre on the D79. Take the second left into the village and stop in the square outside the church.

• *Belloy – Alan Seeger Memorials/0.9 miles/10 minutes/Map Side 1/35*

This powerfully fortified village was taken by the French on 4 July (American Independence Day) 1916, their advance having been made faster and deeper than the British to the north. The famous French Foreign Legion was ordered to carry the position at bayonet point at 0600 hours. The Michelin company produced a series of small battlefield guidebooks from 1919 as a memorial to their employees who were killed in the war, and the Legion's charge is described in the Michelin Somme Guide thus:

> "Deployed in battle formation, they charged across a flat meadow 900 yards broad. When 300 yards from their objective, machine-guns hidden in the path from Estrées to Belloy were suddenly unmasked and a deadly fire mowed down the French ranks. The 9th and 11th Companies sustained particularly heavy losses, all the officers falling. One of these companies reached the objective under the command of the mess corporal. Belloy was captured and 750 Germans were taken prisoners."

Among those to be mowed down was the talented and promising young American poet, **Alan Seeger**, who had been living in France when war was declared and who immediately volunteered. He served with the Legion in the Reims and Aisne sectors throughout 1915 and in the spring of 1916 wrote the prophetic poem *Rendezvous*, that was to guarantee his immortality. Its opening lines are:

I have a rendezvous with Death
At some disputed barricade ....

After the war, his grieving parents paid for a bell to be placed in the belfry of the rebuilt church of Belloy. Its peal represented his voice, still singing over the land he grew to love. In 1940 the church was again badly damaged but a new bell continues to sing out in his name. The village children are taught some lines of their *'poète américain'* and there is a plaque to him on the *Mairie*/school, opposite the church. Seeger was posthumously awarded the *Croix de Guerre* and the *Médaille Militaire*. He is thought to be buried in the French National Cemetery at Lihons (see Itinerary Three). The village war memorial also bears the name of 'Alain' Seeger and honours the French Foreign Legion, July 1916. On the rear of the memorial the fierce defence of Belloy by the 117th RI in May/June 1940 is commemorated. The road is called Rue de Catalogne, and the 'Men from Barcelona' are also commemorated in the church.

Return to the N29, direction Péronne and continue to the junction with the N17. Stop at the French cemetery on the left.

• *French National Cemetery/Chinese Graves, Villers Carbonnel/4 miles/10 minutes/Map Side 1/3*

The cemetery contains 2,285 burials, of which 1,295 are in two mass graves. Fifty-nine men are named in Ossuary 1 and thirty-five in Ossuary 2. Inside the cemetery is the local World War I memorial. In 1941 eighteen French bodies from World War II were exhumed and reburied here. In the adjoining local cemetery there is a plot hidden in trees at the back containing three Chinese CWGC graves from October 1918. The concrete frames of the graves are inscribed *'Concession à perpétuité'*. Normally French graves have a limited concessionary period and signs offering graves for reburials are often seen in

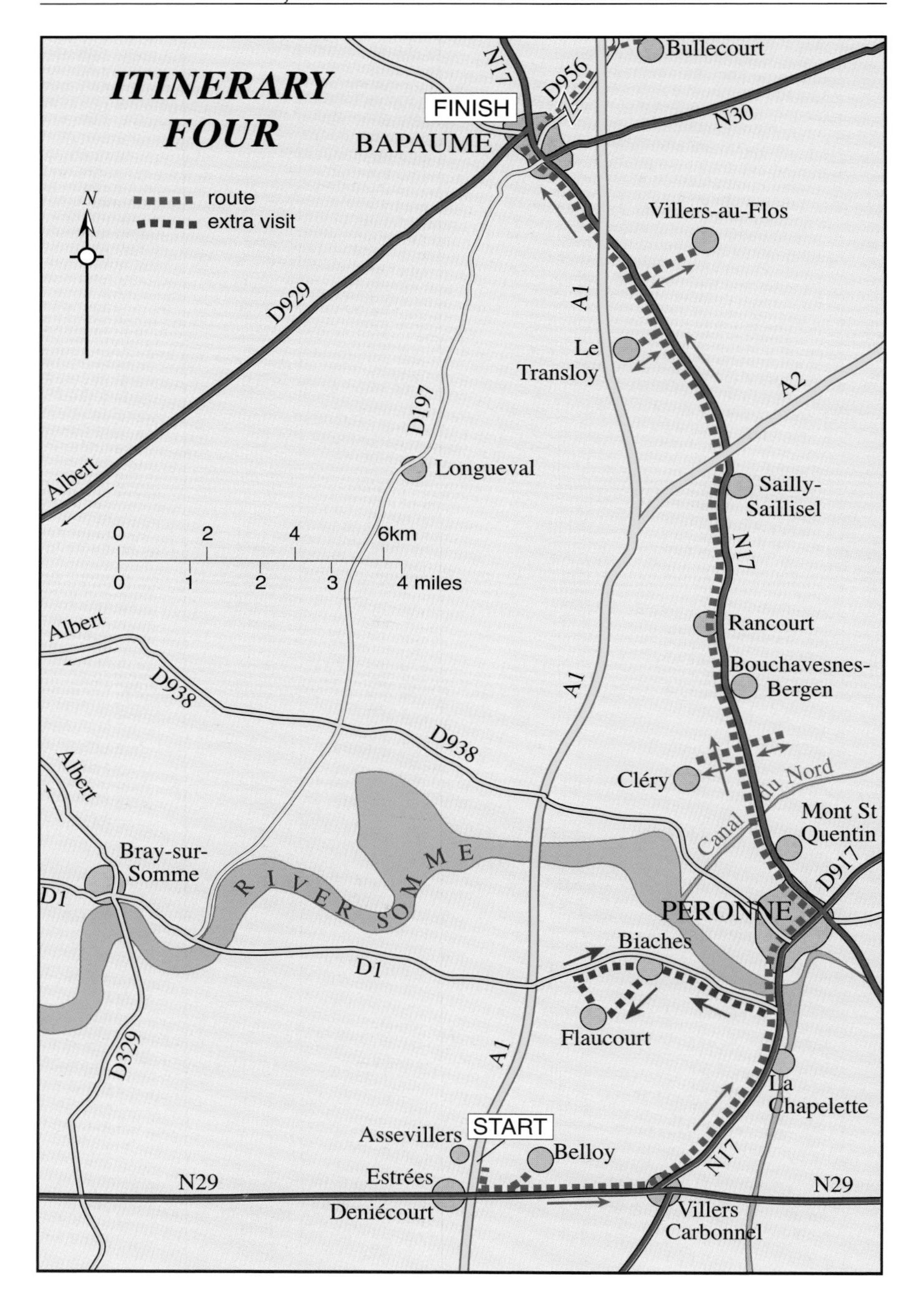
ITINERARY
FOUR
route
extra visit
N
FINISH
BAPAUME
Bullecourt
N17
D956
N30
Villers-au-Flos
A1
D929
Le
Transloy
A2
D197
Longueval
Albert
Sailly-
Saillisel
0 2 4 6km
0 1 2 3 4 miles
N17
Rancourt
Albert
D938
A1
Bouchavesnes-
Bergen
D938
Albert
Cléry
Canal du Nord
Mont St
Quentin
Bray-sur-
Somme
RIVER SOMME
D917
D1
PERONNE
Biaches
D1
Flaucourt
D329
A1
La
Chapelette
START
Assevillers
Belloy
N17
N29
Estrées
N29
Deniécourt
Villers
Carbonnel

Belloy Church and Alan Seeger plaque on the mairie wall

Headstone of Lance Dafadar Jaswant Singh, La Chapelette Brit & Indian Cem, Péronne

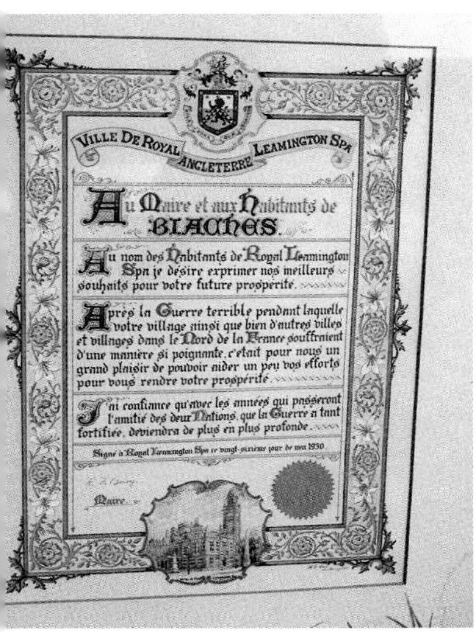

VILLE DE ROYAL LEAMINGTON SPA
ANGLETERRE

Au Maire et aux Habitants de
BIACHES.

Au nom des Habitants de Royal Leamington Spa je désire exprimer nos meilleurs souhaits pour votre future prospérité.

Après la Guerre terrible pendant laquelle votre village ainsi que bien d'autres villes et villages dans le Nord de la France souffraient d'une manière si poignante, c'était pour nous un grand plaisir de pouvoir aider un peu vos efforts pour vous rendre votre prospérité.

J'ai confiance qu'avec les années qui passeront l'amitié des deux Nations, que la Guerre a tant fortifiée, deviendra de plus en plus profonde.

Signé à Royal Leamington Spa ce vingt-sixième jour de mai 1930

Maire.

Certificate from Leamington Spa in Biaches Mairie

French cemeteries. It is pleasing to know that the remains of these obscure Chinese labourers, who came so far to give their lives, will always be preserved here.

Turn left on the N17, direction Péronne and the Historial and stop at the British cemetery some 3 miles further on to the right.

On the left is a Campanile hotel, ☎ (03) 22 84 22 22.

• *La Chapelette British & Indian Cemetery/6.8 miles/5 minutes/Map Side 1/37*

One of the later cemeteries to be completed (it was still listed in the 1929 version of *Silent Cities* as one of the cemeteries which 'for various reasons … have not yet been constructed') it contains approximately 250

British, Australian and 'Christian Indian' graves from 1917 and 1918 and a plot of about 325 Indian Labour Corps from the same period on the left.

Continue to the junction with the D1, just before the River Somme.

Extra Visit to Biaches Local Cemetery, French Colonial Memorial & Tomb of 2nd Lt Brocheriou; Wartime German Cemetery, Flaucourt & French National Cemetery at Biaches Round trip: 9.1 miles. Approximate time: 50 minutes

Turn left and continue to Biaches.

Biaches was occupied by the Germans on 28 August 1914. During the 1916 Somme Offensive, the French advance on Biaches was so rapid that they took the village on 10 July 1916 after an intense and bitter struggle for a strongly fortified position known as the Herbécourt Redoubt, which was taken, when, according to the Michelin Guide, 'a Captain and eight men, with "extraordinary daring" crept up to and entered the redoubt. The garrison, which still numbered 112 men and 2 officers, lost their presence of mind and surrendered without offering any resistance.' Several strong counter-attacks followed, on 15 and 17 July and the Germans temporarily regained the village, only to be driven out again on the 19th. The loss of the village, the last defence along this road before Péronne, was a great blow to the Germans, hence their bitter fight for it. The French remained in the sector until January 1917, when it was taken over by the British 48th (S Midlands) Division, which included battalions of the Royal Warwickshire Regiment. It was a bitterly cold winter, with snow and hard frosts and very intense fighting took place with the enemy. The 7th Battalion occupied part of Biaches, the village green being in No Man's Land, but a pump in the centre was apparently used by both sides. The Germans retreated from the village to the Hindenburg Line in March 1917, leaving it in complete ruins. The Warwicks then moved on and entered Péronne (see Approach One). They retained a strong impression of the village and in January 1922 Leamington Spa held a public meeting (typical of many such gatherings throughout Britain) to vote that because of the 7th Warwicks' connection with Biaches (and as Leamington was famous for its health-giving water and the village pump had provided the Warwicks with water in their hour of need) the town should 'adopt' the devastated village. Members of the British League of Help had already visited the damaged areas and they reported, with the help of photographs, the rubble and the appalling plight of the inhabitants (who had numbered 446 before the war and who were now reduced to 229, living in huts). By August £331 5s 10d had been raised. £200 was spent on fruit trees, £50 on garden and farm seeds and the rest on 'Communal Equipment', which included public weighing machines, fences and gates for the rebuilt cemetery. In June 1930, the Mayor of

Extra Visit continued

Leamington, Dr R. F. Berry, and the Town Clerk, Mr Leo Rawlinson, joined a large group of British local government officials who first visited Paris, where they were greeted by the President of the Republic in the Elysée Palace and hosted to a grand dinner in the Hôtel de Ville. They then moved on to Amiens by train and thence by road to the various villages that they had 'adopted'. At Biaches, Dr Berry and Mr Rawlinson inspected the gifts bought with the money raised by the citizens of Leamington and presented a fine illuminated address (which still hangs proudly in the *Mairie*) to mark the visit. A marble plaque (now in the *Mairie* awaiting a suitable base around the green), stating *'Don de Lamington* [sic] *Spa'*, was attached to the weighing machine, now dismantled, and the school children were granted a day's holiday. Many other Somme villages benefited in equally practical ways. Montauban's water supply and lighting system were supplied with funds from Maidstone, for example.

In the village turn left on the rue de Barleux at the edge of the green in front of the Mairie. Fork right and continue to the cemetery on the right.

On the right-hand gatepost is a **marble sign reading *'Don de Lamington*** [sic]***-Spa'*** (see details of the 'adoption' above). In the cemetery is a well-maintained memorial to 33 Cuirassiers of the 9th Regiment, who fell on 24 September 1914 at la Maisonnette. Next to it is another mass grave to 12 Chasseurs Alpins of 7th Battalion who died at la Maisonnette on 28 August 1914.

Continue to the crossroads and go right again. As the un-made, narrow road descends through a small copse, stop opposite a yellow sign in the bank, on the right at the top of some steps, which directs you to the memorial.

The French Colonial Memorial, set in a glade, commemorates the colonial forces who in 1916 fought in this sector and who died here.

Behind the memorial is the grave, marked by a white cross, of **2nd Lt Marcel Brocheriou**, of the 22nd RI of Lille, *Croix de Guerre, Chevalier de la Légion d'Honneur*, killed on 6 August 1916. (In contrast to the good state of maintenance of this memorial, that to the 56th Battalion Chasseurs à Pied, which was in the nearby hamlet of la Maisonnette, was demolished in 1994 by the farmer on whose ground it stood and no trace of it now remains.)

Continue along the road to the outskirts of Flaucourt.

In a field to the right is a brick shelter with the clear plaque, *'Zur Ehre der Fur Kaiser ond* [sic] *Reich Gefallen Sohne Deutschlands'* ('To the sons of Germany fallen for Kaiser and for State').

Originally this was a **German cemetery**, and until the mid-1970s metal name plaques were still in place on the remains of wooden crosses in a semi-circle round the shelter. This rare German memorial has withstood

Extra Visit continued

the fate of many other wartime German monuments that were often destroyed by resentful civilians returning to their destroyed villages after the war or dismantled by farmers whose ploughing they impeded.

Continue to the crossroads and turn right. Continue through the village, noticing the remarkable painted Poilu (see page 266) by the Mairie on the right and at the junction with the D1 turn right. Continue to the French cemetery on the right.

Biaches French National Cemetery contains 1,362 graves, of which 322 are in two mass graves. It was completely renovated in 1974.

Return to the N17 and rejoin Itinerary Four.

French Colonial Memorial and grave of Marcel Brocheriou, Biaches

French 7th Battalion Chasseurs Alpins and 9th Regiment graves, Biaches Local Cemetery

German Wartime Cemetery, Flaucourt

Continue into Péronne, crossing the Canal du Nord and the Somme and follow signs to the town centre. Turn left following signs to the Historial and park in front of it.

• *Péronne/8.7 miles (For Péronne and the Historial, see Approach One)*

Next to the *Historial* is a hall marked *'Salle Mac Orlan'*. It was named in honour of **Pierre Dumarchey**, born in Péronne on 26 February 1882. Dumarchey was educated at Orleans, then moved to Paris to pursue an artistic and literary life. He became friendly with Picasso and the fellow avant-garde poet (also playwright and critic) Wilhelm de Kostrowitzky, whose nom de plume was Guillaume Apollinaire. (Apollinaire served with the infantry in Champagne, was badly wounded in March 1916 and gassed, and died on 9 November 1918 of influenza in Paris.) Like Apollinaire, Dumarchey took a nom de plume – 'Mac Orlan'. After considerable travels he joined the French Foreign Legion – before the war broke out – and served on the Somme. In 1916 Mac Orlan was wounded at Cléry. One of his most famous war-time works was the poem *Chanson de la Route de Bapaume* ('Song of the Bapaume Road'). Like Charles Sorley's *All the Hills and Vales Around*, the poem hides a bitter message behind an apparently jolly marching song rhythm. After the war Mac Orlan wrote novels, one of which, *Quai des Brumes* ('Quay of Mists'), was made into a popular film.

Return to main road, turn left, passing the town hall on the left and turn left on to the N17, direction Bapaume/A26/Arras/Calais. Continue to Mont St Quentin.

This hill, on the right, 390ft high at its apogée, protected the northern approaches to Péronne. Here the Germans sited their heavy artillery and built strong entrenchments protected by thick barbed wire and chevaux-de-frise. The hill was riddled with underground galleries and huge, well-furnished shelters. Before their retreat to the Hindenburg Line in March 1917, the Germans mined these defence works and blocked the entrances to the underground tunnels, setting light to the wooden props and causing a fire that rumbled on for several days. They re-occupied the area in their March 1918 Offensive, and remained there until the night of 30 August, only to be surprised by the Australian 2nd Division 'bombers' who held the ground despite three fierce counter-attacks by the Prussian Guard the following day. Monash had achieved surprise by building several bridges over the Somme and using them to move his main force against the Hill rather than Péronne itself. As the troops were tired they were issued with rum to lift their spirits and at 0500 hours on 31 August the 17th and 20th Battalions of the 2nd Division charged directly at the hill 'yelling like a lot of bushrangers'. Peronne itself was taken on 2 September, the Australians winning four more VCs and suffering some 3,000 casualties in all.

Three **Australian VCs** won in the area on 1 September 1918 were: **Pte**

Robert Mactier, 23rd (Victoria) Bn, AIF, (buried in Hem Farm Cemetery (qv), Map N6, Itinerary Three); **Sgt Albert David Lowerson**, 21st (Victoria) Bn, AIF, (who survived until 1945); **Lt Edgar Thomas Towner, MC**, 2nd Bn, Aust MGC (who survived until 1972).

Stop at the memorial on the left.

• *Australian 2nd Division Memorial/RB/10.6 miles/10 minutes/Map 1/40a*

This fine figure of an Australian 'Digger' with bronze *bas relief* plaques of Australians in action on each side of the base, is post-World War II. The original memorial portrayed a Digger bayoneting a German eagle and was objected to and destroyed by the occupying German soldiers in 1940. There is a model of it in the Villers Bretonneux Franco-Australian Museum (qv). The French and Australian flags fly to each side of the statue. Behind the memorial is a **Ross Bastiaan** bronze bas relief plaque unveiled by Senator John Faulkner, Australian Minister for Veterans' Affairs, on 3 September 1993. The 2nd Division attack would have been from left to right uphill.

Continue, crossing the Canal du Nord, some 2 miles and turn left on the D149 to Cléry. Continue to the cross on the right at the end of a copse.

• *Memorial to Gustave Fuméry & 132nd Infantry Regiment/13.3 miles/5 minutes/Map 1/40c*

This cross, renovated by *Souvenir Français*, commemorates **Gustave Fuméry**, aged 20, and 150 comrades of the French 132nd RI, killed here on 4 October 1916 and buried the same day.

Turn round and return to the N17. Cross the main road to the rough track straight ahead and drive or walk, depending on the state of the track, to the memorial ahead.

• *Memorial to Aspirant Louis Calle, 106th Infantry Regiment/14.1 miles/10 minutes/Map 1/40b*

This cross commemorates **Officer Cadet Louis Philippe Calle** of the 106th RI who, 'ardent and brave' fell near Bouchavesnes (up ahead) carrying out a perilous mission with remarkable courage and *sang-froid* for which he volunteered, on 25 September 1915. The Bouchavesnes war dead are also commemorated on the monument, several families obviously losing two or, in the case of the Melotte family, three members.

Return to the N17, turn right and continue downhill to the impressive monument on the left.

• *Marshal Foch Memorial, Bouchavesnes-Bergen/14.8 miles/5 minutes/Map 1/40d*

Bouchavesnes marks the furthest limit of the French advance during the Battle of the Somme. On 12 September 1916, Messimy, the former Minister of War, in command of the Light Infantry Brigade, finally took the village. After the war, a francophile Norwegian industrialist called Wallem Haackon asked Marshal Foch what in his opinion was for the French the most significant battle of the Somme offensive. Without hesitation, Foch named Bouchavesnes. Thus it was that Haackon financed the fine statue of Foch here and the village added the name of Bergen, Haackon's birthplace, to its own. The monument commemorates the taking of Bouchavesnes by French forces on 12 September 1916 and by British forces on 1 September 1918, Marshal Foch then being Commandant in Chief of the Allied Armies.

Continue on the N17 to Rancourt. At the edge of the village follow the signs left to the German Cemetery.

• *German Cemetery, Rancourt/15.8 miles/10 minutes/Map 1/41*

This cemetery contains 11,422 burials, of which 7,492 lie in a mass grave. The crosses here are of grey stone, unlike the other Somme German cemeteries which have black metal crosses.

Return to the N17 and continue to the British Cemetery to the left.

• *Rancourt Military CWGC Cemetery/16.3 miles/5 minutes/Map 1/42*

This small cemetery (ninety-two graves) reflects the fact that the village was taken by the 47th (London) Division – fifty-seven of the graves are of the Division – on 1 September 1918. It was begun by units of the Guards Division in winter 1916.

Cross the road to the chapel and cemetery.

• *Souvenir Français Chapel & Museum/16.3 miles/20 minutes/Map 1/43*

There is a **CGS/H Signboard** beside the chapel which was raised as a result of private initiative by the distinguished local du Bos family as a memorial to their son, **Lt Jean du Bos**, *Chevalier de la Légion d'Honneur* and *Croix de Guerre*, age 26, killed on 25 September 1916, and to his comrades of the 94th RI. The maintenance of the monument was undertaken by *Souvenir Français* in 1937. There is a memorial to Jean on the floor as one enters and behind is a photograph of the young man, and a short history of his action. Above the archway of the entrance is an inscription describing how his mother had the idea of erecting the memorial chapel and how his father devoted the last years of his life to realizing her dream. The chapel contains many memorials and plaques which make fascinating reading. One reads (in translation):

> "To the memory of **Josselin de Rohan-Chabot, Duke of Rohan**, Member of Parliament for the Morbihan, Capt in the 4th Bn of Chasseurs à Pied, *Chevalier de la Légion d'Honneur*, decorated with the *Croix de Guerre* and the Medal of China, *Mort pour la France* 13 July 1916 at Hardécourt-au-Bois. A marvellous soldier, loved by all for his profound disregard of

Australian 2nd Division Memorial, Mont St Quentin

General Foch statue, Bouchavesnes-Bergen

Souvenir Français Chapel, Rancourt

British plaques in Rancourt Chapel

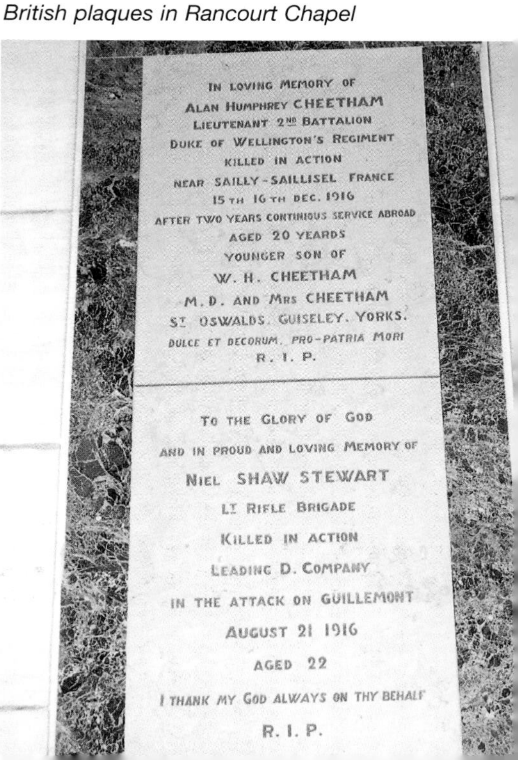

danger, his knightly courage, his beautiful qualities as leader of men, a cavalry officer who transferred to the 4th Bn the Chasseurs à Pied, decorated with the *Légion of Honour* for his magnificent conduct during the first attacks on Verdun when he was wounded. He had only just returned to the front when he was mortally hit on 13 July, a few metres from the German trenches, where he was carrying out an extremely perilous recce for an operation that he was asked to lead."

The body of the duke (among his ancestors was one of Louis XIII's most famous generals) was returned to the family château at Josselin in the Morbihan and buried in the crypt of the chapel. His death was mourned by his friend, Jean Cocteau (see Itinerary Three). To the left of the doorway in the left wall are two British plaques. One is to **Lt Niel Shaw Stewart** of the Rifle Brigade who was killed leading 'C' company in the attack on Guillemont on 21 August, age 22. He is buried in Delville Wood CWGC Cemetery. The other is to **Lt Alan Humphrey Cheetham**, of the 2nd Bn, Duke of Wellingtons, age 20 who was killed at Sailly-Saillisel on the night of 15th/16th December 1916.

Side Chapel, Rancourt

Memorial stained glass windows in the Rancourt Chapel

He is commemorated on the Thiépval Memorial. The locked door leads to a small museum, many of whose exhibits are from local private collections, with items as diverse as the medical instruments that were presented by the Brooklyn Post No 2 Jewish War Vets of the US on 4 July 1918, to a model of the 'Long Max' gun from Laon and models of World War II rocket launching pads in the district. The custodian lives in the house to the right of the chapel and he has keys (which work with a little persuasion) to the museum as well. A perspex-fronted side chapel contains the private memorials that were placed on the French graves in the adjoining cemetery before it was standardized in 1988 (many of them complete with photographs of the soldier), and more plaques including some British ones.

Over the past few years the exhibits in the museum and the chapel have been somewhat depleted.

Walk to the cemetery.

• *French National Cemetery, Rancourt/16.3 miles/10 minutes/Map 1/44*

This is the largest French cemetery on the Somme, with 8,566 burials, of which 3,240 are in four ossuaries. It is a concentration cemetery from all the surrounding battlefields and testifies to the sacrifice of the French from September to November 1916 in the region. It ranks in emotional importance as a focal point of remembrance to the French as do the Thiépval Memorial and Tyne Cot Cemetery in the Ypres Salient to the British. Because of the closeness of the three different nationality cemeteries here, joint Anglo-French-German ceremonies are held on important anniversaries. It also affords an opportunity to compare and contrast the different styles of remembrance of the three nationalities.

Continue into the village.

The Hôtel Prieuré, part of the same group as the Royal Picardie at Albert and La Paix at Bapaume, is on the right, ☎ (03) 22 85 04 43. It has a 'restaurant gastronomique' and makes a convenient base.

Continue on the N17 to the British cemetery to the left on the outskirts of Sailly-Saillisel.

• *Sailly-Saillisel British Cemetery/17.8 miles/5 minutes/Map 1/44a*

Sailly-Saillisel was the scene of desperate fighting on 28 August 1914, when the French Reserves were desperately trying to stop the German rush *'nach Paris'*. The consequences were terrible for the French – see le Transloy below.

The village was captured by the French in 1916 and remained in Allied hands until the German Offensive of March 1918, when it fell on the 24th. It was retaken by the 18th and 38th (Welsh) Division on 1 September 1918. The cemetery records 559 UK, 12 Australian, 7 Newfoundland and 185 unknown burials and 8 Special Memorials. It was made after the Armistice by the concentration of small graveyards, including 'Charing Cross' and 'Aldershot'. After the war the London connection was continued. St Marylebone paid for the *'Salle des Fêtes'* in the rebuilt village.

Continue on the N17/N37 to le Transloy and turn left at the T junction with the D19, following signs to the French 'Monument aux 800 Morts'. Drive to the French Poilu in the village.

• *War Memorial, Le Transloy/21.2 miles/5 minutes*

This commemorates victims from the Franco-Prussian War of 1870-1 and cites the Order of the Day of 24 September 1920 which awards the village with the *Croix de Guerre* for suffering complete destruction in the bombardments, and for always showing dignity and courage in its afflictions under enemy domination. Of the long list of towns and villages thus honoured, many are on the Somme and nearby battlefields, notably Albert, Amiens, Arras, Assevillers, Authuille, Aveluy, Bapaume, Beaucourt, Beaumont-Hamel, Bouchavesnes, Bray, Chipilly, Combles, Contalmaison, Corbie, Courcelette, Dompierre, Doullens, Feuillières, Flaucourt, Flers, Fouilloy, Fricourt, Ginchy, Guillemont, Heilly, Hem-Monacu, Lihons, Mailly-Maillet, Mametz, Maricourt, Montauban, Mont St Quentin, Ovillers, Péronne, Pozières, Proyart, Sailly-Saillisel, Suzanne, Thiépval, Vermandovillers and Villers Bretonneux.

The ridge upon which le Transloy sits was the target of a series of attacks during October 1916 which were opened by 56th Division of XIV Corps on 7 October. Heavy rain turned the fields into liquid mud and the Corps Commander, Lord Cavan, questioned whether the continuous effort was worth the loss in men. French forces were attacking alongside to the south and the British efforts may have been part of the C-in-C's 'co-operation policy'. In any event, the ridge was not taken.

Continue to the cemetery at the edge of the village.

• *Monument to 800 Dead of 28 August 1914/21.6 miles/15 minutes*

There are several memorials inside the gate beside the local *cimetière communal*. On the wall to the left are individual plaques and photographs and there are two major monuments – one a tall column to the 700 braves who fell on 28 August and 26 September 1914, erected by their families (with a plaque on the back saying that the names of the missing are held in the archives in the *Mairie*), the other, a marble wall carrying the names of the missing 792 soldiers *'Morts Pour la France'* at le Transloy on 28 August and 26 September 1914 who rest here. Another stone on a mass grave commemorates ten officers who fell on those same dates and there are individual graves to **2nd Lt Emil Rabache** of the 338th RI from Limoges, 28 August 1914 age 23, *Croix de Guerre*, **2nd Lt Reservist Alfred Grouzillard**, 28 June 1879-28 August 1914 , *Chevalier de la Légion d'Honneur*; a cross to **Capt Anatole Thepernier**, 26th RIT, 26 September 1914 and the tomb of sixteen other named NCOs and soldiers of 26 September.

Individual plaques to two of the '800 morts', le Transloy Cemetery

Memorial Column, Le Transloy

These reminders of this massive slaughter are extremely moving. Even locally, the full facts are little known today. The story is, however, fully documented in a detailed study of the tragic episode called *28 August 1914. Les Combats de le Transloy, Rocquigny, Sailly-Saillisel*, by Maurice Pasquet, grandson of one of the participants, who had been brought up on stories of the massacre told by his widowed grandmother. He uses regimental histories, diaries and personal accounts by survivors to piece together what happened. The story starts at Mons. The British formed the left-hand end of the French line. On 23 August 1914 they briefly held Von Kluck's right wing at Mons and began a three-day withdrawal to le Cateau. Gen Joffre, seeing that his left wing was now exposed, rallied forces to fill the gap left by the British and on 24/25 August, untried French reservists of the 61st and 62nd Divisions were rushed to Arras by train. Their orders were to extend the British line to the west.

Meanwhile the British made a brief stand at le Cateau on 26 August and then began their long retreat to the Marne. Von Kluck declined to follow the British, and sent Von Linsingen's 2nd Army Corps west to Cambrai (where they arrived in the area of Marcoing, which would feature in the 1917 battle) on 26/27 August. The French, now unable to contact the retreating BEF, sat astride Bapaume – the 61st Div to the west, the 62nd Div to the east.

At this point the subsequent actions can be more easily followed by referring to the Michelin map 236, folds 26 and 27.

On 27 August 1914 the German forces, spearheaded by the 49th and 149th Infantry Regiments, headed south-west, roughly along the line of the A2-E19 motorway from Cambrai and reached Sailly-Saillisel (where the motorway crosses the N13). En route they had flank engagements with the French 62nd Inf Div who were in the area between the A2-E19 and A1-E15 motorways south-east of Bapaume. Thus the Germans were south of the French divisions. That night there was fighting at Sailly-Saillisel and Von Kluck, anxious to maintain his advance, yet keen to isolate the French, ordered that the 49th and 149th should manoeuvre to prevent the French from crossing the Somme (which they were vainly and tardily attempting to do in order to block the Germans in their rush *'nach Paris'*). The following morning, in thick fog, the

Memorial to XIV Reserve Korps, German Cem, Villers au Flos

two German regiments moved north along the line of the N17 at le Transloy and hit the flank of the unsuspecting 338th Regt of 123rd Bde of 62nd Div coming, in marching formation, from the north-east in what they thought was pursuit of the Germans. The 338th Regt suffered heavy casualties from the encounter – all its officers were killed or wounded – and the accompanying 278th Regiment, despite attempting to march around the Germans to the north, was also cut down. By 1000 hours the French were falling back to Arras, leaving behind some 1,200 prisoners and a battlefield littered with materiel – much of which the Germans collected. Von Kluck, however, was not pleased with what would seem to be an overwhelming victory. His orders for the 28th had been 'to cross the Somme between Corbie and Nesle'. The French, despite their horrendous casualties, had delayed the Germans by as much as the British had done at Mons and le Cateau.

At the end of the day on 28 August, the normally peaceful fields around le Transloy looked like a vision from the Apocalypse, much as the battlefield of Waterloo had looked on the night of 15 June 1815. It had been a scorchingly hot day and the wounded suffered on the battlefield, lying amongst their dead comrades. There are varied reports of the victors' treatment of the victims. In some places the Germans gave water, basic first aid and an attempt at some shelter from the sun. In others the wounded were put out of their misery – and not for humane reasons. The shocked inhabitants of the village rallied. Farmers brought up their vehicles and carts to move the wounded to improvised hospitals. In the absence of any professional medical help, the women and girls became caring nurses. The next day motor ambulances arrived from Arras and the evacuation of the wounded was completed by nightfall. *'Après les blessés, les morts'*, was the villagers' priority. Their wounded in safe hands, on the third day after the battle they set out to pick up the dead who lay on the plain between Rocquigny, Sailly-Saillisel and Morval. Again with their farm carts and vehicles, they brought the bodies, by now in an advanced state of decomposition because of the heat, to the small cemetery at le Transloy and gently searched for identification. Organized by the curé, M. Blasart, wallets, identification discs and papers, photographs of loved ones, personal possessions – all were lovingly tied up in knotted handkerchiefs and labelled with a name. Then a huge ditch, 10 metres long and 4 metres wide was dug and the bodies were reverently laid, side by side *'comme à la parade'*. Ten officers were buried in a nearby mass grave.

The inhabitants were soon evacuated, and when they were allowed to return in 1919 to find their village – and the cemetery – completely destroyed, the mayor, M. Malet, received a flood of letters from relatives of the dead, wanting to know details of their burial. By 1920, the villagers had found the site of the mass grave and the first landscaping took place, so that on 5 September 1920 relatives and dignitaries were able to join in a ceremony of commemoration. A subscription was raised for a suitable monument and on 25 September 1921 it was inaugurated. From then on a ceremony was held annually on the 3rd Sunday of September and in 1927 marble panels, inscribed with the names of the 800 'braves', was unveiled.

Return to the N17/37. Continue to the junction with the D11 in Beaulencourt. Turn right to the village and then left, following signs along a small meandering road, to the German Cemetery. It is approached down a long brick path.

• *German Cemetery & XIV Reserve Korps Memorial, Villers au Flos/24.7 miles/10 minutes/Map 1/45*

The cemetery contains 2,449 burials under black crosses, but with only two, rather than the usual four, men marked on each. Most of the burials are of July 1916. At the back of the cemetery is a high stone memorial tower to the XIV Reserve Korps, 1914-18 which was orignally in the cemetery at Bapaume. The X1Vth held this area during the 1916 battles (see the Holts' map)

Return to the junction with the N17/37 and continue the Itinerary. Go straight over and continue to Bapaume.

• *Bapaume/28.3 miles*

End of Itinerary Four

OR

Extra Visit to Bullecourt and the Australian/British 1917 Actions: Museum (Map 1/46), Slouch Hat Memorial (Map Side 1/47), Digger Memorial Park (Map 1/48), Memorial to the Missing (Map 1/49).

Round trip: 17 miles. Approximate time: 60 minutes.

From Bapaume take the D956.

To a first approximation the German Hindenburg Line defences ran parallel to your route and some 500m to your left, gradually moving towards you until you reach the site of the Digger Memorial where the Line crossed your road. Thus, in broad terms, the Australian and British attacks of 1917, part of the Battle of Arras in which the Canadians were engaged at Vimy Ridge (qv), were coming from your right during this visit.

Continue into Bullecourt. On the left hand side at No I rue d'Arras is

The Private Museum of Monsieur Letaille (Map Side 1/46). To make a visit it is vital to **telephone in advance: (03) 21 48 92 46**. This wonderful collection contains many personal possessions (including of Sergeant Jack White, whose remains were found near Bullecourt and reburied in October 1995 (qv)) and fascinating accounts, e.g. of **Captain Albert Jacka**, who won his **VC** (the first to be awarded to a Commonwealth soldier) as a Lance-Corporal in May 1915 at Courtney's Post in Gallipoli. In a large barn there

Private Museum, Bullecourt

Extra Visit continued

are collections of entrenching tools, ammunition boxes etc. M. Letaille also conducts tours around the Bullecourt battlefield. Leaflets describing the recommended route are available here or from the Town Hall.

Turn left and stop near the Town Hall. Opposite is

The Slouch Hat Memorial (Map 1/47), a felt Digger's hat which has been bronzed, in *'Square du Souvenir Français'*. The brick base bears the badges of the 1st, 2nd, 4th and 5th AIF, the 58th (London) Division, the 62nd (W Riding) Division and the 7th Division.

'Slouch Hat' Memorial, Bullecourt

'Digger' Memorial, Bullecourt with detail below

Memorial to 2,423 Missing Australians, Bullecourt

The first attempt to seize Bullecourt began on 11 April in driving snow when two brigades of the 4th Australian Division, supposedly led by twelve tanks, set out to take the village and its neighbour, Riencourt. Unfortunately the tanks failed – nine had direct hits and the others had mechanical problems. To compound the difficulties the artillery support was insufficient, due to ammunition shortage and lack of information about the

THE BULLECOURT DIGGER

THE BULLECOURT DIGGER IS THE WORK OF AUSTRALIAN SCULPTOR PETER CORLETT AND MERIDIAN SCULPTURE FOUNDRY OF MELBOURNE, AUSTRALIA. IT WAS COMMISSIONED BY THE OFFICE OF AUSTRALIAN WAR GRAVES IN AUGUST 1992, FLOWN TO THE UNITED KINGDOM BY THE ROYAL AUSTRALIAN AIR FORCE AND PLACED ON THE AIF MEMORIAL AT BULLECOURT BY THE COMMONWEALTH WAR GRAVES COMMISSION (FRANCE OFFICE). IT WAS UNVEILED ON ANZAC DAY 25 APRIL 1993 BY HIS EXCELLENCY MR. KIM JONES AUSTRALIAN AMBASSADOR TO FRANCE AND M. JEAN LETAILLE MAYOR OF BULLECOURT.

THE SCULPTURE PORTRAYS AN AUSTRALIAN SOLDIER WEARING THE UNIFORM AND EQUIPMENT CARRIED BY THE AIF AT THE BATTLES OF BULLECOURT. WHILE THE SCULPTURE IS OTHERWISE AUTHENTIC IN DETAIL, THE FIGURE BEARS THE COLOUR-PATCH INSIGNIA OF ALL FOUR AUSTRALIAN INFANTRY DIVISIONS (FIRST, SECOND, FOURTH AND FIFTH) THAT WERE PRESENT AT EITHER FIRST BULLECOURT 10-11 APRIL 1917, OR SECOND BULLECOURT 3-17 MAY 1917.

REFLECTING THE CHARACTERISTICS FOR WHICH THE AUSTRALIAN SOLDIER OF THE FIRST WORLD WAR WAS BEST KNOWN, THE BULLECOURT DIGGER IS STURDY, ARCADIAN, AUDACIOUS AND RESOLUTE. IMPORTANTLY, AS WELL, THE SCULPTURE EXPRESSES THE HOPE THAT THE DEEDS OF AUSTRALIANS AT BULLECOURT IN APRIL/MAY 1917 WOULD BE OF ENDURING RELEVANCE AND INSPIRATION TO THIS AND FUTURE GENERATIONS.

Extra Visit continued

movements of the forward troops – some 17th Lancers coming up to support came under 'friendly fire'. Despite valiant and determined efforts by the Australians they were unable to consolidate the small gains that they had made and fell back in confusion, though for a brief period they had held one small part of the Hindenburg Line without a supporting barrage. One observer called the 11th "a day of unrelieved disaster": Australian losses were some 3,000.

Continue and fork right on the rue des Australiens following the green CWGC sign to the memorial park on the right.

Digger's Memorial Park (Map 1/48). To the left is a bench with the plaque SEGPA Marquion 1997 and there is a **Ross Bastiaan bronze memorial plaque**. The fine bronze statue is sacred to the memory of 10,000 members of the AIF who were killed and wounded in the two battles of Bullecourt, April, May 1917 and to the Australian dead and their comrades in arms who lie here forever in the soil of France. It was dedicated on ANZAC Day 1992, the 75th Anniversary. On the reverse the sculptor Peter Corlett explains how he has depicted 'the characteristics for which the Australians are known – sturdy, arcadian, audacious, resolute' and that the uniform is authentic.

The second attempt to take Bullecourt began on 3 May and formed part of an overall assault on a front of some 15 miles by 14 divisions, with the town at the right flank. Although the attack had been carefully rehearsed it was, like the first attempt, too complicated. Supporting artillery reduced Bullecourt to ruins and the Australian 2nd Division led off the attack (this time without tanks) later being joined by the 1st and 5th Divisions. The 5th Brigade on the right failed to make any impression, while to its left the 6th Brigade made gains that it resolutely held against fierce counter-attacks by the German 27th Wurtemberg Division. Eventually, on 17 May, the last remnants of Bullecourt fell, a progressive achievement involving troops and tanks of the British 7th, 58th and 62nd Divisions. The Australians lost 7,000 men during the fighting and won two **VCs: Corporal G.J. Howell** (who survived until 1964) **and Lieutenant R.V. Moon** (who survived until 1986).

Continue up the road to the monument in the bank on the left.

Memorial to 2,423 Australians, missing with no known grave (Map 1/49). This cross, with the word 'Remember' was erected in 1982. It is on the Second German Line, on 'Diagonal Road'. On the side of the base are small personal plaques.

Up ahead at the small crossroads where you have to go to turn round was the centre of the fighting by 6th Brigade in May.

Return to the Town Hall, park and, if desired, follow the other points on the recommended route by foot. Return to Bapaume.

The Battles of 1918 on the Somme

Historical Introduction

British visitors to the battlefields covered by this book usually say that they are visiting 'The Somme'. By that most mean that they are visiting the areas associated with the great British offensive of 1916 and assume that the word 'Somme' refers to the river of that name. It does not. It refers to the 'County' or *Département*. The river around which most of the 1916 action took place was the Ancre (see the Holt's Map 2 from square M to square E).

However, in 1918 the Allied counter-offensive to the 'Kaiser's Battle' did drive astride the Somme river and involved all nationalities – British, French, Australians, Canadians, Americans... Some of the memorials visited in Itineraries One to Four of this book already relate to that 1918 action, but in previous editions we had not devoted a specific section to it, especially to the parts played by the Americans, the Australians, the Canadians and the French, though of course where they were involved as part of an allied operation they have been mentioned.

It is, perhaps, little realised that the *Département* of the Somme extends south of Amiens to include Montdidier and, therefore, that the American attack at Cantigny was 'on the Somme'. The Allied Counter-Offensive along the River Somme in 1918, which led to Australian actions at le Hamel and around Mont St Quentin (which is actually in the *Département* of Pas de Calais), may be said to have been 'on the Somme'. When the German March offensive pushed the British forces back towards Amiens and Montdidier, French forces were brought up to help so that they too were 'on the Somme'.

We have therefore decided to extend the coverage of this guide-book to 'the Somme' to include brief summaries of the 1918 actions of the **Americans at Cantigny**, the **Australians at Mont St Quentin** and the involvement of **Canadian and French forces** commemorated along the routes. Thus the coverage of the **Holts' Map** which accompanies this volume has also been enlarged to include these new elements. We hope that this will encourage many visitors to extend their interest beyond 1916 and, it may come as a surprise to many, to find out that Canadian cavalry made a charge 'on the Somme' in which a VC was won.

The additional tour route given below, which traces the 1918 actions south of the Somme river towards Montdidier, follows very closely the final German line of 5 April 1918 (see Map 3), the day on which the German advance reached its peak.

The Americans and The French

America

The United States entered the First World War on 6 April 1917. Relations between Germany and America had been strained by the sinking of the *Lusitania* on 7 May 1915, when over 120 Americans died and, by indiscriminate German use of submarines against unarmed merchant shipping. Things were brought to a head by the publication of the 'Zimmerman Telegram'. Supposedly sent from the German Embassy in Washington to the German Embassy in Mexico, it proposed, that, in the event of war between America and Germany, an alliance be formed with Mexico and that Mexico should be allowed to 'reconquer her lost territory in Texas, New Mexico and Arizona'. Feelings in America ran high against Germany, despite theories that the telegram was a fake engineered by British Intelligence, and finally President Wilson declared war.

On 26 May 1917 Major General John J. Pershing was appointed to command the American Expeditionary Force and he landed at Boulogne on 13 June 1917 with a small advance party. Two weeks later elements of the First Division ('The Big Red One') began to land at St Nazaire. (After the war a splendid memorial was erected to commemorate the Division's arrival but it was destroyed by the Germans in the Second World War. A full size replica was erected in 1989.)

America had no experience of the 'new' war that was being fought in Europe and units were distributed amongst Allied formations in order to gain experience. (e.g. see *Carey's Force*). The first American deaths occurred at Bathlemont (south-east of Metz) on 3 November 1917 when three men serving with the French were killed. However, it remained a key part of American policy that their forces should operate as a whole, as an 'American' force.

In March and April 1918 the German attacks generally known as the 'Kaiser's Offensive' hammered against much of the Western Front with large gains along a line from Péronne to Montdidier (see Holts' Map and in-text Map page 247). Pershing put all American troops under General Foch in order to help to counter the German threat and the American First Division entered the front west of Montdidier, the first time that a complete American division had been so used. Given the task of taking the high ground around Cantigny the Division's 28th Infantry attacked at 0645 on 28 May 1918 taking the town that day and never losing it, despite heavy German counter-attacks over the next two days. The American action was acclaimed as a great success and its significance is remembered by two memorials at Cantigny – one commemorating the National significance of the event and the other remembering the First Division (see 1918 Itinerary below).

France

The Kaiser's Battle opened early on the morning of 21 March 1918 and in the south was directed along a rough line from Péronne to Amiens against General

Byng's 3rd Army and General Gough's 5th Army. Both British Armies fell back, the 5th in the south suffering particularly badly. As the German drive towards Montdidier developed during the day General Pétain gave orders that French troops should support the British right and forces under General Humbert, part of General Fayolle's Army Group (he had commanded the French 6th Army that attacked south of the Somme on 1 July 1916), were rushed forward in lorries, joining the battle the following day.

The German advances continued and on 26 March at Doullens (see Approach Two) all Allied forces were placed under the command of General Foch, superseding Pétain. Two days later General Pershing told Foch, '...all we have is yours'. On 27 March Montdidier fell but the German progress had been stalling as French resistance south of the Somme gathered pace and now, almost forty miles from their supply bases and exhausted, the Germans stopped to gather breath.

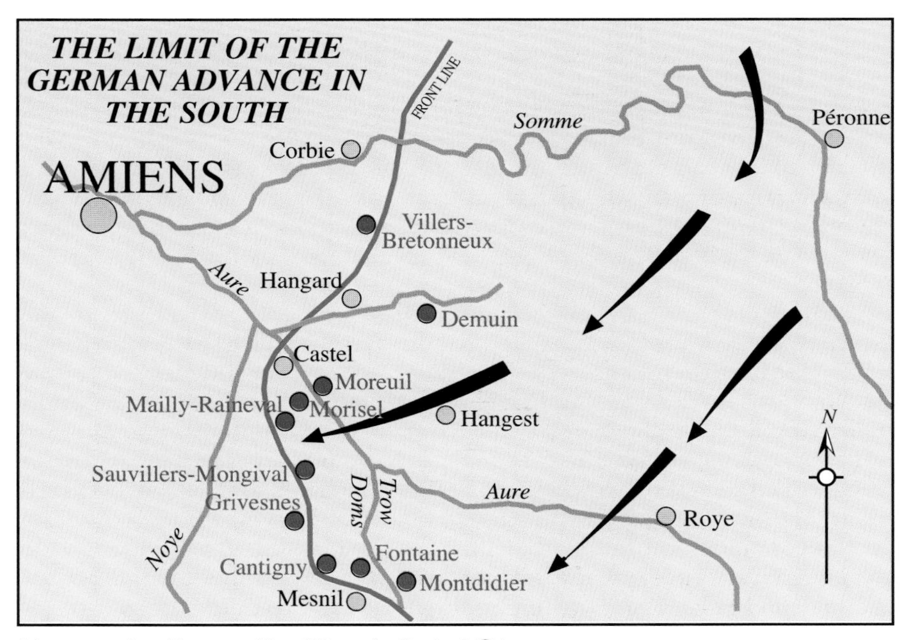

Map covering Itinerary Five (Stops indicated ●)

ITINERARY FIVE

THE AMERICAN, CANADIAN AND FRENCH 1918 SECTOR

The tour starts at Villers Bretonneux, continues to Montdidier via Crucifix Corner (Map 3/1), Demuin (Map 3/2 & Toronto (Map 3/3) CWGC Cems; French 31st Corps Mem (Map 3/4); Capt Aubry Mem (Map 3/5); Morisel Ger Cem (Map 3/6); French Mems, Auvillers Mongival (Map 3/10/11); Cantigny US Mems (Map 3/13/14); French Mems, Fontaine-sous-Montididier (Map 3/15/16); 19th Div Mem (Map 3/17), return to V' Bretonneux.
Round trip 39 miles. Approximate time: 2½ hours

Take the D23 south from Villers Bretonneux. After 1.4 miles Crucifix Corner CWGC Cemetery is signed to the right.

During this itinerary it is broadly accurate to say that German attacks came from your left and Allied responses from your right.

Crucifix Corner became renowned in April 1918 when the German advance on Amiens was halted. The village was recaptured by the Australian 4th and 5th Divisions with units of the 8th and 18th Divisions. The cemetery was begun by the Canadian Corps in August 1918. The original plot contained 90 graves and French troops were also buried here. After the Armistice it was greatly enlarged and there are now over 650 burials, including 158 known UK, 236 known Australians and 70 known Canadians. The French, Americans and Germans originally buried here have since been moved. The ruined crucifix which gave the area its name is still near the entrance.

At 3.2 miles a cemetery, easily missed, is passed on the right.

Demuin British CWGC Cemetery. The village of Demuin was taken by the Germans on 29 March and changed hands several times in 1918 until it was finally recaptured by the 58th Canadian Battalion in August, when the cemetery was made by the 3rd Canadian Battalion. It contains 40 WW1 burials (mostly from the 13th and 16th Can Inf from 8 August) and two WW2.

In this area the French forces of General Debeney's Army initially took over from the British, the two forces often co-operating at tactical level with British tanks aiding French infantry. German attacks, coming from your left, continued until August but these were not advances, these were savage struggles for the small villages and hilltops between here and Montdidier.

Almost immediately after another cemetery is signed to the left.

Toronto CWGC Cemetery. This cemetery was begun by 3rd Canadaian Battalion, the Toronto Regiment in August 1918. There are now 70 identified Canadians and four unknown and five UK known and 17 Unknown and one Australian.

Continue to the large memorial to the left at the junction with the D28.

French 31st Army Corps Memorial. The impressive memorial displays the date 8 August 1918, and lists the 64th and 65th Infantry Divisions, the 108th RAL and the 31st Aviation. The land on which it was erected was the gift of Monsieur le Comte de Rouge in 1926 and it was raised by contributions from the officers and men of the Corps, commanded by General Toulorge. The legend translates, 'Here on 8 August 1918 the Corps broke the German lines, chased the enemy as far as Houdroy where, on 7 November, the German plenipotentiaries negotiated the Armistice'. A plaque on the wall below the obelisk notes that the monument was destroyed by 'the soldiers of Hitler' in 1940 and rebuilt by *Souvenir Français* in 1955.

The road down which you have just driven was bitterly contested ground, with features and high ground changing hands sometimes several times in a day. On 26 March two French divisions brought up by lorry from the south (i.e. they came towards you) were driven back to Moreuil, the village ahead, by the fierceness of the German attack. Another division, the 163rd, arrived just in time to meet a two-division attack on the night of 29 March but could not stop the enemy from taking Moreuil. Attack and counter-attack continued around the villages that you will pass through on the route ahead, sometimes involving a mixture of French and British forces.

On 8 August, the first day of the British Picardy counter-offensive, 66th Division of General Toulorge's 31st Corps re-took Moreuil. Other divisions listed on the memorial, the 37th and the 42nd, cleared the areas to the east up the D28 towards Mezières. It was the start of the 'Hundred Days' that led to final victory.

Continue to the sharp turn to the left at 7.7 miles signed (visible once you have turned!) to Le Plessier Rozainvillers. Continue to the far end of a small wood that straddles the road and immediately up a track to the left is

Memorial to Capitaine Aviateur Aubry, Chasseurs à Pied, Squadron C43, who was killed here, gloriously, on 26 March 1915. It is sadly neglected.

Turn round, return to the main road and turn left. Continue into the main square of Moreuil.

In it is an exuberant Art Deco church, a splendid *Poilu* memorial and a highly recommended patisserie.

When the Germans took the village on 29/30 March, after struggles that had seen it change hands several times, it seemed possible that a major breakthrough could follow, unless the high ground to the north and west of the village could be held. Barely 2 miles to the north, in the area of the village of Castel (see Map page 247), was the Canadian Cavalry Brigade under General Jack Seely. After consultation with the French, Seely galloped his Brigade into action. The Royal Canadian Dragoons heading the charge suffered heavy casualties and Seely followed them up with Lord Strathcona's Horse, impressing upon the leading squadron leader, **Lieutenant G. M. Flowerdew**, the urgency of the situation. Flowerdew charged the enemy, his troopers killing many with the sword and, despite losing some 70% of his force, stayed the German advance, an achievement for which he was awarded the **VC**. Sadly he died from his wounds and is buried in Namps-au-Val British Cemetery some 16 kms south west of Amiens. In Flowerdew's squadron was **Lieutenant F. M. Harvey VC** who had won his award almost exactly one year to the day earlier at Guyencourt. Harvey survived the war and went on to become a Brigadier

Follow the signs to Ailly on the D920 to a cemetery on the left

Monument to French 31st Army Corps, with detail

Memorial to Capt Aviator Aubry, le Plessier Rozainvillers

German Cem, Morisel

Machine-gunner Poilu Memorial, Sauvillers-Mongival

American Memorial, Cantigny

German Cemetery, Morisel. This forlorn cemetery with a large black cross in the centre contains 2,640 burials of 1918. In the top right hand corner is a mass grave. The town was taken by the Germans on 4 April and liberated on 8 August.

Continue and turn left signed Mailly Raineval on the D14 to the local cemetery on the right just before the village sign.

On the wall by the gate is a metal **Anchor in Memoriam May/June 1940 4D.I.C.** which matches the anchor at le Hamel (Itinerary Three).

Turn left on the D14E to Sauvillers Mongival. Continue to the memorial on the left.

It is to **Volonteer Sous-Lieutenant Jean de Séganville, Sergeant René Antoine and Léon Hochet of the 29th Bn de Chasseurs.**

The men commemorated here of the 29th Chasseurs part of 36 Corps, died on 4 April 1918 when the Germans, attacking from the west (i.e. from the other side of the road to the memorial), took a large stretch of the French line including Mailly-Raineval, Morisel and as far north as Castel.

Continue towards the village passing the local cemetery with a green CWGC sign on the wall.

In it are the graves from 15 April 1943 of **Sergeants Buxton, McLean and Hancock and Sqn Ldr Latimer DFC**

Monument to the US 1st Division (the Big Red 1), Cantigny

and Lt Muttrie RNVR of HMS *Daedalus*. Mailly-Raineval. The village itself was taken by the Germans on 4 April and liberated on 23 July.

Continue to Sauvillers-Mongival.

The village was retaken from the Germans together with Mailly-Raineval, through which you have just passed, and Aubvillers a village about 2 Kms ahead. It was a considerable success for the French who took over 1,800 prisoners and some 300 machine guns.

Turn left signed Grivesnes.

On the right is the local war memorial, the statue of a determined **machine-gunner *Poilu***. On the church wall behind is a memorial to the **Men of the 87th RI** who fell in July 1918 in the liberation of the village, erected in 1959.

Continue to the right fork to Grivesnes on the D84.

On the right is a large **memorial to the 325th and 125th RI, 1918**.

Enter Grivesnes.

German attacks began here from the direction of Malpart to the east (i.e. your left) on 30 March, five unsuccessful assaults being made on that day alone. The next day the 1st Division of Prussian Guards took the town, apart from the Château where the Commanding Officer of the 350th RI defending the town held out with a few men. Writing a message asking for help and ending it with the words, 'I am in the castle and shall hold until death,' he sent a cyclist off to seek help. Extraordinarily the man got through the German lines, support arrived including two armoured cars, and after house to house fighting the town was cleared. Further attacks followed by the Guard on 1, 3 and 5 April but stubborn resistance by the 67th RI and 25th Chasseurs held the line.

Continue and turn left on the D26 on rue de 31 mars 1918. Enter Cantigny and stop by the church.

In front of it is a ***Conseil Régional de Picardie* signboard** describing the Memorial opposite with a picture of the unveiling. It describes how on 28 May 1918 (when the Germans were re-occupying the Chemin des Dames and retaking Soissons) the Americans launched their first large-scale operation on the Western Front to free this village. Under the French Xth Corps of French General Marie Eugene Debeney's 1st Army, the 28th Inf Regt of the American 1st Division (known as 'The Big Red 1') were told that the village (which had twice been unsuccessfully attacked by the French) had to be retaken at all costs. The 28th had been chosen as the assault force largely on the reputation of its commander Colonel Hanson E. Ely, said to be 'as hard boiled as a picnic egg.'

The assault was carefully prepared and was launched at 0645, backed by 32mm guns, Stokes mortars, tanks and flamethrowers, though according to some records none of the twelve French tanks allocated in support actually made it into Cantigny. The Americans, easily recognised by their distinctive uniforms, attacked against heavy machine gun and artillery fire. They took 225 prisoners (including five officers) 16 machine guns, 2 mortars and 500 rifles. The village had been evacuated, save for an ancient lady who insisted on remaining. The Germans responded with intensity after losing 600 dead and

400 wounded, shelling the village for 72 relentless hours. But the Big Red 1, whose motto was 'No mission too difficult, no sacrifice too great: duty first', did not concede one inch. The victory was psychologically important, as it was the first assault on French soil by a wholly American Army and demonstrated that the Americans could fight just as well as the other Allies - something that some British and French Commanders had had doubts about.

The Americans under their new General, Robert Bullard (who later led the 1st Army) whose HQ was at le Mesnil St Firmin, barely 3.5 miles south-west of Cantigny, were warned of the coming task on 15 May. This launched the Division's staff (including one Lieutenant-Colonel George Catlett Marshall who was to play such a major role in the next war) into two weeks of planning. On 23 May the 28th moved into a back area to begin rehearsals for the attack. The ground had been chosen for its similarity to that at Cantigny and trenches had been dug to match aerial pictures taken of the German lines.

After the war, Colonel Robert McCormick who lived in Wheaton, Illinois, near Chicago, and had commanded the 1st Battalion of the 28th, founded a museum in his house, which he renamed 'Cantigny' and had as gates replicas of those at Cantigny Château.

Opposite is **The American Monument** and as you walk across the road towards it you are moving directly towards the advancing Doughboys of 1918. The memorial was designed by Arthur Loomis Harmon and inaugurated on 9 August 1937 and commemorates the 199 men killed and the 867 wounded and gassed here. The elegant white stone shaft is surrounded by a beautifully tended park. At the entrance is an **American Battle Monuments Commission plaque** describing the Cantigny operation, the first attack by an American Division in the First World War. The street behind the park is rue 1ière Division USA.

Continue down the hill to the memorial up the bank on the left.

'Big Red 1' Memorial. This handsome column surmounted by an eagle (sculpted in 1919 by Jo Davidson) has plaques around bearing the names of the Missing in Action and the message of 10 November 1918 from the Commander in Chief acknowledging the Division's esprit. Its famous red numeral on a brown tabard was adopted just before it went into battle.

The Division had come into the Cantigny area some 6 weeks before the battle and suffered greatly from German shell fire and gas attacks, though in its counter artillery fire it was said that the Division despatched over 10,000 shells every 24 hours onto the German lines. However, the Americans found the gas attacks particularly troubling and some 60 years later Sergeant George Krahnert of the 26th Infantry remembered his encounter with mustard gas - 'I went out into this field one morning to do you know what and I made the mistake of using some grass to clean up. Christ did it burn. My rear end still looks like it's petrified! As for the other part of my body well I fathered eight children after the war so it couldn't have bothered me permanently. I never did report it as a wound - just kept bathing with GI soap.' (*Make the Kaiser Dance*, Henry Berry).

Continue downhill to Fontaine sous Montdidier

Memorial to 49th Chasseurs, 1918

Monument to 'Le Beau Dix-Neuf' – the French 19th Division

The German 9th Division occupied the village on the morning of 28 March. An immediate counter-attack by the French 132nd Infantry Regiment recaptured the village and fighting in the area around Montdidier surged backwards and forwards over the coming months until the Allied offensive of 8 August.

Take the first left and just before a dip fork left downhill along a narrow road. Take the first small track to the left (past the last house) and continue to a memorial on the left.

Memorial to Capt Rene de la Lande Calan, 49th Bn Chasseurs à Pied who 'fell gloriously at the head of his men having held the enemy for seven hours on 30 March 1918.'

Continue to the churchyard outside of which is

Memorial to the 49th Chasseurs who stopped the German advance on 30 March 1918 and below a **plaque to André Morel** who fell on 15 March 1945 in Russia and **Pierre Graval**, 6 March 1945 in Weimar.

EITHER *Return along the route you have come*

OR *continue to Montdidier* where there is a variety of restaurants and a German Cemetery, with 4,351 known and 3,700 unknown burials, on the N329.

Follow signs to Amiens on the D935. Continue past the airfield on the right and on the left is

Monument to 'Le Beau Dix-Neuf'. The monument bears the insignia of a trumpet and has an inscription in Latin, detailing the actions of the 19th Division from 1854 in the Battle of the Alma, through the Great War to 1945.

Continue on the D935 to Moreuil and thence to Villers Bretonneux.

ALLIED AND GERMAN WARGRAVES & COMMEMORATIVE ASSOCIATIONS

COMMONWEALTH WAR GRAVES COMMISSION

All the British and Commonwealth Cemeteries and Memorials on the Somme battlefield are lovingly and beautifully maintained by the Commission.

Their Head Office is at 2 Marlow Road, Maidenhead, Berks. ☎ **01628 634221. Fax: 01628 771208**. Website: www.cwg.org E-mail Casualty & Cemetery Enquiries: casualty.enq@cwgc.org. Their Area Office, in France, is at rue Angèle Richard, 62217 Beaurains, ☎ **(03) 21 21 77 00. Fax: (03) 21 21 77 10**. E-mail: france.area@cwgc.org (See Itinerary One for details of the various workshops that are housed there.)

The Commission holds information on all the 1.7 million Commonwealth servicemen and women killed in the two World Wars as well as some civilian casualties of WW2. The records are now computerised and the launch of the Commission's website has considerably enhanced the services offered. The website provides general and historical information on the Commission, current news and details of publications. Information sheets, including *The Thiépval Memorial* and *The Battle of the Somme,* can now be downloaded from the Publications Section. Details of individual casualties can be found

Headstone of Pte George Nugent, whose remains were found at Lochnagar Crater and who is now buried in Ovillers CWGC Cem

Work in progress: temporary grave marker, St Etienne au Mont Cem

on the search-by-surname **Debt of Honour Register** which allows enquirers to carry out their own traces at no cost. Information can be obtained from the Commission's offices and the Enquiries staff at Head Office (direct line ☎ 01628 507200) are still happy to offer a personal service. It will speed your enquiry to have as much information about the person you are seeking as possible, e.g. name, rank, number, unit, regiment, date of death. No charge is normally made for an individual casualty enquiry but researchers making multiple enquiries may be charged £2 per name and are encouraged to use the website register.

The old-style cemetery registers are no longer published but the computerised system can produce tailored reports, including lists of those buried in individual cemeteries, together with historical notes and plans, details of those killed on particular dates, e.g. 1 July 1916, casualties with the same surname and from a particular regiment. Prices for Cemetery Reports start at £10 and the more bespoke reports from £20. Such has been the interest generated by the website, which now receives as many as half a million hits a week (compared with 40,000 a year before its introduction), that the Commission is currently putting more resources into improving the information available, though there is some debate as to the true ownership of the material held on the database. However, the improvements will enable researchers and others to obtain more detailed and comprehensive information from the site.

Those wishing to visit a particular grave or name on a memorial on the Somme are strongly advised to contact the Commission - or access its website - to find the precise location of that grave or name before setting out. There are well over 150 CWGC cemeteries on Side 2 of *the Holts' Battle Map of the Somme* alone. Their purple dots mark the poignant mosaic of death which clearly defines the old front line. Trying to visit a grave without a precise location is like looking for a needle in a haystack. The Cemetery Reports produced by the Commission are a mine of information. They summarise the burials by nationality and then list them in alphabetical order, reproduce the citation from the London Gazette for Victoria Cross winners, contain a map and often a historical background to the battles in the area of the cemetery. Although the Commission aims to have a Cemetery Report in each of the bronze register boxes they can, sadly, go missing. This makes prior research even more important. At many of the cemeteries the Commission has also placed stainless steel historical notices giving a summary of the campaign and notes on the cemetery. A programme of replacing this notice with smaller notices in bronze will begin in the next few years.

The Commission's Annual Report, published each November, makes engrossing reading. It summarises the main refurbishment work carried out during the past year and it is a task that resembles the maintenance of the Forth Bridge in its continuous nature to keep the cemeteries and memorials in the immaculate condition that visitors appreciate and have come to expect. It details the vast budget required to carry out that work. It lists the 140+ countries from A (for Albania) to Z (for Zimbabwe) where there are graves or memorials to maintain, and the number of graves and names recorded for the

United Kingdom and for each of the Commission's member governments: Undivided India, Canada, Australia, New Zealand and South Africa. The report is now also available on audio tape. A 47-minute VHS video, entitled a *Debt of Honour,* showing the world-wide work of the commission is available for £9. A shorter video, *Memorial and Memory*, aimed at a younger audience, is available free to schools.

The Commission, originally known as the Imperial War Graves Commission, was established by Royal Charter on 21 May 1917. Its duties were, and still are, to mark and maintain graves of the members of the forces of the Commonwealth who died in World War I and, later, World War II, and the memorials of those with no known grave. It was the inspiration of a volunteer Red Cross commander, Major Fabian Ware, who became the Commission's first tireless and enthusiastic Director-General. The Commission's Chairman was Lord Derby and Rudyard Kipling was amongst the first Commissioners. (It is sad and ironic that his close and energetic ties with the Commission failed to help him to identify his son's body after he had been declared 'Missing' at Loos. It was not until July 1992 that a researcher at Maidenhead believed he had identified John Kipling's body under a headstone in St Mary's ADS Cemetery at Loos and that headstone was then inscribed with his name. It was a decision challenged by the authors of this book - see *My Boy Jack?, The Search for Kipling's Only Son*)

The Commission chose a uniform headstone (2ft 6in high, 1ft 3in broad) bearing, when known, the regimental badge, name, rank, number, date of birth and death, religious emblem and a personal inscription which the family could choose. At first the Commission actually charged the bereaved family 3 $^{1}/_{2}$ old pence per letter for this inscription, but Ware was sympathetic to the plight of some families who were unable to afford even this modest fee and the charge became 'voluntary'. The choice of the headstone, which has proved immensely suitable for the large amount of information which can be inscribed upon it - a unique feature of the British and Commonwealth markers - was not an easy decision. Many mothers were vehement in their wish for the religious symbol of a cross. The headstone has the advantage that upon it may be inscribed the Latin Cross, the Star of David, Hindu or Muslim characters - or in the case of an atheist or an agnostic, for whom a cross would have been inappropriate, no emblem at all. The stones were laid out, for the most part, in straight lines, 'giving the appearance of a battalion on parade'. In some cases, war-time graves were left in their original haphazard pattern. Horticulturalists and architects worked together on the overall design of the cemeteries. The concept was to create a sentimental association between the gardens of home and the foreign fields where the soldiers were to lie. Sir Edwin Lutyens, a principal architect, used the ideas of his horticultural mentor, Gertrude Jekyll, to give the effect of a garden rather than a cemetery, with the use of cottage garden plants and roses in the borders in front of the headstones and protecting shrubs and avenues of trees. Other prestigious architects like Sir Herbert Baker and Sir Reginald Blomfield

Personal tribute on a grave

Cross of Sacrifice, Ovillers CWGC Cem

were also commissioned to design the cemeteries and memorials. The famous trio of Baker, Blomfield and Lutyens were described respectively as 'gentle', 'temperamental' and 'brilliant'. Two monuments are common to most cemeteries: Blomfield's Cross of Sacrifice bearing a bronze Crusader's sword upon its shaft (in areas where climactic or atmospheric conditions are poor for bronze, or the bronze is liable to be stolen for its intrinsic value, glass reinforced plastic (GRP) is used for replacements): in larger cemeteries, Lutyens' Stone of Remembrance, designed specifically to commemorate those of all faiths and none, upon which are inscribed the words from Ecclesiasticus, chosen by Rudyard Kipling, 'Their Name Liveth for Evermore'.

He chose, too, the words, 'His Glory Shall Not be Blotted Out' which is inscribed on the headstones of graves that were originally known to be in a particular cemetery but which were destroyed by later action. These memorials of bodies 'known to be buried in this cemetery' are called 'Kipling Memorials'. Each sizeable cemetery has a bronze box containing the Visitors' Book and, provided it has not been stolen, the Cemetery Report.

The future maintenance of the cemeteries (to be preserved, according to the Commission's Charter, 'in perpetuity') will depend upon the support of future Governments of participating nations – the United Kingdom about 80%, the rest being distributed proportionally according to the number of their burials between Australia, Canada, India, New Zealand and South Africa. Pakistan has already opted out. The UK funding is now influenced by the Defence Vote and it was reassuring that, in November 1995, the Secretary of State for Defence made a statement to confirm that it was indeed the intention to maintain the war graves and memorials for ever. The number of signatures in the Visitors' books and 'hits' on the web-site indicates the high level of interest today. The gardeners, too, appreciate your personal comments, so please sign if you can. It is always interesting to read details of a family or regimental pilgrimage that has visited a particular grave.

In many cases, in the Somme district, the area superintendents and gardeners are descendants of the ex-servicemen who came out to work with the Commission after the war and settled in France. In 1920 400 British gardeners were working in France and Belgium and this had risen to more than 1,300 by 1924. At first they worked in 'Travelling Garden Parties', driving out with tents and three-days' rations and drinking water, as well as their tools. Their initial task was to prepare ground, establish levels, fence cemeteries and mark plots and rows. It was dreadful work, the creation of today's glorious cemeteries from the war-scarred land, full of much volatile, unexploded material, and they were men of extraordinary devotion to endure the conditions. The logistical problems of such a vast task were enormous. Contracts were made for the main construction work with major building firms and many monumental masons were kept busy producing the thousands of headstones. 700,000 tons of stone, brick and cement had to be quarried or made, for instance. The gardeners were helped by Chinese labourers, who insisted on cutting the inscriptions on the headstones of their own race. By 1935, fourteen planned cemeteries had still to be completed – three of them on the Somme: at Assevillers, Contalmaison and Redan Ridge. Eventually the local offices, like that in Albert which had bustled with the activity of architects, draughtsmen, engineers, horticulturalists, directors and supervisors, shut. But the work of maintenance continued, organised from the area offices, as it still is.

For many years each gardener was assigned to his own particular cemetery (or cemeteries, in the case of the tiny ones, and gardeners in the case of large ones). This led to an intense personal pride in the care and appearance of that cemetery. In recent years financial pressures have led to the rise of more sophisticated machinery, pesticides and fungicides and cuts in manpower. Once more the cemeteries are tended by 'Travelling Garden Parties', and

The remains of Sgt Jack White, 22nd Bn AIF, who was killed at the Battle of Bullecourt on 3 May 1917, were buried with full military honours at Quéant Road Cemetery near Bullecourt on a foggy 11 October 1995

cemeteries are maintained on a rotational basis, sometimes with fairly lengthy gaps between visits. Today's gardeners, working from purpose-built base sites, are 'all-rounders', with a wide range of skills and equipment to tackle every job – from mowing and border maintenance to large-scale cemetery renovations. They still maintain the high level of commitment of their predecessors.

A surprising, and it seems ever-increasing, number of human remains from the Great War are still being found. On 11 October 1995 Sgt John James ('Jack') White of the 22nd Bn AIF, age 29, whose body, with full identification, was found by a local farmer, was buried with military honours and in the presence of his daughter Myrle (who was 10 months old when her father went off to war on 4 April 1916) his grand-daughter, Patricia, and grand-son, Keith, who all travelled from Australia especially for the burial, at Quéant Road Cemetery near Bullecourt. Jack had been killed in the Battle of Bullecourt on 3 May 1917. The CWGC made a special dispensation for Jack to be buried at Quéant, a cemetery that was 'officially' closed. When the foundations for the new museum at Delville Wood were being dug in 1984-5, other human remains were found which were buried in Delville Wood CWGC Cemetery. From January 1999 to June 2002 seventy-one remains have been discovered, working out at about 20-30 per year in France and Belgium. The remains of Pte George Nugent, for example, found at the Lochnagar Crater (qv) were reinterred in Ovillers CWGC Cemetery (qv) on 1 July 2000.

Unfortunately, few are found with any identifying artefacts and they are quietly buried with due decorum by the local area office and the Military Attaché at the relevant British embassy. When any positive identification clues are found this is where the work of MOD PS4(A)NWG Cas/Comp comes in - see below.

MOD PS4(A)Non-War Graves Casualty/Compassionate Cell

Working closely with the CWGC, MOD PS4(A)Cas/Comp, operating from Upavon in Wiltshire (contact PS4(A) NWG, ☎ 01980 618824. Fax: 01980 615563 E-mail: cascomcoord@hotmail.com) is now responsible for identifying the newly discovered remains of British Army personnel from the two World Wars and other past conflicts when sufficient evidence is found with the remains.

This may consist of a variety of factors, such as regimental and army insignia and personal artefacts, and the remains are examined in order to estimate the soldier's height, physique, age at death, etc. This information is then used along with that contained within any surviving documentation, such as Service records (which have written physical details of the soldier that can be compared against the forensic archaeologist's report). Sadly, this is where work on many cases of trying to identify remains comes to an end, as many Service records from WW1 were destroyed during the 1940 blitz. War diaries, pension records, and books on relevant battles and regimental histories, are also recalled and read. All evidence is then submitted to the head of PS4(A)Cas/Comp and a decision on whether the individual can be identified is arrived at, based on the balance of probability. DNA testing is not used.

If a soldier is identified the NWG Section then becomes involved, not only in co-ordinating a military funeral, but also in trying to trace any surviving family of the soldier. This is done using the records of births, marriages and deaths held by the Office for National Statistics, surviving parish records, wills and National Census returns held by the Public Records Office.

When sufficient supporting evidence is found with a set of remains for an attempt to be made to identify them as those as that of a specific soldier, the CWGC area office (who will have been informed of the find by the relevant local authorities and in some cases the individual who has made the discovery) then contacts MOD PS4(A)Cas/Comp. Initially the CWGC will supply the NWG Section with a report stating both what has been found and the location of the find, as well as a list of those whose remains they could potentially be. In such cases the NWG Section will then task a forensic archaeologist to examine the remains. No details of the circumstances of the discovery and the possible identity of the soldiers are made known to the archaeologist, who will compile a report on each skeleton which gives details of height, stature, age at death, evidence of dental health, and other physical details. The examinations always take place in the country in which the remains have been found and there is no entitlement to repatriation for soldiers killed in the two World Wars. Their remains are now always re-buried in a CWGC cemetery near to where they are found, as described below.

The most famous and well-documented recent find was at St-Laurent-Blangy near Arras, when in January 2001, excavations began for a business site called Actiparc over the sector where, in 1917, five different British units were facing the Germans during the April offensive. Then human remains were discovered, notably a trench containing twenty-three soldiers, with badges of the Lincolnshire Regiment (the Grimsby Chums). Poignantly their arms appeared to be linked together. The CWGC at Beaurains were informed and working with the Arras Archaeological Service and a forensic scientist from MOD PS4 stringent efforts were made to further identify the men. Unfortunately, no identifications could be made and the soldiers were buried in nearby Point du Jour CWGC Cemetery in June 2002. (This cemetery still has space, as the French remains originally buried here in a significant plot were later removed.) A video for television was made of the incident called *Bodyhunt Search for the Unknown Soldier.*

In the case of remains found at Athie, near Arras, in June 2001 all five sets had 15th Bn Royal Scots insignia found with them. Two sets of remains also had identity discs and one set had a ring with the initials GW inscribed. The CWGC area office, by looking at its own 'Debt of Honour Register', was able to ascertain that the two identity discs belonged to soldiers who were still recorded as missing - Cpl William Gunn and Pte Archibald McMillan who were both killed in action on 9 April, the first day of the Battle of Arras. It was also able to supply a list of missing soldiers from 15th Bn Royal Scots whose initials were GW. Research by MOD PS4 traced the family of Pte McMillan and on 20 June 2002 his 87-year-old son, Archie McMillan, his grand-daughter and great-grandson attended the re-interment. The Regiment buried their sons with full military honours on a grey and wet morning in Point du Jour cemetery in a ceremony of tremendous dignity and tenderness. The most recent reburial, with full military honours, of an identified soldier was that of Pte William Ewart Gladstone Crompton of the 1st Lincolns in Peake Wood Cemetery on 20 Sept 2002.

Their work is done meticulously and with great sensitivity.

SERVICE DES SÉPULTURES DE GUERRE

The French organization for the maintenance of wargraves and memorials comes under the Ministry of *Anciens Combattants et Victimes de Guerre*. Details of the *Nécropoles Nationales* can be obtained from their head office at 37 rue de Bellechasse, 75007 Paris. ☎ (01) 48 76 11 35.

A law was passed on 29 December 1915 to give the rights to a free, and eternally maintained grave to every French or Allied soldier who was killed in the war. Another law was passed on 18 February 1916 to set up a service to deal with pensions, to give information to families and to cope with the thousands of burials of the enormous casualties that were being incurred. On 25 November 1918 a National Commission of Military Graves was set up which undertook to progressively make landscaped cemeteries, each with a flagpole (and it is marvellous to see the French *tricolore* proudly flying), and to mark each grave with a concrete cross or headstone (for Colonial forces, agnostics, Jewish burials etc). The marker bears the soldier's rank, name, regiment and date of death and the words, *'Mort Pour la France'*. As with the CWGC, there are differently shaped markers for each nationality. The Treaty of

French Colonial headstones, St Acheul National Cem

Pattern of crosses, French National Cem, la Targette

French experimental headstone, Louvencourt Cem

Versailles of 28 June 1919 specified that each signatory country should respect and maintain the graves of military foreigners on their land. On 27 January 1920 the Ministry of Pensions absorbed the *Service des Sépultures* and regional teams were set up. The immediate post-war task of identifying bodies and helping relatives to find their loved ones' burial sites is movingly depicted in Bernard Tavernier's award-winning 1989 film, *La Vie et Rien d'Autre* ('Life and Nothing But'). On 31 July 1920 the cemeteries became 'national' and many small front-line cemeteries were concentrated into these larger national burial grounds. By the end of 1925, 960,000 reburials had been made and the bodies of 22,000 *Poilus* had been repatriated from Germany. Between 1926 and 1935 more than 122,000 French and German bodies were found, without graves, on the battlefields. On 11 July 1931 the treasury voted funds to embellish the cemeteries and the larger ones, like Notre Dame de Lorette (France's largest military cemetery with 20,058 graves and 20,000 in mass graves, on a 25 hectare site) were quickly completed.

Like the CWGC, the French decreed that there should be no distinction because of rank or status in the burials, following the Constitution's principal of equality. No 'sumptuous' decoration could be placed on the graves and only cut flowers. Unidentified bodies would be buried in mass graves (*ossuaires*) which should be surrounded by a wall and bear a memorial plaque. The erection of individual monuments was permitted by families and regiments. At first only 'sterile' material, like gravel, was allowed round the lines of graves and on the mass graves. But in 1950 lawns and polyanthus roses were permitted. It is very evident that this concept has been emphasized in the past few years and the somewhat stark appearance of the French cemeteries is now giving way to the more garden-like aspect of the British, with more flowering shrubs and sheltering trees. Maintenance is organized in sectors, with a technical service which has an annual budget. There is a box inside the entrance gate of most cemeteries, with the cemetery register and, a recent addition, a Visitors' Book. Other recent additions are explanatory boards just within the cemetery gates which describe the historical background of the Somme battles and show the national cemeteries in the area. The *Ministère des Anciens Combattants et Victimes de Guerre* publishes an *Atlas des Nécropoles Nationales,* which is obtainable from the *Historial de la Grande Guerre* at Péronne. It describes the 265 national cemeteries in France, and divides them in sectors, each with a map. There are some twenty in the Somme battlefield area.

Souvenir Français

This association was founded in 1872, after the Franco-Prussian War and revived after World War I. Its aim is to keep alive the memory of those who died for France, to maintain their graves and memorials in good condition and to transmit the 'flame of memory' to future generations. Their Head Office is at 9 rue de Clichy, 75009 Paris. There are active local branches in Albert, Amiens and Arras. Signs of their attentive care can be seen on many of the local *'Poilu'* memorials, and on private memorials, French and British, in the area. Often their red, white and blue roundel insignia is attached when refurbishment has taken place. Representatives lay wreaths at many ceremonial and commemorative ceremonies. One of the most dedicated local Presidents over many years is André Coilliot of the Arras branch. The young members he inspires often say the Exhortation in French at joint ceremonies (as, for example at 0730 each year at the Lochnagar Crater). André has the most incredible private collection of World War I and II artefacts, uniforms and ephemera in his private house at 71 rue Raoul Bricquet, Beaurains, 62000 Arras, ☎ (03) 21 71 46 25. André welcomes visitors, but please do not call unannounced.

Volksbund Deutsche Kriegsgräberfürsorge

The German War Graves Welfare Association's Head Office is at Werner-Hilperts Strasse 2, D-34117 Kassel, Germany. The organisation is similar in function to the Commonwealth War Graves Commission in that it maintains the war cemeteries and memorials to the German War Dead from World War I onwards, and assists relatives in locating and, in many cases, visiting the graves.

The German cemeteries are not as standardly uniform as the British and French. The markers vary from flat tablets, to upstanding squat stone crosses, to black metallic crosses. Jewish soldiers are marked with a headstone, which bears the Star of David. The markers bear scant information, sometimes only a name, with occasionally a rank, regiment and date of death. Most cemeteries have a mass grave, the names of the unidentified, missing soldiers probably buried therein being listed on bronze panels. Under the majority of markers two, four or even more soldiers will be buried. There are two reasons for this. It signifies 'comradeship in death' and also, on a practical note, the Germans were not allocated as much territory in which to bury their dead as were the Allies. In some German cemeteries there is a small memorial chapel, and often there will be some statuary – normally of bereaved parents or comrades. There will be a register in alphabetical order and sometimes a Visitors' Book to sign. Oak trees, symbolizing strength, are a frequent feature. There is a marked lack of flowers and colour in most German burial grounds. They are sad, sombre, mournful places – but then the death of a soldier is sad and mournful.

The maintenance of the German cemeteries in France is administered by the Service for the Care of German Cemeteries (SESMA), whose regional office is at rue de Nesle prolongée, 80320 Chaulnes, ☎ (03) 22 85 47 57.

There are thirteen German cemeteries on the Somme Battlefield of 1916-18 including (number of burials in brackets): Sapignies (1,550); Achiet-le-Petit (1,314); Villers-au-Flos (2,491); Fricourt (17,026); Rancourt (11,422); Bray (1,122); Proyart (4,634); Morisel (2,642) and Vermandovillers (22,600). Individual leaflets are available for each of them, but all German War Cemeteries in France, Belgium, Luxembourg and Holland are described, with maps, in the *Atlas Deutscher Kriegsgräber,* available from the Head Office in Kassel.

Association Internationale des Sites et Musées de la Guerre de 1914-1918

This association has been formed to guarantee that the memory will be kept alive. It groups all the major museums and battle sites in the north, north-east and east of France and will preserve and promote them and provide explanatory tourist literature. Its head office is at the *Historial,* Château de Péronne, 80200 Péronne.

The Durand Group

For Historical Research Into Subterranean Military Features

This 'fraternal association of individuals who have voluntarily undertaken to work together' comprises former and current military personnel and civilians with skills as historians, archaeologists, technicians, explosives and munitions experts, engineers, archivists, surveyors, cartographers, mountain and cave rescuers, IT, film production and medics. In just a few years they have become a pre-eminent authority on what might be described as 'underground battlefields' using highly sophisticated and technological equipment and methods in a most responsible manner.

The work that triggered the later formation of the group was initially organised by Lt Colonel Phillip Robinson in the late 1980s at the behest of the Director of the Vimy Memorial Site. The Royal Engineers investigated the La Folie mining system, and found two armed mines, one of which, the Durand Mine (the abandoned *fougasse* mine which gave the group its name), contained 6,000 lb of ammonal and was located under a public area. Research also suggested a much larger charge at the end of a blocked tunnel close to the Broadmarsh crater.

In 1996, upon return from extended service abroad, Phillip Robinson organised a volunteer team to access the Broadmarsh mine. Fortuitously, it was found to have been neutralised but further investigation of the Durand mine by Lt Col Mike Watkins, a serving officer of the Royal Logistic Corps and a leading EOD expert, indicated that it was fully viable and a potential threat.

Renovated Poilu at Flaucourt

Poilu Memorial, Chaulness

Working in arduous and dangerous conditions Mike Watkins disarmed it.

Following from this Mike Watkins and Phillip Robinson formed and constituted the Durand Group. Working with Veterans Affairs Canada, Durand have investigated over 4km of tunnels under Vimy Ridge and after removing some 40 tons of spoil blocking the way to another mining system, are investigating a neigbouring deep fighting system. They are also involved at Beaumont Hamel, where they have made many significant discoveries, with the Pas de Calais and Arras Archeological Services, and the Thiépval project.

A video of the Group's work called *One of Our Mines is Missing!* is available from Fougasse Films Ltd, 7 Essex Close, Eastcote, Middx HA4 9PX at £12.99/Euros 22 plus £1 UK, £2/Euros 3.25 Europe p+p. It is a highly professional and fascinating production by Group Secretary Andy Prada using a crew from the Services Sound & Vision Corporation, and vividly portrays the thorough, responsible and dangerous work the Group undertakes. This was highlighted by the tragic death of Lt Colonel Mike Watkins in 1998, when the excavation into a tunnel at Vimy collapsed upon him. The group's base and workshops are in a farmhouse near St Pol and it is mostly self-funding, but as their costs are extremely high donations are accepted. **Contact** Lt Colonel Mike Dolamore, MBE, RLC, Deputy Chairman. 5 Wentworth Avenue, Temple Herdewyke, Southam, Warks CV7 2VA. E-mail: mike@dolamore.demon.co.uk.

Numbered point on Australian battlefield tour (ABT)

Lozenge-shaped sign to site of village of Fay

THE SOMME ASSOCIATION

Based at the Somme Heritage Centre at 233 Bangor Road, Newtownards BT23 7PH, Co. Down, N. Ireland, ☎ 028 91823202, Fax: 028 91823214, **website: Irishsoldier.org E-mail:** sommeassociation@dnet.co.uk, the Association is dedicated to co-ordinating research into Ireland's part in the First World War (e.g. of the 10th and 16th (Irish) and 36th (Ulster) Divisions). It supports WW1 veterans, has research and education programmes, sponsors publications, organises anniversary commemorations and battlefield tours. Much of their information comes from the records of the Ulster Patriotic Fund (an endowment fund for widows and families provided by well-to-do business men, one of whose projects was the building of the Ulster Tower) which is still under the Official Secrets Act. Their database lists every man who served in an Irish Regiment from 1914-1921 and can be searched by name/regiment/details of next of kin/place of commemoration etc. It also maintains the Ulster Tower and its Visitor Centre (qv).

CONSEIL GENERAL DE LA SOMME/HISTORIAL/CIRCUIT DE SOUVENIR

The *Département de la Somme* is working with the *Historial* Museum at Péronne to preserve and promote battlefield sites in their area. Notable are the acquired sites of the preserved trenches at Soyécourt (Map 1/31), the Gibraltar bunker at Pozières (Map G48) and the site of the vanished village of Fay (Map 1/27a). Routes for a *Circuit du Souvenir* are marked by a stylised red poppy on a brown sign and there is a booklet and leaflet describing it. Descriptive signboards are progressively being placed at the entrance to sites of historic interest (signified by CGS/H - *Conseil Général de la Somme/Historial* throughout this book). They are at: Australian Memorial, Villers-Bretonneux; Australian Memorial, Mont St Quentin; Newfoundland Memorial, Beaumont-Hamel; New Zealand Memorial at Longueval; South African Memorial, Delville Wood; Ulster Tower; Thiépval Memorial; Lochnagar Crater, la Boiselle; Canadian intervention at crossroads of D23 Villers-Bretonneux-Moreuil; P'tit Train, Froissy; Lochnagar Crater; Souvenir Français Chapel, Rancourt; Tank Memorial, Pozières; Bazentin; Frise; Combles; Mametz (to the Welsh

Memorial); Maricourt; Maurepas; Sailly-Laurette and four signboards that relate to Manfred von Richthofen, the 'Red Baron' – at Cappy, Vaux-sur-Somme (near the brickworks), Bertangles and Fricourt.

Ross Bastiaan *Bas Relief* Commemorative Plaques

The series of beautifully designed, durable, informative plaques that can be seen at sites on the Somme - at Bullecourt, Digger Memorial; Le Hamel, Town Hall; Mont St Quentin, by Digger Memorial; Mouquet Farm, by roadside; Péronne, *Historial* entrance; Pozières, Windmill site and 1st Div Memorial; Vermandovillers Town Hall (non-standard, to McCarthy, VC); Villers Bretonneux Town Hall and at Australian Memorial – are the inspiration of Australian dentist, **Ross Bastiaan** (qv). Ross received no support (and at first little acknowledgement) from the Government in his dedicated work of designing, researching, creating, erecting and finding sponsors for these magnificent plaques which are gradually being placed around the world wherever Australian forces were engaged with distinction. They were first introduced in Gallipoli in 1990 and are now sited as far afield as Johannesburg and Damascus. Ross is now properly recognised in Australia for his dedicated work and has been appointed to the Council of the Australian War Memorial by the Prime Minister, whom he guided round the Gallipoli and Somme battlefields in 2000. **Website:** www.plaques.satlink.com.au

The Trench

Over the Easter 2002 period three episodes of a well-intentioned but inevitably controversial TV programme entitled *The Trench* were shown on BBC2. It aimed to recreate the everyday life of Tommy in a WW1 trench in as authentic a manner (except of course to undergo real enemy fire) as possible. Although the well-respected Khaki Chums were among the 25 volunteers who trained for, and were eventually chosen to act as, the Hull Pals there was some fear that the programme would trivialise what the men of '14-'18 had endured "for real". After undergoing some hard training at Catterick the men moved to France and after another week's training in situ, alternated between the recreated trenches and a simulated behind-the-lines environment for three extremely hard weeks of iron rations, cold uncomfortable nights, often in the company or rats, boredom, primitive latrines and other '14-'18 harsh realities. Perhaps the major achievement of the experiment was as an educational tool and it will inevitably stimulate interest in the Great War and the sacrifices of those who really took part in it. The trenchline at Flesquières (near Cambrai) where the programme was filmed has been purchased by the Flesquières Tank Association, a French group, with a view to opening it to the public in the future. The IWM mounted an exhibition, sponsored by the BBC, to coincide with the programme.

Tourist Information

It is the ironic and inevitable fate of a guide book that some information given in it will have become out of date by the time it is published. For instance, the reader may be surprised to see how many new Visitors' Centres and memorials have been erected on the Somme since the first edition of this book in 1996. New roads and the ubiquitous roundabouts appear, road numbers change. The personnel mentioned in hotels, restaurants, museums and tourist offices retire or move. Opening hours for these establishments often change. The tourist information in this guide is, therefore, as the cliché goes, 'correct at the time of going to press' and we apologise in advance for any changes that may have occurred since.

Our best advice, if you have obtained this book before you leave home, is to go through it carefully in conjunction with the accompanying *Major & Mrs Holt's Battle Map of the Somme*, marking the sites or itineraries that you intend to follow, then obtain the relevant tourist documentation from the addresses below:

French Tourist Office, 178 Piccadilly, London W1V OAL, premium-rate hotline ☎ 0906 824 4123, Fax: 0207 493 6594. They produce an excellent booklet entitled, *Reference for the Traveller in France*, up-dated every year, which contains just about all the basic information you need to know before going to France: on currency, passports/visa, medical advice, electricity, metric measurements and sizes, banking and shopping hours, phoning, motorways, driving, caravanning, camping, hotels, self-catering, *Gîtes de France*, local tourist offices (*syndicats d'iniative*) signed 'i' for information, food and drink etc, how to get there by car, ferry, rail, tunnel, air, car hire, with relevant phone numbers. It is absolutely essential. Send a large SAE and £1 in stamps.

You can also contact the following local tourist offices for more detailed information on hotels, restaurants, general local tourist information, holidays and calendar of events – the serious student of the battlefields may well wish to avoid the latter as local hostelries will be full and roads congested.

Départmental Committee for Tourism in the Somme (Director M. Vermersch), 21 rue Ernest Cauvin, 80000 Amiens, ☎ (03) 22 71 22 71, Fax: (03) 22 71 22 69. E-mail: acceuil@somme-tourisme.com

Albert, 9 rue Gambetta, BP 82, Albert 80300, ☎ (03) 22 75 16 42, Fax: (03) 22 75 11 72

Amiens, 6 bis, rue Duseval, BP 1018 Amiens cedex 1, ☎ (03) 22 71 60 50

Arras, Hôtel de Ville, Place des Héros, Arras, ☎ (03) 21 51 26 95.

Péronne, Place du Château, 80200 Péronne, ☎ (03) 22 84 42 38.

Where to Stay & Where to Eat

Hotels and restaurants that are conveniently on the routes are mentioned as they occur in the Itineraries. In most cases the comments about them reflect the authors' subjective views. For comprehensive lists see 'Tourist Offices' above, and consult 'Hotels' and 'Restaurants' in the Index.

Circuit de Souvenir Sign

Sign to German Cem, Bray sur Somme

The CWGC cemeteries are well signposted

Telephoning France from the UK and the UK from France

From the UK dial 00 33 followed by the new prefix (probably 03) and then the eight-figure local number. From France, dial 1944, drop the first '0' of your local code, then dial that local code followed by your number.

The Somme Past & Present

A Brief History to the Outbreak of World War I

The *Département* of the Somme was created in 1790 when France was reorganized administratively. It incorporated the major part of the ancient Province of Picardy and its character remains 'Picard' to this day. The region has been inhabited and invaded by many different peoples. Recent advances in aerial archaeology show the distinct traces of Gallic fortified camps (*oppida*). Julius Caesar occupied the area in 57BC, overcoming the indigenous Belgic tribes. Evidence of the Roman (Gallo-Roman) era are found throughout the *Département* in the form of temples, baths, theatres and farmsteads. Christianity came to the area at about the end of the third century AD. The first Bishop of Amiens was Firmin, who was martyred for his faith in 287. Another famous Christian was Martin, the Roman soldier who divided his cloak and shared it with a naked beggar in Amiens, was converted, and died in 397 as Bishop of Tours.

The era of the *Pax Romana* was a relatively calm period, but at the end of the fourth century a series of invasions began. The Vikings, in the ninth and tenth centuries, were perhaps the most feared, until they were beaten by the Carolingian King Louis III at Sacourt-en-Vimeu. In the Middle Ages, abbeys and châteaux flourished under the feudal lords, resulting in local power struggles. Agriculture and the cloth industry expanded in the twelfth and thirteenth centuries. Towns grew up as trading developed, but the increasingly prosperous land continued to be fought over – by the rival counts of Amiens and Flanders and the kings of France. In 1185 the *'Comté'* (the land ruled by a count) was taken over by the Crown.

In 1297 the *Comté* of Ponthieu came under English domination, when Edward III married Eleanor of Castille, who had inherited it. In 1328 Edward staked his claim on the French throne, and the Hundred Years' War began. In 1329 Philip VI persuaded Edward (as Count of Ponthieu) to come and pay homage to him in Amiens Cathedral. But the following year Edward landed in Normandy and marched through the Somme, making a defensive stand at Crécy en Ponthieu. The English and Welsh longbows routed Philip's army and the flower of French knighthood was destroyed.

Henry V was the next English King to march through Picardy, in 1415. He encamped at Corbie, where he publically hanged one of his soldiers for stealing a golden vessel – an incident featured in Shakespeare's *Henry V*. Crossing the Somme at Ham, Henry led his weary army right across the area which was to be the setting for the 1 July 1916 battle, through Beaumont Hamel itself, on his way to Agincourt. It was another disaster for the French. *'Voulez-vous voir la France, allez à Londres'*, was the saying after Agincourt, for in London were the only remaining knights and lords of French extraction, who had come with the Norman invasion of Britain in 1066.

The Somme then passed to Anglo-Burgundian rule until 1477, when Louis XI retook the area.

The Spanish were the next invaders. They took Amiens in 1597, but it fell again to Henry IV of France after a siege of six months. In 1636 they took Corbie, which in its turn was retaken by Henry. In 1653 the Santerre (qv) was devastated by the Great Prince of Condé, allied with the Spanish, in the Civil War known as the *Fronde* (meaning 'wind of revolt'.)

Then a period of peace eventually ensued and gradually prosperity returned to the province once more, especially in agriculture and the cloth industry.

1870 saw the arrival of the Prussian Army in the Franco-Prussian War. Amiens was taken in 1870 after the Battle of Dury (south of Amiens). General Faidherbe had some limited successes with his army of the North – notably at Pont Noyelles near Querrieu (qv).

Forty-three years later came the outbreak of World War I. Amiens was again occupied, on 31 August 1914. Picardy was once more to become a battlefield and this time the devastation was so terrible that it was thought it would never be cultivated again.

The Aftermath of the Great War

After the war, the parts of the Somme most frequently and bitterly fought over – in the area of the Ancre around Albert and in the Santerre around Villers-Bretonneux – were officially described as a *Zone Rouge* (red zone). It was considered uninhabitable and uncultivatable for evermore as, indeed, were great tracts of land around the Verdun battlefield. These latter were designated as national parks, afforested and then left for nature to perform her own slow healing process. Villages completely disappeared.

Not so in Picardy. Although it was said of Albert after the war that *'Il ne reste que le nom et la Gloire'*, the townspeople insisted (as did the citizens of Ypres in

Flanders) on returning to their sad ruins and recreating their town. The Picard, so deeply tied to his land, returned to till the impossible mess that had been made of his smallholding. It hardly seemed possible that normal life could ever resume. Even before the war ended, John Masefield walked 'The Old Front Line' and described it in vivid terms. 'It is as though the place had been smitten by the plague', he wrote.

The *Berliner Tageblatt* described the region as a 'desert incapable for a long time of producing the things necessary to life'. The precious upper covering of fertile soil, from which the agricultural economy drew its living, had almost completely disappeared and the limestone substratum was laid bare. The huge mine craters gaped. The great one at la Boisselle was 200ft in diameter and 81ft deep in 1919. Wooden crosses marked the mound of British graves in its depths, a skull guarding them for years. Even as long after the war as 1928 it was thought that Serre could never be rebuilt. Thiépval, whose economy depended on its wealthy château (which was not rebuilt) was also slow in its rebirth, and never attained its former size.

The gradual rebuilding of the villages and towns took place in the Twenties, when the style known as Art Deco (from the exhibition of *Arts Décoratifs et Industriels Modernes* in Paris of 1925) was at its short-lived apogée, leaving an extraordinary architectural legacy. Its trade marks of geometric shapes, sunbursts and zig-zags can be glimpsed in the wrought iron gates of farms and cottages, the designs of windows, the proud new station at Albert, and the incongruous church spires, like the somewhat bizarre concrete fretwork of Lamotte Warfusée.

The rebuilding was done using the reparation money voted to the ruined villages by the Treaty of Versailles. This was augmented by funds raised by subscription in many British cities and towns. The British League of Help inaugurated an 'adoption' scheme (see Biaches above), and, for instance, Birmingham adopted Albert (hence the street name 'Rue de Birmingham'); Sheffield – Bapaume, Puisieux and Serre (where so many of her 'Pals' fell); Maidstone – Montauban; Wolverhampton – Gommecourt; Derby – Foncquevillers; Llandudno – Mametz (where the Welsh fought so gallantly); Stourbridge – Grandcourt; Ipswich – Fricourt; Tonbridge – Thiépval; Canterbury – Lesboeufs and Morval; Hornsey – Guillemont; Brighouse – Courcelette; Gloucester – la Boisselle and Ovillers; Portsmouth – Combles and Flers; Folkestone – Morlancourt and Leamington-Spa — Biaches (qv).

Imported Polish labourers helped to clear the battlefields, and the scrap-metal merchants prospered. The 'iron harvest', however, seems to be eternal, and Picard ploughs turn up tons of it each year (qv).

The Picard

That the Somme presents today a peaceful, prosperous, bucolic face, with the Santerre's fertile fields that once were the granary of the Roman army, producing their habitual record harvests; that the Somme flows through tranquil, verdant banks; that the pastures of the little farmsteads around la Boisselle and Beaumont Hamel are calmly grazed by fat, sleek stock – are all due to the character and personality of the Picard.

They descend from the Belgae – a mixed race of Celtic and Teutonic stock. Their traits are a fierce pride in, and loyalty to, their land; resistance to change; quickness to defend liberty and rights; inherent honesty and courtesy. They are hard-working and independent of spirit, and they were determined to coax their battered land back to life.

One can imagine what torments the war must have caused to such people. Until ordered to leave by the military authorities, they would cling to their shell-torn homes and farms. They also had the humiliation of peremptory requisitioning to bear. Yet most of the personal accounts one reads by Allied soldiers talk of comfortable billets, much fraternising behind the lines, and families who kept their promise to look after the tragic crosses which marked pals' graves. There are far fewer reports of profiteering from the captive market of the soldier here than on other areas along the front. After the war, a number of Tommies came back to Picardy, married their wartime sweethearts and settled down on their old battlefield. The daughter of one of them, Marie Baudet, née Salter, served her father's country with the ATS in World War II.

The ancient language of Picardy, a dialect with 'Romano' origins, is unfortunately dying out with the older generation. But the pilgrim will still hear its mysterious tones in isolated villages along the Somme and in folk songs and recipes.

Districts of Picardy Fought Over in the Somme Battles

The Amiénois

The real heart of the province includes its capital city, Amiens, which was known by the Romans as Samarobriva (Bridge over the Somme). Its strategic position as the gateway to Paris and its situation on the great river made it an important distribution centre for local products. These include linen (woven from local flax) and woad (the blue dye used by the ancient Britons). Amiens was much damaged in the two World Wars, but some typical Picard houses remain in the picturesque and increasingly restored Old Quarter of St Leu. The city boasts an interesting stone Circus (opened by its famous citizen Jules Verne, who is buried in la Madeleine Cemetery and whose house at the corner of Bvd Jules Verne and rue Charles Dubois has been preserved), the Museums of Picardy and of Local Art and History, and a Costume Exhibition.

The Amiénois is a region of great natural beauty: of water and woods, hills and valleys, and heavy morning mists. It includes: Doullens (qv) with its Citadelle, planned by François I in 1525 and completed under Louis XIV, in the north; Bertangles (qv) with its imposing eighteenth-century château; Corbie (qv); Bray (qv) and the whole Valley of the Ancre, from Albert to Hamel. It therefore encompasses the greatest section of the British Front Line of 1 July 1916 and was part of the post-war *Zone Rouge* (qv).

In the Amiénois the traditional farm, with its courtyard and distinctly rural odours, (what Bairnsfather called 'a rectangular smell') still exists — and many of them were rebuilt to the old format after the war. You will hear the skylarks singing over the scores of beautifully kept cemeteries and memorials, and Roses of Picardy bloom everywhere – as does the 'Flanders' poppy. Farm cottages have become exceedingly popular with British expatriates, fascinated by researching the battles of 1916 and 1918, who often buy them and convert them to B & B establishments.

In this region one sees evidence of a phenomenon which was widespread, but is now dwindling. It is the strange terraced formation of steep slopes, known locally as *rideaux* (literally 'curtains') or *remblais* ('lynchets'). Contrary to popular belief they have nothing to do with viniculture. Wine has not been produced in Picardy since the Middle Ages, soon after Henry V's invading troops got drunk at Boves on local wine. It was with their backs to a three-tiered slope of *rideaux* that Edward III ranged his batailles at Crécy – with devastating results for the French. Masefield, on his wanderings along 'The Old Front Line' in 1917, noted them (he always referred to them as *remblais*) near Hébuterne, near Matthew, Mark, Luke and John Copses at Serre, in the outskirts of the village of Beaumont Hamel, near 'Y' Ravine. You will see them on the right of the road from Amiens to Querrieu. Masefield speculates that 'they are made ... by the ploughing away from the top and the bottom of any difficult slope', and this is a theory subscribed to by some local historians. The manifestation is also seen in Kent.

Throughout the region restaurants, from the simplest to the most sophisticated, serve delicious local dishes: *Poissons de Picardie* (Picardy fish – normally eels, river trout or turbot, in sorrel sauce, or with leeks and cream), duck, veal and pork, *e.g. Le Caghuse* (pork cooked in onions, butter and white wine) or flavoursome and tender *Pintadeau* (young guinea fowl). Perhaps the most popular dish is the *Ficelle Picarde* (a savoury pancake with ham, cheese and cream). Follow any of these with the famous macaroons or *Tuiles* (made of chocolate and almond) from Amiens or the rich *Gâteau Battu* (made with a large quantity of egg yolks and butter) or *Galuchon* (a sweet currant bread) – delicious!

Poppies on the Somme

Fishermen at Feuillières on the River Somme

The River Somme

The Somme is a river which meanders, changing its aspect at every bend, from a wide expanse of fast moving water to a myriad of secret pools (*étangs*), branches and canals, shaded and secluded by lush foliage. These pools are the delight of the weekend fishermen and hunters, whose cabins throng the banks. The river yields a variety of fish, the greatest delicacy being the eels, which are caught in *Anguillières*. From them is made *Pâté d'Anguilles*, or *Anguilles à l'Oseille* (eels in sorrel sauce), *Anguilles du Hourdel* (eels in a sauce of onions, parsley, egg yolks and vinegar), *Anguilles au Vert* (eels with spinach, sorrel, mint, sage, etc). In these tranquil pools, duck, snipe and other game birds are stalked by the hunters, often with colourful decoys. Duck pâté, therefore, is another local speciality, as is *Canard Sauvage* (wild duck) with a variety of sauces. Boat trips may be made along the Somme, which, with no great stretch of the imagination, will conjure up pictures of the hospital barges which plied from the battle area to Amiens after the 1 July 1916 battles. Apply to the local tourist office or direct, ☎ (03) 22 92 16 40.

Remember that the Somme was very muddy in 1914-18 – and can still be so today

The Hortillonages

The name for these small gardens, made in the rich mud and silt of the marshy banks of the fragmented rivulets of the Somme above Amiens, comes from the Latin *Hortus* – garden. They have long been a picturesque tradition, now sadly dwindling. They are tended from the flat-bottomed black boats, *Bateaux à Cornet* that, until 1976, transported the crops to the market at the Quai Parmentier in Amiens. Leeks, onions, carrots, radish, cauliflower, crisp lettuce and many other varieties of vegetables and salad stuff grow to perfection in the dark soil. They are the ingredients for *Soupe des Hortillons* (mixed vegetable soup with chunks of bread) and other soups, and an array of savoury flans and quiches, known as *Flamiches*, for example, *aux Poireaux* (with leeks and cream), *des Hortillons* (vegetables and ham) and many more variations. Guided visits by boat may be made to the *Hortillonages* – apply to the local tourist office or ☎ (03) 22 92 12 18.

The Santerre

As the origins of its name implies (from the Latin *sana terra* – good earth) this is an extremely fertile plain, broadly bounded by the Somme in the north and the Avre in the south. It encompasses Villers-Bretonneux, the site of bitter fighting in 1918, but otherwise mostly covers the French sector of the 1 July battle. Because of the carnage and destruction which took place on the rich soil, it too became part of the proposed *Zone Rouge* after the war. But the land was recultivated, and now sugar beet, wheat, salsify, spinach, potatoes (brought to France by Parmentier, citizen of Montdidier), sweet corn, tender little peas and *flagiolets*, flourish in the expansive fields of the Santerre. It is the centre of the vegetable canning industry, producing the perfect accompaniment to the rich game dishes of the region, or as the basis of soups, such as *Potage Crécy* (carrot soup) or *Soupe aux Endives* (chicory soup). During the hunting season, local farmers and 'weekenders' from Paris and other regions beat the fields and woods, shooting hare, rabbit and game birds. Be vigilant when walking across fields in the autumn. The sound of shots can often be too realistic and close for comfort. *Lapin Farci à la Picarde* (stuffed rabbit with beer, cider etc) and *Lapin aux Pruneaux* (rabbit with prunes) are among the tasty results.

The Somme is a region to be enjoyed, not only for its history, but for the many delights of its picturesque landscape – but beware, it can be very muddy!

ACKNOWLEDGEMENTS

We wish to acknowledge the wealth of information that we have gleaned from those who travelled regularly with us, too numerous to mention, on Major & Mrs Holt's Battlefield Tours in over a quarter of a century of touring the battlefields. Other large debts of gratitude go to Jean-Pierre Thierry, recently-retired Research Officer of the *Historial* at Péronne and Curator of the Franco-Australian Museum at Villers Bretonneux, for his indefatigable investigations on our behalf, to Dominique Frère of the *Historial*, for some fine photos, to Anne-Marie Goales, recently-retired Director of Tourism for the Somme, for her continuing support and friendship over the years, and the same to Tom and Janet Fairgreave, curators of Delville Wood. Thanks, too, to the succession of officers of the Commonwealth War Graves Commission at Maidenhead and Beaurains for answering our numerous queries with alacrity, in particular David Parker, Tim Reeves, Roy Hemington, Judith Donald, Kim Loizou and all the staff in France for continuing to tend the graves and memorials with such loving care; to Nick Smith Chief Information Officer of MOD Media Operations; to Lt Col Phillip Robinson and Lt Col Mike Dolamore of the Durand Group; to Lt Col George Forty, Tank Museum, Bovington; to Capt Simon Mann of 82 Sqn RE; to Professor Peter Simkins; to Brad (Aviation) King of the Imperial War Museum; Kiri Ross-Jones of the National Maritime Museum; Sir Frank Sanderson of the Thiépval Project; Arlene King, director of the Newfoundland Memorial; to Carol Walker of the Somme Association and Teddy & Phoebe Colligan of the Ulster Tower; to Ian Alexander of the War Research Society; to Avril Williams of Auchonvillers; to Christopher Marsden-Smedley; to Col Bob Sayce, Australian High Commission; to Ross Bastiaan; to Ron Austin of Slouch Hat Publications; to Ronald Cameron for Gaelic translations; to the staff of Dover and Leamington-Spa Libraries and to the managers and staff of the Novotel, Amiens-Est for their hospitality during our researches.

INDEX

FORCES

MEMORIALS

Museums/Exhibitions/Visitors' Centres

War Cemeteries

General Index